2-10-07
To Jim Schmitz
Hope you enjoy this
unique book about NW
fly angling!
Frank W. Amato

"The waters know their own, and draw

The brook that springs in yonder heights.

So flows the good with equal law,

Unto the soul of pure delight."

John Burroughs

D E D I C A T I O N

To my dear wife who says she
Wishes she were a trout so
That I would love her more.

Published in 2006 by
Frank Amato Publications, Inc.
PO Box 82112 • Portland, Oregon 97282 • (503) 653-8108

Illustrations by Blaine Hallock
Book Design: Leslie Brannan

Softbound ISBN: 1-57188-386-X   Softbound UPC: 0-81127-00220-7
Hardbound ISBN: 1-57188-387-8   Hardbound UPC: 0-81127-00221-4
Limited Hardbound ISBN: 1-57188-388-6   Limited Hardbound UPC: 0-81127-00222-1

Printed in Hong Kong

1 3 5 7 9 10 8 6 4 2

TABLE OF CONTENTS

INTRODUCTION

The worn manila envelope lay unpretentiously on the dining room table, where I would not have given it a second thought, except that it was the only item present on a surface usually covered with printed material of one kind or another. It was an old manuscript discovered in my mother-in-law's basement years ago by a family friend. Curious about the contents, I settled down with the envelope after dinner. The manuscript was held between two pieces of cardboard, employing a binding mechanism of two metal prongs passed through holes at the top of each page. I opened the front cardboard cover and began to read. I was enthralled.

Humor, fishing, and life in the 1890s to the 1950s encompassed me. I asked my wife Annie for details of the author, her grandfather, and learned that Mr. Hallock wrote several articles that appeared in fishing magazines in the thirties and forties. The *Pendleton Sun*, his childhood newspaper, became part of the collection of children's literature at the Smithsonian Museum. Over the next several days I finished reading the manuscript, and wondered why it was never accepted for publication. I thought any fisherman would embrace it, as well as those interested in Oregon history, or life in the West during that time.

The manila envelope found a bookshelf, and there languished until I became interested in digitizing it and sending it around to family members, friends, and fly shops. The response was less than overwhelming, as few had the patience to read a computer document of what is essentially a picture of the typed page — a yellowed, fifty- to seventy-five-year-old document written on a Courier typewriter with occasional penciled-in notes, not easily read.

The manuscript, now replete with shiny CDs, again returned to the bookshelf. There it awaited resuscitation until a conversation I had at a dinner party. A bright, engaging man there described his self-publishing process and the resultant product which was very impressive. Desktop publishing became my new passion, and I began work to produce a more reader-friendly version. I continued to labor along for several months on the contents of the manila envelope.

One evening while visiting my in-laws, my sister-in-law Miriam Holley commented that her daughter Ann (the author's great granddaughter) was given a box of her grandfather's things, stored in the barn. I shall long remember the trip to the barn. We found the red wooden box in excellent condition. Among other things, it contained two copies of the manuscript, a few additional chapters, and a set of matching pen-and-ink drawings by the author himself. The box also preserved much correspondence, including letters from William O. Douglas and fishing-rod maker first name E.C. Powell. Upon sharing details of the red box finds with family, the author's grandson Matthew Blaine Wells provided an additional treasure trove of pictures he had inherited.

As I began thinking about approaching a publisher, Frank Amato Publications first came to mind as the outstanding publisher in the fishing world, and it was located in Oregon, the author's home. I had a cordial initial phone call with Kim Koch at Frank Amato Publications indicating that they would look at the manuscript. I assumed that they looked at many documents, so I started my letter with "found in the red box in the barn" in hopes that would catch Mr. Amato's eye. That was both foolish and unnecessary. The manuscript stands on its own without assistance from me. Mr. Amato called in two weeks to accept the manuscript for publication.

The manuscript, and many of the pictures, were made available by the author's daughter, Mary Hallock Sargent, the "Mary" frequently referred to in the book. Her enthusiasm and continued support are deeply appreciated. The text, drawings, and pictures then came together in a digitized manner, with great assistance from my daughter Paige Hamilton. Another daughter, Anne Hamilton provided invaluable help with her knowledge of the publishing world and with this Introduction.

I did tie and fish the Hallock Killer fly described in the book, but with less success than the author. Despite what fishermen say, a full creel is more dependent on skill than on the rod, the line, the fly, and the moon. The old adage regarding truth and fishermen is probably the only thing about fishing that could be considered a "law".

My only regret through this process is that I was never privileged to know the author. One can glean from his writing that would be a very worthwhile relationship. Read this book. Then you will know of what I speak.

Richard Hamilton, M.D.
Denver, Colorado
26 May, 2005

CHAPTER

Earliest Recollections

I shall not pretend that I remember the darkened room in the little frame house where I was born, nor, for that matter, anything at all about my early babyhood. Unlike some autobiographers, I confess that I have no recollection of the joy which must have shone in my mother's eyes at the sound of my first feeble wail, or the remark of the midwife who must surely have murmured, "Ah, a very fine boy indeed." No doubt my proud parents did promptly confide in one another the conviction that someday I would become president of these United States. But if so, they never communicated that understandable prediction to me. I later learned, though only through hearsay, that my advent into the world meant the serious problem of another mouth to feed at a time when my older sister, the first-born, was already taxing the resources of my young parents. They, like their neighbors of those far-off days, were very poor. I learned, also upon hearsay, that the momentous event of my birth occurred in the little frontier town of Heppner out in the rolling sagebrush hills of eastern Oregon.

But a time did come when something happened that I can relate without recourse to secondary evidence, for it is indelibly impressed upon the tablets of my memory and has contributed much toward my belief that the world is a grand place to live in and that good things often do come in miraculous ways.

The shades of evening had gathered. On a round center table covered with a dark cloth, a lamp burned brightly shedding a soft circular glow. It had a porcelain shade, green on top and white beneath. I was sitting on my father's knees. There were several papers scattered on the table.

"Sometimes" said Father, "when little boys are very good the fairies bring them presents." I had heard of the fairies before but was not much impressed.

"Look under the papers," continued Father, "and see if you can find anything."

When I lifted one of the papers, what should I find but a little piece of white candy. Wide-eyed with wonder and excitement I gulped it, and feverishly examined the table under all the other papers. My search was minute and complete, but there were no more candies.

"Now look again," said Father. Lo and behold, there was another piece of candy! Again I made a diligent search, but I found nothing.

"Try once more," my Father urged. A third piece lay under the very paper which only a moment before had concealed nothing but the table's cover.

"How can the fairies be here on the table when I can't see them?" I asked.

"Well," he explained, "they are invisible." I didn't know just what that meant, but I was satisfied then that fairies really did exist and that when a boy was very good they were apt to reward him.

Another experience with the fairies occurred no great while later. One day Father explained that fairies sometimes made toys come to life. I was the proud possessor of a little tin monkey painted in bright colors which climbed a string when it was pulled, but never until that day had it performed this acrobatic feat without human aid. I loved this toy and when not playing with it, I would pin the top of the string to a window curtain where I liked to see it dangling. While this explanation regarding the activities of the fairies was going forward I glanced at a little doll buggy on the floor, a prized possession of my older sister. Suddenly it began not only to move but actually to roll along the floor. I was spellbound. Hearing a faint click I glanced up at my monkey dangling on the curtain, and it too suddenly began to move, climbing steadily up the string. Had any doubt lingered in my mind about the prowess of the fairies, it was that moment completely dispelled. What pains my father had taken to attach these toys to invisible threads, and how he was able to make them perform with no movement my young comprehension could detect, remains one of the unexplained mysteries of my life.

The fairies kept a watchful eye on my fortunes for a long time thereafter. When I began to lose my baby teeth I showed my father one day that a tooth was quite loose. He very deftly plucked it out with thumb and finger, and I experienced no pain.

"My little man," he said, "if you will put that tooth in a glass of water by your bed tonight the fairies might change it into money." Surely enough the next morning a shiny nickel lay in the bottom of the glass.

My recollection of our home in those days is hazy indeed. In retrospect I see a faint picture of what seemed to me a very long back yard with a picket fence all around and a straggly shade tree in one corner.

I can recall my first velocipede. Mother had promised me a present, and Father took me for a long walk somewhere which terminated in a store. I can see myself astride this little velocipede riding I knew not where. My father walked behind, and suddenly out of a strange unfamiliar world I found myself at our very front gate. The unerring instinct which had headed me in the right direction from the store to our home, probably a block or so away, I can only credit to my father's encouraging instruction that I should "Just keep riding along."

When the curtain of memory lifts again there are three of us children, my older sister, myself, and a brand-new baby girl. We are living with my grandmother in a rambling, old white house with green shutters and a big yard in Salem. I can hear the rain dripping from the eaves, and smell the pungent odor of damp moss on the oak sticks that sputtered in the open fireplace through many gloomy days. Violets bloomed against the damp brick walls on the north side of the house, and under a great oak tree out by the barn, there was a soggy accumulation of deep brown leaves where I could occasionally find little tough-skinned balls that grew on the under sides of the leaves. But when the sun did shine on the long yellow grass that sloped down past the moldering wall to Mill Creek on the south, and spilled through the leaves and onto the purple clusters of grapes along the arbor extending from the back porch out to the old barn, the world was a delightful place.

To me the house seemed enormous. It was one of those old-fashioned structures, rarely seen anymore, with the lower floor and living quarters half below and half above the ground level. A short flight of steps under the front porch gave access to the living room, another flight up to the front porch led into the parlor, used only on rare occasions. The round-backed, deeply carved oak chairs were upholstered in black horsehair. On a marble-topped table under a glass bell was a heap of artificial fruit. Brilliant lithographs of comely young women, toying with birds or feeding deer, adorned the walls, in dark oak frames, with the ends of the moldings crossing and extending beyond the common margin. Interspersed with these were cross-stitch mottoes worked out in gay colors, carrying the slogans: "Welcome," "God Bless Our Home," and the like. On both sides leading off the long hall back of the parlor, were several bedrooms, all somewhat similarly furnished. A very long flight of stairs led to the top floor bedrooms, but I rarely got that far from the big semi-basement living room, which occupied half of the entire lower floor. The other half was a huge combination kitchen and dining room. Daylight was let into these lower quarters through windows that were set in damp brick-lined light wells around which the violets grew. Against the front window in the big living room, innumerable tin cans of brilliant geraniums, begonias, fuchsias and plants with multi-colored leaves were displayed on an A-shaped bamboo rack with shelves. Grandmother tended these flowers with the greatest care, and they filled the old house with spicy fragrance. Among other knick-knacks on the broad mantel above the fireplace was a little keg or barrel with a tiny faucet, suspended on a rack where dangled a half dozen little cups from hooks. This was probably intended for liquor or wine, but on the few occasions when we children were permitted to play with it the faucet spilled into the cups nothing more potent than water.

Near the spreading oak in a hollow toward the end of the backyard an egg plum tree kept it company. This tree produced in astonishing profusion. When the plums ripened, the whole neighborhood gorged on the succulent fruit, Grandmother converted vast quantities of it to plum butter, and still when the overripe plums fell to the ground they filled the grassy hollow with a pool of gold. One day my older sister conceived a great idea. She had me sit on a gunny sack which she pulled by running down the slope over the slippery yellow grass, whereupon I would be precipitated with a great plop and splashing of rotting plums into the hollow beneath the tree. But when we came in to supper that night, our clothes generously splattered with plum juice and fiber, Mother put a prompt stop to that diversion.

The back porch was dark and shadowy, being completely enclosed in cross lattice. In the gloom of one corner we discovered a marvelous contraption, an old-fashioned water-flushing toilet. The only thing that concealed the user from the common gate was the darkness of the shadowy corner, but what a thrill we would get when we used the device! Unoccupied, the seat stood up at a slight angle from the rear hinge; but when one sat on it, the marvel started to work. The gurgle of water would be heard, and one's bottom would be treated to a fine spray of cold water. For this reason I much preferred it to the conventional old two-holer out in the back yard, which was reached by a sloping plank walk. When it rained this was always slippery and apt to precipitate one onto the seat of his pants, which would thereby get a good wetting before even being pulled down.

The slope of the grassy yard was broken half way to the creek by a low brick wall, and above this a weather-beaten outbuilding moldered in the rain, or steamed when the sun shone. A cluster of tall pink and white hollyhocks and flaming red poppies grew at the foot of the wall. Peering between the stalks I discovered a hole in the wall and promptly contacted my sister and my Uncle Jake who was only a year or two older than me.

"Do you want to see a pirate cave?" I whispered.

Down the hill we went and a little prospecting around the ancient edifice disclosed that a small boy, his small sister and his small uncle could crawl underneath it without difficulty. When our eyes became accustomed to the gloom we discovered that some of the bricks were loose.

"Let's make a secret hiding place in the wall," said Jake.

With a rusty nail we scraped away the mortar around one of the bricks and were soon able to dislodge it. A marvelous place to hide pirate secret writings!

"Pirates write their secrets in blood," I volunteered.

"But we haven't any blood," murmured my sister in a hoarse whisper. A great inspiration possessed me.

"Give me that pin out of your hair ribbon," I demanded.

With some trepidation she produced the pin and with one bold prick of my thumb a drop of red blood was at hand. Not to be out-done Jake too pricked his thumb and then sister, with some hesitation, also submitted to the ordeal.

"Make an X right here," I said, producing a crumpled piece of paper from my pocket. We each left our bloody mark, pushed the paper into the hole, replaced the brick and swore a holy oath that we would never, never reveal the secret. As far as I know that great confidence has not been violated to this very day. A narrow strip of flow-ered meadow lay between the wall and the creek.

One day while lolling in the grass at the edge of the stream I dis-covered that it contained schools of minnows. Hurrying back to the house I induced Mother to provide me with fishing tackle which con-sisted of a willow switch, a short piece of twine and a bent pin. With bread crumbs for bait I fished in the minnow pool for hours at a time, but the fates decreed that the thrill of catching my first fish must be deferred until we moved to Herman Creek.

CHAPTER

Little Boy
and His Trout

H erman Creek, during the early years of the gay nineties, was but little fished. It was hidden away in the mighty folds of the Columbia River Gorge remote from any large town and rather inaccessible, although a rough country road did lead to a point not far from its mouth. One ambitious to reach its higher waters must toil up a rude trail along the "hogbacks" for several miles. But at the time of which I write, the fishing right in front of our camp was quite good enough for a small boy.

The stream sprang from the rugged heights of the Cascade Mountains south of the great river. It hurried between granite walls, plunged over steep cliffs, with many a sparkling waterfall and somber rock-ribbed canyon until it reached a saucer-shaped basin where, in hesitant and uncertain manner, it found its way through high boulders, then on between mossy banks under an arching forest of great hemlocks and cedars. In this wooded stretch the shadows were deep, and in spring the pale trilliums and delicate blue anemones thrust up through a soft carpet of fir needles and moss. It chattered down a hill around water-worn stones and over sparkling gravel bars past the old Conley farm where pink-headed clover blended with acres of fern, and finally arrived at the grove of maples and oaks under which gleamed the white walls of our tent. Just below camp the creek slipped beneath a railroad bridge, left the confining hills, traversed a strip of yellow sand and reached the embracing arms of the lordly Columbia. When this great river was at high stage, its lapping waters washed the very foot of the hill, but in late summer the creek ambled across a sandy beach for nearly a quarter of a mile before it joined the river.

Here and there among the cedar and hemlock trees on the upper reaches of the stream which I visited in later years, for I was too small then to know anything about it, staunch oaks and maples reached for the sun. On the south sides of the trunks and hanging from the larg-er branches were thick rolls of dry moss. What marvelous beds they made! We would gather great armfuls, spread them on the soft earth, top the heap with a covering of flat cedar boughs, and try to count the stars as the glowing embers of our campfire faded into the night.

Those were the days to which my parents later referred as "the hard times." Jobs and money were scarce. The government was build-ing locks on the river at a town appropriately named "Cascade Locks" and massive granite slabs required for this work were quarried along Herman Creek. In order to get them out, a spur track had been con-structed from the quarry to a connection with the main line of the old Oregon Railway & Navigation Company, now the Union Pacific Railroad. The so-called "Stone Train" had to make periodic trips over the main line to the site of the locks and return to the quarry.

My father was the telegrapher and dispatcher for this operation.

How vividly I remember our home of those far-off days, and how contented and happy we all seemed to be. If my parents were over worried or concerned about our situation, they either concealed it from us, or I was too young to remember it. There were six of us in the family, Mother, Father, and four children. In winter we lived in a little one-room frame house beside the tracks. It had a double window in one end and on a counter just under the window Father had his clattering telegraph instruments and his records and stationery. A small sheet iron stove served both for heating and cooking. Against one wall was a rude board table and above it were shelves for dishes, a few groceries and supplies. At the end of the room, opposite the window, were double-decked beds made of fir poles and equipped with bough mattresses. Father and Mother occupied the upper bed and we four children slept crosswise in the lower one. Several hours each day were devoted to "school work." Our parents alternated as teachers. I distinctly recall learning to spell five words: multiplication, division, addition, subtraction and chocolate. Just what connection there was in my mind between chocolate and mathematics I have long since forgotten. The Youth's Companion arrived each week and during the long winter evenings Mother would read it to us from cover to cover. When she had read the very last word, Father would take over. Of the books in his meager library I remember Dickens, Shakespeare, Bryant's Library of Poetry and Song, Goethe, Arabian Nights, the Bible, a big atlas, and a seven-volume set of Byron, Hood, Pope, Cowper, Tennyson, Milton and Moore, each book bound in a different color. There were probably some other books in the collection, but of them I have no recollection.

Father read aloud *Old Curiosity Shop*, *Great Expectations*, *Bleak House*, *David Copperfield*, *Oliver Twist* and many other stories. A lot of it I did not fully understand, but I do remember how I loathed old Fagin for his treatment of Oliver Twist and how I cried for poor, hungry little David Copperfield when he had to sell his only "weskit" for but nine pence. For Washington's Birthday, Mother dressed me in a blue George Washington suit and cocked hat, which she had made for the occasion, and Father took our picture with me whacking away at a sapling with a little hatchet. This important ceremony had been planned for days. The entire audience consisted only of our parents, with us children as the actors. Father had taught us a little song which we included in the program. I think it actually went something like this:

> "What a pleasure there is dancing in the sunlight
> When all this earth seems to smile,
> It gives a merry ringing to your laughter
> You don't know care or guile."

But we children must have had scant appreciation for the sentiment because, to us, as we sang it. In lusty discord, and as I remember the words to this day, they ran:

"What a pleasure there is dancing in the sunlight
When Aldrich seems to smile.
It makes a merry ringing in your ear
You don't know Paragile."

In our imagination Aldrich who smiled so readily was a character to be emulated, while Paragile, whom it seemed to us, we were not even to know, was a villain of the deepest dye.

In summer we lived in the tent down under the maple trees, cooking and eating our meals under a canvas fly and storing the rest of our worldly goods in a bough-thatched lean-to. The creek ran just in front of the tent, and as a little boy I marveled to see my father catch trout in our very "front yard." It could not have been more than one hundred yards through the woods from our tent on the stream back to the road, but I never had the courage to make the trip alone, for dark shadows lurked beneath the trees and around the hazel bushes where Paragile might show up at any moment, and there was always a strange chatter of birds and squirrels; although once I did catch a chipmunk not too far back of the tent in a little box trap that my father made for me. The world seemed very large and full of mysteries.

One day my father let me trail along with him up the wooded bank of the stream while he fished. I remember that he used two flies and caught a trout and sometimes two in almost every likely pool. After awhile he sat down to clean the fish and allowed me to take his rod and dangle the flies over the water. I shall never forget what happened then. It is as vivid as though it occurred but yesterday. The creek was small and crystal clear and the bank at that point was free of trees. The end of a big log extended a few feet out over the water, partly damming the stream above, causing the current to scoop out a shallow pool in the bright sand and gravel below the log. In the clear water I saw a school of trout minnows, the largest not more than two or three inches long. I worked my way out on the log and dangled the flies on the surface of the pool. There was a rush of minnows and I gave the rod a jerk, but without reward. Again and again I repeated the maneuver with the same result, but finally a minnow did impale himself upon one of the flies. I gave one mighty yank and he flew over my head and landed on the bank. I dropped the rod and rushed to my prey. The tiny fish flopped about on the grass until I was able to clutch him in my hot and trembling hands. My first trout — and what a beauty! It was all of two inches long. I can still see the amber tint of his tiny transparent fins, the fine lines of his gill coverings, the round shiny eyes, the square little tail and the lovely opal par marks down his gleaming sides. All the king's horses and all the king's men couldn't have wrested my prize from me, though I do not recall that anyone was interested in such a project. After I had duly fondled the fish, Father considerately put it in the creel with his own, and back to camp we went. Although I had become a little tired following him up the creek I fairly flew back to the tent to display my catch. From that moment I knew that I must be a trout fisherman come what may, and that is what I am today. I have found the law a means by which to live, to live that I may go fishing again. So it follows that this book will contain much about that gentle diversion.

Not long after that memorable day, Father made me a fishing outfit for my very own. He cut a small dead fir sapling, trimmed off the branches and dressed it down with a chip of glass. Then he twisted a few guides along the rod with copper wire, and made a reel from a spool. The reel had a little peg for a handle and was pivoted on a nail driven into the end of the rod. The line was heavy black thread with a small plain hook tied on the end. My creel was a salt sack hung from my shoulder on a cord. I have since owned many rods, have tied thousands of flies, have picked up fancy tackle in odd places throughout the world, but I have never owned an outfit which I loved more dearly than the tiny rod with its spool reel. After that I spent many happy hours up and down the stream near the camp, and would often come in with wet feet and proudly display two or three trout, some as great as five or six inches in length.

A day came when the miracle happened. As I walked down the stream, wishing that I owned a trout fly with which to replace the bait hook, I saw a patch of white, shining on a shingly bar. I ran up to have a look, and what should it prove to be but a flour sack, lost by some fisherman. In it I found a fly book containing half a dozen flies, some Professors and some Grizzly Kings! My delight knew no bounds! They were snelled flies which gave me at least a semblance of leader. I tied one of each on the line and became a fly fisherman then and there and rarely ever used bait again. Knowing little, if anything, about other patterns of flies and caring less, I fished for years thereafter with the Professor/Grizzly King combination. Even after I originated the "Hallock Killer" about which more appears between these covers, I still find this first combination very effective.

As the summer advanced, the creek became lower. I would wade over the shallow bars, and one day, without difficulty I crossed at a point a little below camp and discovered a fern-girthed brook emptying into the main stream over yellow sand and bright pebbles. I promptly named it Sand Creek and followed it up through the woods. Here and there in the deeper pools carved under the overhanging banks I caught little trout which were nearly black because their lives had been spent in the deep shadows. The brook came down between the ferns from a slightly higher elevation and when I scrambled up a hill I found a mountain meadow through which the tiny stream meandered in a channel so narrow that I could step across it. Long grasses hung down on each side and when I dropped a fly over the little exposed patches of water I was surprised to learn that I could catch larger trout and that some of them in the sunnier stretches were quite brilliant.

The discovery of Sand Creek suggested interesting possibilities to all of us children, although it sometimes proved quite a task to get little brother Joe across the main stream where we had to splash through several inches of water as it flowed over a gravel bed. At the head of the clearing we found a cabin and discovered that an Indian girl, slightly older than any of us, lived there with her father. She introduced us to a rare delicacy, the first of the kind that I had ever tasted — sandwiches made of thin slices of homemade bread and fresh cucumbers soaked in vinegar. Just why this should have made such a profound impression upon me I cannot say, but I do know that even today when I eat cucumbers I think of the rude cabin in the green mountain meadow and our young Indian friend.

In winter we lived in the little house, sometimes almost buried in snow and in summer we camped under the trees for two years. It was in the second summer that my father took me with him to fish a nearby stream, locally known as Dry Creek. Dry Creek was hardly more than a brook, but where it dashed over the cliff in a snowy waterfall it had scoured out a deep pool with always a spray of mist blowing across it. That made damp work of trying to fish, but I was able to get my fly out on the pool and in a moment a cutthroat trout almost nine inches long rose and took it — the deeply speckled beauty was by far the biggest fish I had ever caught.

Wild blackberries were abundant in the late summer and on an open sunny hillside where an old burn had left much downed timber and whiten snags, we found them in goodly measure — clusters of big, shiny, deep-purple jewels full of fragrance and tang. They are hard to come by in these later days, for but few of the wildwood lots are left, but to anyone who has scrambled over logs and through brambles to gather them I am sure they are the most delicious berry in the world. Here and there a stately tiger lily lifted its soft brown head, peppered with black spots, and on the granite boulders and warm dry logs little gray lizards with bright blue tails slept in the sun, their shiny sides flashing and iridescent. When we approached them they would disappear with a whisk. We used to imagine that if we could catch them they would change into footmen as they did in the story of Cinderella. One day as we gathered berries under the brilliant blue sky, I heard the faint whistle of a train pulling up the grade. What is there about such simple experiences that impress us so profoundly? The sound of a cow bell at dusk, the faint barking of a dog, the smell of burning leaves in the fall, the aroma of frying bacon and wood smoke, these are the makers of memories. Even today when I hear the distant whistle of a locomotive I think of wild blackberries warm on a flowery hillside, and I experience a feeling of loneliness and nostalgia.

Down the road which lead toward the Columbia there was a tumble-down farm where a solitary old Scandinavian by the name of Skar eked out a lonely existence. He had a cow, and every afternoon, lard pail in hand, we children would amble down the dusty road and return at dusk with the family milk. Sometimes in the fall Mr. Skar would give us apples, which we were reluctant to take until he would assure us in his thick English, "Eat, eat, they will not hurt you." One day when we were munching apples he sat before his doorway and began to whittle a piece of tongue-and-grooved flooring with his big bone-handled jack knife. His gnarled hands were sure and strong and soon before my wondering eyes appeared a real cross bow. "It is for you," he said, holding it out to me, "and I will make you some arrows too." Thereupon he split a shingle into a generous pile of shafts and thus I was equipped to cope with Paragile or any other danger that might be lurking in the venerable woods.

It was in Mr. Skar's pasture that I found my first prunella, an odd little flower with the bloom made up of a cone-shaped arrangement of stiff cup-like petals, carrying a few purplish-blue blossoms here and there, as though stuck in at random. These flowers have a ragged look as though most of the blossoms had been knocked off, but through all the later years whenever I found them on hillside or in grassy meadow, their appearance was always the same. Apparently one has about as much chance of finding a prune in perfect bloom as of finding a coconut palm with a straight trunk. But I love them more than any other flower. You may have the glorious yellow chrysanthemum of late fall, the long-stemmed red rose developed to the last degree of hothouse perfection, or the dainty corsage of delicate orchids — the prunella for me!

Mr. Skar was a strange old character, and we children invented many stories about the secluded life he led. When I went to bid him goodbye as we were leaving our forest home he put his arm around my shoulder and said, "You make me think of another little boy," That was all we ever knew. God rest his soul!

Barefoot Days

he eastern Oregon city of Pendleton, now of Roundup fame, was a typical western frontier town in the mid [18]nineties. The streets were mud wallows in winter and spring, but in summer the Indian cayuses kicked up great swirls of dust as their dusky skinned, blanket-clad riders came into town from the nearby Umatilla reservation. What few sidewalks Pendleton could boast were made of planks, about every tenth one extending to the wooden curb. They rattled as an occasional cyclist rode down the street in knee breeches and woolen stockings, perched astride an enormous wheel, behind which, at the end of a down-curving goose neck, a little wheel enabled him to maintain his precarious balance. Nails stuck up here and there through the boards to the sorrow of us barefoot boys, who suffered many a stubbed toe. Planks were missing in places, and often we peered between the cracks in the hope of finding nickels lost by pedestrians. Hitching posts stood before the square-fronted frame stores, and Indian ponies switched their tails at the swarms of pestering flies. Farm wagons drawn by big sleek horses clattered down the streets with children lolling in the straw among the boxes and sacks, while the black-and-white sheep dogs trotted along under the wagons in the shade. Occasionally Mrs. DeSpain, wearing a ruffled black silk dress with a "gold watch and chain," rode by in her victoria. She carried a doll-sized black parasol which she could tilt from side to side, but she often disappeared from view in the clouds of dust. It was years later that Mr. Judd brought the first automobile to our town.

In those days social obligations presented no problem. Families took their recreation together. They met their neighbors at "ice cream sociables," or drove out to Byers Park, a grove of cottonwoods down by the river to enjoy fried chicken, lemonade, ice cream and cake. Nothing that I know of yet can equal the custard ice cream which we would churn to hardness out in the woodshed before the picnics. We could never wait until it really froze, but kept peeking into the freezer, solacing ourselves with small slivers of salty overflow as the grinding went on. But the finished product was superb, and nothing like it can be purchased today.

Cooking must have been a chore during the scorching summer days. Like our neighbors we prided ourselves on the ownership of a "Majestic" range and in the cool of the morning Mother would bake pies or cakes or roast meat for supper, and later we would sit down to eat in the darkened dining room. We always enjoyed the great bowls of red lettuce sprinkled with sugar and vinegar, or cold sliced cucumbers. But if it was necessary during the day to build a fire in the range, we would fan our brows till after sunset when the refreshing breezes from the nearby Blue Mountains extended happy relief. We thought little of the innumerable flies which buzzed and circled around the middle of the room, though we were well supplied with Tanglefoot fly paper. We played marbles and spun tops, went to Sunday school, took part in amateur theatricals, chivareed the newly-weds and stole gates on Halloween. The local fire brigade kept in good trim to compete with any challenge from the neighboring towns. In short, Pendleton at that time depicted a phase of American life which has now largely passed from the scene.

Like all small boys I was always poking about in out-of the-way corners and one day I discovered many odds and ends of type in a heap of rubbish behind the *Tribune* office, where my father then published a

Republican newspaper. A little exploratory prospecting disclosed a veritable type mine. It had accumulated through years of sweeping the composition room and was generously mixed with sawdust, cigarette butts and miscellaneous refuse. But after much digging I salvaged enough to make up the polyglot composition of a boy's newspaper whereupon I became a journalist. The paper, which I called the *Pendleton Sun* was made up of four pages, and was printed on a little hand press. After school and in the evenings of the first two or three days of each week I set up and printed the first half of the paper, exhausting my meager supply of type in that process. Then redistributing the type I devoted the latter days of the week to making up the other half of the paper, and on Saturdays peddled it on the streets at one cent per copy.

Most children take a fling at publishing a newspaper some time during their young lives, but the *Sun* evidently was in a class by itself, for during its brief career a number of metropolitan papers carried "quotes" from it. I received regular exchanges, and it had an out-of-town subscription list; to mention but two entries,

> "The Sun is getting quite a circulation, for we
> now have little boy way back in Topeka, Kansas."
> and again,
> "Last Tuesday I received a paper "The Reflector,"
> from way back in Marshall Town, Iowa, which
> shows pretty well for the Sun."

To this day guests at our home enjoy perusing the yellowed pages of the little bound volume which contains each issue with its jumbled type, terrific spelling and high moral tone. With rare good judgment my parents refused to contribute or to correct any entry, so the paper bore the unmistakable mark of its youthful editor on every page. Because it reflects the atmosphere of those faraway days I should like to quote some of it, although I regret that it cannot be done in facsimile for as here presented it loses much of its piquancy in dress and spelling.

As will be seen, the editorials were both moral and constructive.
"FLYS

> The flis are coming out as thick as spatter and
> everybody has to put on their screen doors to keep
> them out, but they get in in spite of all. They eat up
> the meat and sugar and every other thing, and one
> has to plaster their house with fly paper and some-
> times you put your hand down and accidentally
> get it on some fly paper. Flis have their places out
> of doors, but not in the house. It seems like that
> after the hard winter we have had that the flis
> would be frozen out, but there are a lot of them

coming out and before long the kitchens will be full of them. Flis are always a sure sign of summer."

"INDIANS

Pendleton has more Indians than any other town I ever saw. They come in from the agency like bees and hitch their wagons in every vacant lot in Pendleton, only what are fenced in. About noon they are thickest for most of them bring their lunch."

"SALOONS

It is very bad for Pendleton to have so many saloons. Every other building down on Main and Court Street is a saloon and the keepers do all they can to attract attention of the men.
Some poor hardworking men who just have to dig for a living will.
On Saturday nights spend all their scanty wages for liquor and their families are at home without half enough food and clothing.
I have seen Indians get so crazy for beer and whiskey that they would pawn off their blankets, saddles and even their hats to get money to buy drink with while the poor squaws have to do all the hard part of the work. An old squaw came past our house Saturday with a sack of flour strapped to her back, and her arms full of other bundles, while her husband I suppose was in some saloon. I think it is dreadful and should be stopped."

"SIDEWALKS OF PENDLETON

The sidewalks of Pendleton are in a dreadful con-dition. The nails project out so far that it is impos-sible to walk quietly along without stubbing your toe, and making quite a show of yourself by falling down. It is quite time they were being fixed before they are so badly gone up that it will be a life long job to fix them. Ladies and children beware of the nails."

"THE BUILDINGS OF PENDLETON

Pendleton is said to be the liveliest town for its size in eastern Oregon which no doubt is very true, but I think if a town is lively it must have some decent buildings to make it lively, for how can a town be lively if there are no buildings to work in. Pendleton surely cannot be bragged on its buildings, for if some of them were torn down it would be much better. The old Golden Rule Hotel is one of them, and some of the buildings around it are about the same, and it would be a great deal better for Pendleton if they were nice brick buildings in their place. Some night the town of Pendleton will be alarmed by a terrible fire, and half the town will go up in smoke and ashes, take heed what I say and look out."

Following the publication of this article, my father came to me and in a very serious vein, explained that he had been called upon by a delegation of property owners, including particularly the proprietor of the old Golden Rule Hotel. He urged assurance on my part that I had no thought either of encouraging or attempting incendiarism. The following items are taken at random from several issues of the *Pendleton Sun* and are typical of what was carried under the general caption "News."

"If the weather is profitable tomorrow a crowd of young people are going out kodaking.
They have been putting it off for one or two Sundies now, awaiting for a pleasant day."
"The fire engine was out last Tuesday for exercise."
"The tramps swarm into town over day like so many bees."
"Most of the people of Pendleton were out buggy riding yesterday, as it was fine weather."
"There is going to be a pie social at the Congressional Church tonight, admission 15 cents."
"The hose team ran last Saturday evening and they got water pretty quick. There is a man in this town who says that when the turnament comes the Pendleton team will not even get a smell, but I don't think that way."

"Frank Light's buggy team ran away last Sunday afternoon and caused great confusion among the people around Light's woodyard."
"Hot weather always brings hives, so most everybody has got them and it keeps you scratching and digging at them all the time."
"There is quite a number of stray dogs and cats around town and at night they rase cane generaly. They howel and fight and nook over slop cans, and

when you get up in the morning and find your slop
can nocked over I tell you it isn't very pleasant."

"Glenn Bushie has a very cute little cub which
he has around town. It is about 15 in. long &
afoot high."

"The road to the agency is now fine for wheels, and
the only drawback is the rocks and chuck holes."

"The strawberry peddlers say the reason the
strawberries are so cheap is the rain. Strawberries
are now down to 5 cents a box, which tells that
they are very plentiful."

"Mrs. Shull has 3 cows and 3 calves, and the cows
give so much milk that the calves have all they
want and she still has a good sized dishpan left. If
all the cows in the U.S. were as good as these, milk
would be down to about 5 cents a gallon. Most
cows with calves don't give very much milk."

"The Pendleton Hose team had their picture taken
last Sunday afternoon with their suits on down on
Water Street."

"That man down in front of the saloon that sells
speks prophesied that today was going to be the
worst day that Pendleton ever saw because his
leg hurt him so he could not sleep a wink and it
came true."

Under date line July 17, 1897, the *Sun* announced the arrival in
Pendleton of William Jennings Bryan. The article proclaims that
"about 1 o'clock in the afternoon the band went
down to the depot, headed by 6 horses all fixed up
in gawdy colors" and concludes, "then Mr. Bryan
made quite a long speech which I suppose was
very interesting to the democrats and poppulists."

We children attended school up on the hill and for our benefit
arrangements were made for us to hear the Great Commoner. Our
teacher herded us into a nearby wool warehouse where we were
perched on wool sacks arranged tier on tier and, in an atmosphere
heavy with the odor of raw wool in the grease, were told all about
free silver. The speaker employed an illustration which I have never

forgotten. He said that the inside of a good egg was silver and gold but that the inside of a rotten egg was all yellow. I suppose he intended to convince us that with only a gold standard the country was in a rotten condition but that with a bi-metal standard of part silver and part gold we could live in well-fed comfort.

I composed and printed little verses covering whatever occurred to me about the various members of our citizenry. The following verses did not appear in the order here shown but have been gleaned from several issues of the *Sun*:

"Mr. Bruce keeps that Golden Rule
That place is clean and neat
He has the sweetest little wife
That ever I did meet.

Mr. Ely peddles fruit
All through the summer long
And oh the boys they swipe the things
While to each house he's gone.

A. D. Thompson has a beard
And he's a goodly man
He makes all kinds of furniture
The very best he can.
And now to Tommie we will go
 To little Tommie Nye you know
Although he is a little lame
He is a good boy just the same.

Mr. Jackson looks like Lincoln
I guess its cause he's always thinkin
Mrs. Borie sings so sweetly
That she wins our hearts completely.

Babe DeSpain is very jolly
She did like a boy named Cholly
But now she goes with Mr. Stine
And Master Choly's left behind.

Jim Lipscome is a little man
With a captyvating face
He strolls around about the town
And girls he does embrace."

Just why there were no protests from the suffering public or actions for slander or libel I am unable to say, unless it was that my financial status was not conducive to litigation.

My time was not sufficiently taken up with these activities to enable me to forget about fishing when the trout season opened. The *Sun* abounds in references to angling which was really never out of my mind. In those days I had outgrown the little rod which my father had made for me. My tackle then consisted of a bamboo cane bought at a local variety store for five cents, about twenty feet of green cutty-hunk line, half of which was twisted up the rod from the grip and firmly tied at the end, and a half dozen plain hooks to which I fastened miscellaneous fragments of wool yarn and feathers, the product of my first venture in fly tying. Water from the Umatilla River was diverted to Mr. Byers' flour mill as a source of power, and then flowed under ground until it spilled out into Hartman's pond and on through the levee back to the river. The pond was one of my favorite fishing spots and at the end of a long summer day I often came home with a half a dozen "shiners," a few chubs and sometimes a trout. In the issue of the *Sun* under date May 8, 1897, I find:

> "It is now a good trout season and lots of the boys
> go fishing.
> The trout are mostly in Hartman's pond. This
> time a year a fly hook is used. A dark hook is
> good for Spring."

I caught the big trout on May 15. In the issue for that date this item appeared:

> "The manager of the Pendleton Sun went fishing
> yesterday and caught the biggest trout that he ever
> caught in his life and as he was coming home he
> was offered 25 cents for it but he would not take
> it because he wanted to eat it for supper."

I remember to this day that the fish lacked one quarter of an inch of being twelve inches long.

The urge to go fishing was too strong to resist, and this notice, immediately following the outburst on "Summer," tells its own story.

NOTICE!!
> "This will be the last issue of the Sun until
> about a month and a half as the editor of the
> Sun is going to the Springs. Anybody that wishes
> their money back I will pay it to them."

So the publication was discontinued, not for about a month and a half, but for all time. Some of my subscribers must have been left holding the sack, for the issue of May 29th contains this novel item:

> "The manager of the Pendleton Sun traded a life-
> long subscription of the Sun for a little lamb."

and in the issue of June 5th:

> "I forgot to mention that the boy I got the lamb of
> was Fred Vincent."

I do not recall that Fred ever received any further consideration for the lamb, but I do remember that I broke it to lead and one day a sheep man bought it for the fabulous sum of three dollars. With this fortune, and following my return from camping at Teal Springs, my interest in journalism fizzled out. I went into the poultry business instead and kept detailed books on the large turnover, and a diary of day-to-day transactions. There I find, fully indexed and cross-indexed several items such as these:

"June 18th,	Mrs. DeSpain, 3 eggs	5 cents
Jan. 6th,	Labor	5 cents
May 13th,	Labor	5 cents"

A recapitulation recites that my hens laid 1234 eggs in 1897, with a production increase to 1516 eggs in 1898. There is an elaborate calculation reflecting that out of 224 eggs set, 96 chicks were hatched with an average of 2.33 eggs per chick, or 14.3 chicks per egg, all worked out without benefit of logarithms or calculating machine. The index leads to property inventory where this entry appears under date of Sunday, March 12th:

> "A dog or something killed old Whitey."

and the diary entry of Monday, March 13th reads:

> "I got up at about 7:30 and had mush for break-
> fast started to school again and I hated to go the
> teacher gave me a lecture about smiling my seat is
> changed 3 back from where I sat. I buried the Old
> white hen down in the corner of the yard and Put
> a big tumb stone on her grave. I buried a hen on a
> summer's day. Out in the yard not far away. And
> on it I placed a monstrus stone. So there lays poor
> Whitey left alone. I carried in some wood and
> played with Trixie. Got my Youth's Companion. In
> the evening Mamma read and Jim came over. I
> got my spelling lesson for Tuesday and read a
> story in the Companion called the "Adventures of
> Antone and Peare" then went to bed about 10."

Eggs sold for a little as ten cents a dozen, and twenty-five cents would buy a good fat hen for the stew pot. But chicken feed was cheap, for I find upon consulting those ancient books that I bought culwheat from Mr. Byers for only a few cents a sack. The business was carried on for a couple of years by which time I had the back yard pretty well filled with chicken coops made out of dry goods boxes, and pens constructed from odds and ends of cast-off chicken wire which I had picked up here and there and from cull lathe purchased at Mr.Burrow's planing mill. The closing entry on the chicken business for the second year reads:

"Income, $28.70   Expense, 17.55   Profit, 11.15"

A big flowering locust tree grew in our front yard, and on summer nights its fragrance, which still lingers in my memory, drifted into my attic bedroom through the open window. I was afraid to go to sleep for fear I would not wake up at the peep of dawn for my Saturday fishing trip, but while I slept the profound sleep of a tired boy, I needed no alarm clock. My anticipation was always too lively to permit me to slumber too long and I was up at dawn.

When the chickens were getting along fairly well without need of personal supervision, I would be up with the first streak of morning light, ride out on my bicycle over the dusty roads to McKay or Birch Creek and spend wonderful hours fishing for little trout. Mr. Ely and other nearby farmers grew delicious watermelons and, with a companion or two on these excursions, we would often gorge ourselves on the succulent juicy red fruit, surreptitiously appropriating a melon from the shadiest and most concealed corner of the patch.

With the outbreak of the Spanish-American War in eighteen ninety-eight excitement ran high. A group of our gallant young men, dressed in light khaki cotton uniforms with leather puttees and wide stiff-brimmed hats crushed to a peak at the top, debarked for somewhere, to the accompaniment of our local band playing "There'll be a Hot Time in the Old Town Tonight," the waving of many flags and much cheering. The slogan in those days was "Remember the Maine."

We knew nothing then about machine guns, armored tanks, or jet bombers, but a martial spirit was abroad in the land. I became interested in gun powder and learned that it was made of sulphur, saltpeter and charcoal. My research did not extend to ascertaining just how these ingredients should be blended, but I mixed them together according to my own fancy and was ready for action. I wadded this compound and a few pebbles into an empty shot-gun shell and wedged it through a knothole in the woodshed. Leo Karsig was my first assistant in this venture. We held a lighted match over the "touch hole" and stood back to await results. A fine spurt of foul-smelling smoke shot up through the hole and Leo, apparently feeling that the pressure should be increased, clamped his chubby thumb over the opening. Thereupon, with a muffled "poof" the charge exploded, pebbles going forward, shell kicking backward and striking Leo in the very center of the forehead. He sprang up from the vile dust in which he fell with blood pouring down his face and ran yawping home. He was the first casualty of the campaign, and I imagine carries to this day the imprint of that shell on his aging brow.

I was not discouraged by this experience but I made no mention of Leo's wound to my parents. Rather, I launched out on a more elaborate campaign. Somewhere in the trash about town I had found an iron housing from the hub of a wagon wheel. From this and various other paraphernalia I made a cannon that looked like business. Numerous children gathered around to watch and admire as the work went forward and when all was ready and the cannon trained on the rear of the house, everyone backed away. I applied the match, the gun roared and rocks banged against the wainscoting while at the same instant my small brother in his excitement fell into the woodpile and bashed in his head. He screamed and raced toward the house with gore flowing over his white ruffled collar, just as Mother and a bevy of ladies whom she was entertaining at whist came running out the door. There was a definite misunderstanding as to exactly what had happened, but one thing was perfectly clear. I would not be shooting off any more cannons in the immediate future.

Long afterwards Father let me accompany him on grouse hunts. My fowling piece then was an old-fashioned single-shot twenty-two Flobert rifle, with an enormous odd-shaped hammer block. It required all of the strength I could muster with two hands to cock it. Occasionally he would take me on little excursions up the Umatilla River or along Meacham Creek above Pendleton. In the brushy brakes at the foot of the hills, or through the flaming sumac patches near the streams we would flush coveys of ruffed grouse which were very abundant.

In trade for a battered cornet, a mangy dog named "Fidget" who never quite got over an attack of distemper, and fifty cents in money I acquired my first shotgun, a loose-jointed, rust-pitted single-barreled semi-hammerless Remington twelve gauge, with three or four brass shotgun shells, and so equipped I sallied forth on my first duck hunt. I can't remember ever having seen any ducks around Pendleton prior to that time, but a divine Providence must have led me to them because, without rhyme or reason I decided to hunt along Tutulla Creek, a little rivulet that wound through the hills and shoestring meadows some three or four miles from town. When I arrived at the stream I slipped forward and peered over a clump of bushes and lo and behold, there were three ducks swimming on a small pool! I thought of them then as a mother with her brood of two, but I realize now that it was a gadwall or widgeon and two teal. At any rate I sneaked through the brush until within twenty or thirty feet of the birds, but not content to fire until I was certain of my quarry I waited until they had lined up. Only then did I train the gun on the row of birds and pull the trigger. The shock of the explosion flung me flat on my back and a great cloud of smoke rose to prevent my seeing the result immediately, but when the air had cleared, to my delight I found all three ducks kicking belly up on the surface of the pool. My first shot with three hundred per cent score: I was sure than that duck shooting was a cinch, but I think it was some ten years before I killed another duck.

It was while we lived in Pendleton that the foundation was laid for what later became, in my mind, "Slumber Cave." In one of my rambles down the river when I was far from home, it started to rain. My shoes and overalls were soaked to the knees, my back was chilled and the rain dripped from my hat down the back of my neck. In summer I wore only a cotton shirt and a pair of overalls, and ran barefoot with the rest of the boys in my group through the long dusty days. But because of the rough going and the long trip I wore shoes on this occasion. As the rain increased I worked my way along a sagebrush hillside near the river and out across an alfalfa field through the lush wet growth. Then I climbed a fence, stepped across a little irrigation ditch and wandered down to the river bank at the foot of the hill through a sparse clump of cottonwood samplings. There I found the cave. The floor was covered with a thick layer of dry sand and at its entrance laid a heap of faggots, some of which, under the protecting roof, were crisp and dry. High water of many seasons had deposited them there. I built a fire and while drying out my scanty raiment I lay on the warm sand and dozed off to sleep. I was evidently profoundly refreshed for the recollection of that experience has remained very vividly in my mind for more than fifty years. I recite these details only because they have become a sort of incantation which I use when I wish to invite illusive slumber, but I must rehearse the whole journey without deviation or the charm is broken.

In those days I had no trouble with insomnia, always falling into a sound sleep the minute my head struck the pillow. But in later years, particularly at the end of a strenuous day in court, with substantial property rights or on occasion, even a human life at stake, I would often find it difficult to go to sleep. It was then that I discovered that I possessed a magic formula, a real "Open Sesame" to a cave of dreams for I had but to imagine myself walking to that old shelter in the rain and lying out on the dry sand with the warm fire crackling at the entrance when I would fall into a peaceful slumber and "the ravel'd sleeve of care" would soon be knit.

CHAPTER

Serious Days

W e moved to Portland in time to see the Lewis and Clark Exposition held there in 1905. It was a small town in those days, but it seemed quite a metropolis to me crowded as it was with visitors. I was fascinated with the cable cars and the more modern electric street cars, but it took me a long time to become accustomed to the radical change in climate. At Pendleton the skies were always deep blue. The sunshine was brilliant, the air was keen and crisp and distances were foreshortened so sharply that it seemed as if we could almost touch the nearby hills. In Portland all this was changed. It rained a great deal, the skies were often gray and overcast and frequently the surrounding timbered hills were mothered in fog or mist. In patches where the mists lifted, the dark firs appeared like silhouettes in an etching. Many times I felt that I could smell the sea, and although it was nearly one hundred miles away, seagulls wheeled about the water front uttering their plaintive calls. Until the novelty wore off I used to stand on the old Morrison bridge and pitch fragments of bread to the questing birds. They never failed to snatch these morsels before they touched the water. Even in summer there was a soft haze on the horizon, the sky looked pale. At dawn and sunset the embracing hills were bathed in soft pastel shades. What passed for a bright sunshiny day in Portland would have been called a hazy one at Pendleton.

But I was delighted with the beautiful Willamette River on which time had then left "no track or trench." For two summers we lived in a houseboat on the river, enjoying many a splash in its cool waters and moonlight parties on its sloping grassy banks under huge oaks. The river was much more primitive then than in these days of factory and mill. It flowed on its quiet journey to the sea in great part through vast stretches of unbroken forest, and we never tired of watching the old stern wheel steamers plying back and forth with their bridal veils of water cascading out behind. It took all day to travel up the river some fifty miles to Salem, and the steamer would make innumerable stops on right bank or left to take on cord wood for fuel, deliver a parcel or pick up a lone passenger who could be seen, bag in hand, waving at the boat to flag it down. The very last word in elegance was the big side-wheeler *T. J. Potter*, furnished luxuriously in the best rococo style of the gay nineties. Somewhat like its forerunners, the Mississippi steamboats, it had several decks protected by ornate railings; its commodious lounge was upholstered in rich red velvet and its funnels belched great clouds of smoke as the busy stokers fed cord wood to its steam boilers. It made weekend excursions down the Willamette and Columbia rivers to the beaches along the Washington coast, giving us a night and almost another full day at any of the many little seaside resorts served by a narrow-gauge railroad. The train, made up of a string of open flat cars equipped with wooden benches and drawn by a tiny tea pot locomotive wound its way along the sand spit from Ilwaco near the mouth of the Columbia, to the sleepy little weather-worn oyster town of Nahcotta on Willapa Harbor. The bay was simply paved with delicious Olympia oysters, now such a high-priced delicacy, but then available at any restaurant in Portland. A generous cocktail cost ten cents. The same quantity now would cost more than a dollar if at all attainable.

We often picked up a row boat at Nahcotta, paddled out over the oyster beds toward the end of ebb tide, and let the boat settle on the bottom. As the receding water left it stranded, all we had to do was reach over the side, pick up the oysters which were cemented together in big slabs and with a nail or jack knife open the shells and gobbled down as many as our young appetites and good health would demand.

On one of my rambles along the waterfront shortly after we moved to Portland, I was delighted to run into an old boyhood friend, Pete Allen, who had formerly lived in Pendleton. He was in the act of stowing an eighteen-foot canvas-covered Racine canoe into a dilapidated river-front shed.

"Gosh, Pete," I said, grabbing his hand, "how good it is to see you again."

"You look pretty good to me, too," grinned Pete.

We walked uptown arm in arm, and drifted into the old Hazlewood lunchroom, where over a dish of strawberry ice cream we eagerly discussed past, present, and future. I told him of my efforts to learn show card writing, that I was pretty well discouraged, that I wanted to take a rest — do some strenuous relaxing. Pete in turn explained that he had been working on a small Willamette Valley farm which his a father had taken in a trade and that he too wanted a vacation.

"Well, Pete," I asked, "coming down here from Pendleton, what do you think of this beautiful river?"

"Onward ever, lovely river flowing softly to the sea," mused Pete who was a staunch admirer of Simpson.

"That's it," I suddenly exploded, "your canoe — the river — let's see where it comes from and what it looks like up near its source."

"A swell idea," agreed Pete enthusiastically.

The next Sunday afternoon we were in Eugene, then a small college town about one hundred and seventy-five miles by river south of Portland. We had come by rail had shipped our canoe and duffel by express. After a brief altercation with the express man who was supposed to be off duty on Sunday, we finally secured our canoe and with the aid of a bevy of small boys, got it and our duffel to the river, and were shortly adrift on its lapping waters. What a contrast to the river as we knew it at Portland! There it was wide, deep, and placid. Here it was hardly more than a big creek wadeable at most points with innumerable riffles, white water stretches, and clear swirling eddies. With soft blue skies above, a swift-flowing stream beneath, and two carefree weeks before us, we were a happy pair.

The second day out, pulling, pushing, and dragging the canoe a mile or so up the Mackenzie River from its confluence with the Willamette, near Harrisburg, we found unbelievable fly fishing, catching plump rainbow trout up to eighteen inches in length. In the main river, lusty bass were plentiful and would readily strike a spinner. The thickets and brushy patches along the shores, particularly at the mouths of small tributary streams, afforded excellent ruffed grouse shooting and we gorged on fish, fowl, and wild blackberries. Warm hazy days followed one another in delightful succession as we loitered down the quiet stretches or shot rapids that tossed white water into our laps and splashed our fascinated, sunburned faces. Rocks and logs whirled by when we sped through the swifter flows; and where the water slipped over shallow gravel beds, the bottom of the stream often threatened to and sometimes did scrape the keel of the canoe. Although we were in the very heart of the Willamette valley, even then rather thickly populated, long sections of the river appeared as wild and primitive as though their shores had never felt the tread of human foot. What a contrast to today here around every bend factory and mill are adding their contribution of pollution and municipal outlets are dumping their burden of slime into this once-lovely stream.

Lumbering was then the principal industry of the Northwest and time and again we ran between or around great numbers of logs which were being driven down the river to tidewater. One such experience nearly proved fatal to our happy excursion. A little below the village of Buena Vista we overtook a logging crew, some twenty or thirty men with their horse and equipment following the straggling tail of a log drive. With team and pike poles they would pilot the logs through the main channel and dislodge those that had been stranded on shallows and gravel bars. A big mess tent on a staunch log raft brought up the rear. Here the stream appeared pretty well choked with logs, men, horses, and equipment. But as we sped by we shouted inquiry to a man on the raft: "Which way through?"

"Keep well to the left of the logs," he bawled with a wave of his arm.

In a moment we entered a swifter stretch of water with rolling and plunging logs all about us, and as we passed a lower group of loggers, they called out something to us which we could not understand.

Then as the current carried us on they all stopped their work and stared at us in apparent amazement. As directed, we kept well to the left, but we suddenly found looming dead ahead a great log jam which almost completely blocked the channel, causing the current to meet the opposite bank almost at a right angles where it flowed directly into the shore, uprooting a stand of big trees in a swirling caldron. Down this wild shoot the logs were racing singly or in groups. Upon striking the shore they would batter at the uprooted trees, by this time completely stripped of bark and foliage, jamming in the process. We could not stop, could not reach the shore, and apparently we could not go on. The bouncing, churning logs were all about us, and the quickening current was carrying us on at an alarming rate.

"Swing hard to the right," yelled Pete over the roar of the waters. He was handling the stern paddle and I was in the bow. How we did it I do not know — sheer desperation, I guess. We dug our paddles into the water. We strained every muscle of back and arms, beating against the current, but being dragged along with it we spun through the chute and, missing the cauldron of logs and tangled roots only by inches, cleared the last log and shot into quieter water — seconds before the jam closed against the tangle of roots. It was some while before either of us could utter a word.

Lack of camping experience plus youthful appetites resulted in a definite shortage in our food supplies when we were still two days out of Portland. Thinking to replenish our stock we put in at a rickety little wharf which we thought marked the location of a village, but we found that it was only a boat landing where river steamers occasionally stopped for cord wood. A solitary old fellow with tobacco-stained gray bead was sitting on the dock fishing with a cane pole and a bobber. He looked us over for some time and then drawled, "D'ja come from sumwher?"

"Yes."

After another interval of quiet inspection, "Ya goin' sumwher?"

Again being advised in the affirmative and apparently well satisfied with the information thus elicited, he picked up his pole, sauntered slowly along the bank and disappeared among the trees. Fortunately a little further down the stream we were able to talk a farm wife out of half a loaf of bread and seven fresh eggs, which by dint of careful rationing, saw us to the end of our journey.

The trip provided material for my first attempt as a writer. I wrote up the story, embellished it with sketches and Kodak pictures taken on the trip, and sold it to the *Portland Oregonian* for thirty five dollars, which just about cover the expenses of the trip. And I had the satisfaction of seeing the article in the Sunday *Oregonian* of August 20, 1905.

Because of my father's sudden death in an accident in 1906, and the serious business of earning a living, coupled with my studies for admission to the bar, I found far less time for fishing, which then became a luxury.

Finding work was a matter of definite necessity, so I got a job as clerk in the Tax & Right-of-Way Department of the old Oregon Railroad & Navigation Company. On the side I made a few extra dollars painting window cards and signs for two department stores. I had always been interested in drawing and lettering for those were the days of the Gibson Girls and when Elbert Hubbard's mottoes hung in every parlor. I had copied a good many of them so when I was seeking work I had told the store management that I could do lettering. One day the telephone rang. It was for me.

"Is this Blaine Hallock, the card writer?" came over the wire.

I had never painted a real window card in my life, and knew almost nothing about what paint ingredients to use of how to go about it. Nevertheless, I sensed this was the opportunity for which I had been waiting.

"Yes," I responded, for that was partly true — I was Blaine Hallock.

"This is Mr. Bannon of Roberts Brothers. Our card writer has gone off on another of his periodic jags, and we fired him for the last time. Come down to the store right away."

I promptly presented myself, was ushered into the basement studio, given a lot of copy and was told to go to work. I had no brushes, paint, or other materials and had no notion of what I needed to launch out in that business. I thought lamp-black should make a good medium, so I bought a little bag of the fluffy greasy stuff and two or three brushes and hurried back to the basement. But when I tried to mix that pigment with water it merely floated on top and remained as dry as ever. In the meantime my employer was clamoring for bargain-day price cards. In sheer desperation I rummaged about and found some empty glass containers on a shelf and then discovered that a certain kind of water color paint was called tempera. I hustled out again and purchased a jar of this material, hopefully thinned it with water and was delighted to find that I had what I wanted. So far I was in luck. I went to work with trembling hands painting the cards and price tags. Why those people ever kept me on the job during those early days I do not know, for my work was conspicuously amateurish and crude. But perhaps they were impressed with my earnestness and zeal for I remember that as I struggled through the first day of this undertaking I kept repeating to myself, "I cannot fail, I cannot fail, and I will not fail." I might have actually voiced this sentiment to the point that it was overheard by some of the store people. At any rate, I kept the job and to this day I can make a creditable show card.

I must have acquired some proficiency during these weeks of struggle, for in my scrapbook I still have a letter from the store manager reading:

"TO WHOM IT MAY CONCERN: This is to advise
that the bearer Mr. Blaine Hallock, is the best card
writer we ever had, and he is also a gentleman."

But all this was merely earning a living. I was aiming higher as I was obsessed with the idea that I must be a lawyer. In those days the law school of the University of Oregon consisted of night courses and lectures held in Portland. So I enrolled, bought the required textbooks, and began the serious pursuit of that jealous mistress. Summer and winter for some three years I would get up about five o'clock in the morning, and with law book in hand, eat a hasty breakfast at a nearby lunch counter. Then I would hurry down to the railroad office in the old Wells Fargo Building, in the winter time long before daylight and pour through my textbooks until the other members of the force arrived. At the stroke of noon I would rush from the office, gulp a glass of milk with a doughnut and paint what window cards I could for one of the stores until one o'clock. Precisely at five thirty-one I would be at the other store and paint cards there until time for supper, completing the work for that day in a little attic room at home which I had equipped as a studio; then in to the law books until about eleven o'clock, when I would tumble into a very welcome bed. There were lectures twice a week in the evenings, and I kept up this program until I received my sheepskin.

I mention all this feverish work, partly because it emphasizes such a strong contrast to the prevalent present-day attitude of free help for everyone. In those days it never entered my mind, or the minds of my friends, that we either needed, or had any right to expect help, although I had two wealthy uncles. I knew that any success I might achieve depended solely upon my own efforts. As I view it now, in retrospect, I think it may have been too full and exacting a schedule for a boy of my age, but I also look back with the definite realization that it gave me an invaluable point of view which has served me well throughout my life. The best gifts of this earth are those which we earn by our own efforts. Yet in spite of my busy life I could always find a little time for reading. Not withstanding my heavy schedule and the necessity for dividing my thoughts between the railroad company's interests, show card writing, and the law, the subject of fishing would inevitably creep into my thinking. I would dream of catching a fish while trying a case or practicing law on a trout stream. My state of mind in those days is pretty well exemplified by what I composed in verses:

LEX DE PISCIBUS

Whereas to divers sundry streams,
The lusty trout his fate resigns,
Himself, his spouse, his next of kin,
His heirs, successors and assigns.
Now, therefore, go the anglers forth,
Inheritance of trout or dace
They would demand pursuant to
The ancient rule in Shelly's case.
Encumbered with deceitful lure
Of fly and spinner, plug and bait
They thrash along the sedgy banks
Or for a bite, but sit and wait.
But the aforesaid fish, to-wit:
These false inducements all decline,
Preferring nature's grub or worm,
To feathered hook or baited line.
Said anglers summon all their guile,
The weighty problem they discuss,
At last to get the fish they try
A writ of ha'-beus cor'-pus.

But contra to the angler's plan,
According to their native lights,
Said fish decide the thing to do
Is stand upon their Bill of Rights.

And so said fishes do prevail.
Each angler to his home retires.
Further deponent sayeth not,
Are fish or only lawyers liars?

But I did get in some nearby fishing, for we occasionally spent weekends at our little cottage on Neahkahnie beach near Nehalem, and when time permitted I could catch trout and bass in the clear waters of the Willamette River a short distance above Portland. By April, when trout season opened, there were still little rusty patches of snow lying on the higher levels. In the broken glades white trilliums glistened against the deep-green moss, and the first anemones had pushed up round heavy buds full of promise. There was a little stream flowing into the Columbia River not far from Portland called Young's Creek. I think of it as one of the prettiest, coolest, and most delightful little brooks I have ever known, and it was well supplied with small brilliantly spotted cutthroat trout. The stream tumbled down through the rocky defiles of Sheppard's Dell near Bridal Veil, and after a short trip through the quiet firs found its way to the Columbia. In places the brook plunged sheer for many feet, and the footing was uncertain. I used to fish it very slowly and carefully, keeping well out of sight of the little trout. On days when the fish did not bite readily, I could always bring home a creel full of wild flowers.

The Deschutes River, famous throughout the west for its many fighting rainbow trout, pursued its turbulent course through deep rocky gorges, and emptied into the Columbia about a hundred miles east of Portland. A night's run by rail would bring me to the fishing waters. Since I was a railroad employee then, I could get a pass, but I could not afford a sleeper, so I traveled both ways in a day coach. Now I would find two hot nights in a cramped and stuffy chair car, with a strenuous day's fishing in between, a tough proposition, but in those days it meant nothing. It was no trick at all to fill a number six basket with heavy, broad-backed, deep-bellied, rainbow trout from a foot to eighteen inches in length. Even as I write, I can smell the pungent sage, and feel the cool of the morning as I stepped off the train at North Junction. I can see the flash of blue on the mallard's wing, as he pursued his solitary flight up the lonesome canyon. Such things are impressed on the tablets of memory, though without conscious thought, and I am richer for them. But how much more vivid are the scenes and impressions of the actual angling. Every minute detail of this or that thrilling experience, with the straining rod and struggling trout, is caught and faithfully retained in the mind's eye.

One of my experiences on the Deschutes can never be forgotten. I stood in the shallow, hurrying water, where it broke at the head of a little gravelly island. A clump of snake grass had found footing in the meager slit between the larger stones, and I discovered a company of tiny grey flies clinging to the grasses. Now and then some of the insects, dislodged by the light breeze, floated out above the water. My discovery suggested a change of tackle, and I rigged a light tapered leader with three midget dry flies, size sixteen, of a pattern resembling my little neighbors of the grass. A few preliminary tries at the head of the riffle gave me the distance, and the flies were allowed to float down to the choppy, foam-flecked eddy, where something told me, there was sure to be a response. The flies were lost in the fretful wavelets, but the line indicated that they were quartering in from the edge of the riffle. I took up the least bit of slack, by slightly elevating the tip of the rod. There! A great, swirling, unmistakable lump stirred the water. I caught the gleam of red and silver. The line straightened, and a tiny hook was set hard in something that sent a quiver through eight and a half feet of seasoned bamboo. The water was clear, and deliciously cold blue-green out where the tightened line disappeared.

Across the canyon, great rugged hills, daubed with the blue and red of wild flowers, were brushed by white puffs of cloud.

I would drink in the scene, but there was no time to lose. The trout was not given to reflection, and already he had the situation well in hand. He rushed down with the current, and there was nothing to do but let him go. A size sixteen hook and a 3X leader were not designed to check the headlong rush of three pounds of fighting rainbow headed down stream in the center of the Deschutes River.

Away went the line to the accompaniment of an angry reel. Most of the backing had cleared the guides, and I put the leader to the test, by tightening the thumb pressure. This set the big fish nose up, and he cleared the torrent a full two feet. A hundred diamonds were flung from his broad tail, and I could not suppress a yell. The sound was caught and flung back by the high lava rock walls, a mocking challenge. This monarch of the roaring stream belonged to it and to the rocks and crags that guarded its wild journey. Again he was off, and I applied what drag the delicate leader would stand. A second and third time the great fish displayed his gleaming sides in two more mad somersaults. Each run brought him into swifter water, and the backing was all but gone. The fish had to be checked then if at all, and I braced against the pull of the straining rod, held upright, and bending dangerously. There was a moment's pause in the wild rush. A raven winged across the canyon and laughed derisively. The tip of the rod trembled like a living thing. I felt two or three premonitory tugs, and then the fighting trout, in a manner truly splendid, again threw himself high into the air, shook his lithe body from stubborn nose to speckled tail, and I was left to reel in two flies, and to find such solace as I could in my faithful pipes.

After Father's death and breakup of our household, Mother made her home with my married sister and for a year or so I lived with 0. S. Jackson and his family in Portland. I had been delivering the *East Oregonian* when Mr. Jackson published that paper in Pendleton. After moving to Portland, Jackson became the founder and publisher of the *Oregon Journal* which grew into a great metropolitan daily and produced a fortune for its owner. While I was at dinner with the Jackson family on the day they had just returned from an automobile trip across the continent, Mr. Jackson said to me, "Blaine, set a goal for yourself, aim at it constantly. Never let it out of your mind. Think of it not as a hope but as an assured conviction. See yourself attaining it. Know that it is going to come true."

I know that miracles could happen but it had never before occurred to me that I might have anything to do with their actual realization.

"That's a very interesting philosophy," I replied, "but how can a poor boy with no capital but his head and his hands get very far with such a program?"

"Just try it and see," said Mr. Jackson. "I've just returned with my family from an automobile trip of more than five thousand miles. That's part of the goal that I had set for myself when I too was a poor boy. I used to say to myself and I never once let go of the idea. By the time I am fifty I will own a big newspaper — I will have $50,000, I will travel five thousand miles, and I will spend $5,000. I have just passed my fiftieth birthday. I own a big newspaper; I have more than $50,000. I bought a big Lozier car, have completed a trip of more than five thousand miles, and I have spent more than $5,000. That's the way it works."

Well, then and there I set the same goal, except that I substituted the law for journalism. Those were busy days marked by pressure of necessity; but hardships, if such they were, became lighter. My goal was clearly before me. There were bar examinations taken with heart in mouth, eventually a position with the law department of the Union Pacific Railroad Company, marriage to the girl who wished she were a trout so that I would love her more, World War I with a stretch at a field artillery training camp and ultimately a law partnership in Baker, Oregon. Then my opportunities for fishing increased, and I found sufficient leisure to see a little of the world.

My first law office in the old Wells Fargo Building in Portland was a narrow little cubby-hole, just wide enough for a window at one end and a door at the other but under my name on the door appeared the magical word "Lawyer." I called it the Promised Land.

The Interstate Commerce Act required that railroads charge for their service no greater, smaller or different rates than were found in their duly published tariffs. Every so often an overworked rate clerk would quote to a prospective passenger or shipper a rate for the service different from that provided in the tariffs. Usually, long after the transaction had been concluded, the auditors would discover the error and under the law it became the duty of the particular carrier in question to collect the undercharge. That job fell to me. I read every statute and court decision on the subject and took my job most seriously. I could usually effect collection merely by writing a letter to the disgruntled patron explaining the situation; but occasionally when a substantial sum of money was involved, the shipper or passenger would resist the demand. One day, the chief clerk threw a file down on my desk and called attention to the fact that within the next few days I was to try a case against one of the more prominent shippers of flour who had paid the rate quoted by the rate clerk, a rate which actually reflected a substantial undercharge.

This was my first case in court. I had never even seen a case tried before and was definitely nervous and excited. Nevertheless, I reviewed all of my authorities and on the day of the trial I literally loaded down a taxicab with innumerable law books which I piled on the counsel table to the obvious dismay of the trial judge. When the case reached the point for argument I said to the judge — with some trepidation, "Of course, Your Honor is quite familiar with the rule of law involved in this case; but in as much as the authorities are numerous I may be able to refresh the court's recollection by referring to some of the more recent decisions."

With that the court responded, "Well, young man, let's not have any misunderstanding. The court doesn't know anything at all about the law of this case, so I have no recollection to be refreshed. Just go ahead and outline your position. Proceed as though the Court had never before heard a case of this kind, which incidentally, is the fact. But I will say this; if you are going to contend that after an agent or representative of the railroad company has demanded a particular rate and that rate has been paid and the transaction closed, that the railroad company is then justified in trying to collect more moneys you are going to be confronted with a mighty high hurdle in this court. Now, go ahead."

Opposing counsel who was defending the case on the ground of estoppel* bowed approvingly to the judge, smiled on his client, and with a triumphant grin in my direction settled himself comfortably in his chair.

What should I say now? For that matter, with the unaccustomed lump rising in my throat could I say anything at all? How would the fellows in the office greet me when I came dragging back to replace my books on the shelves?

My books! — That was it! — My precious books! With a preliminary gulp or two I was able to swallow the lump and start on the books. I knew every case almost by heart, and I read from one after another. It soon became obvious that the judge was impressed. In about two hours I had got through nearly a third of the books when the judge stopped me.

"Now, what say you?" He nodded to opposing counsel. The grin had long since faded from his face for anticipating his position. I had completely shattered his defense of estoppel. In fact there was no respectable law for such a contention under the transportation act.

My opponent got to his feet and spoke for about ten minutes without submitting a single supporting case.

"Have you authorities for your position?" asked the Judge.

"There are none!" I made so bold as to interject.

"I am standing on the broad principals of estoppel," said the defense lawyer.

*Estoppel: A legal bar to alleging or denying a fact because of one's previous act or statement to the contrary.

"If that is all", said the Judge, "you may as well be seated. Those principals are not broad enough for you to stand on in a case like this."

The judge then went on at some length to lament the fact that contraty to his former position he found it necessary to find against the defendant, even though it seemed to him quite inequitable. And he concluded, "Plaintiff may take judgment as demanded with statutory interest, costs, and disbursements. Court adjourned."

As opposing counsel and his witnesses filed sadly out of the courtroom, several newspaper reporters promptly surrounded me and began to ask questions. I felt very important.

The next morning, after returning the books to their shelves in the big central library, I entered my tiny office with a broad smile, but it was short-lived.

W. W. Cotton, a small man with a round face, a bald head, and sharp piercing eyes, was the chief of then law department. When I entered my cubby-hole I found him pacing back and forth between the door and the desk.

At first I was flattered to think that he had called to compliment me on my great victory. He had entered my office only once before on the occasion when I had just been installed in my new quarters, at which time he had given me a broad smile, dropped a little calendar on my desk, and said, "Give me an answer to that." On the calendar appeared a little verse readings:

> "An answer to this question
> Is what I simply wish.
> Does fishing make men liars,
> Or do only liars fish?"

It was with much satisfaction that I was able to respond in verse, returning the calendar the following day with this:

> "In answer to your question
> I fain would volunteer
> A plea for humble fisherman,
> So lend me, pray, your ear.
>
> The river stretches to the sea,
> The mountains reach the skies.
> The angler sees the universe
> Expand before his eyes.
>
> The atmosphere of fishermen
> Is big, and broad, and high.

And if perchance, they stretch the truth,
Why call the yarn a lie?

What though the facts expand a bit
As circumstance requires.
All liars are not fishermen
Nor are all anglers liars."

But it was not in any such mood that Mr. Cotton favored me with a visit the morning after my victory in court. His face was flushed and he angrily flung on my desk a copy of the *Morning Oregonian*. On the front page of the paper in glaring headlines appeared the following:

COURT SCORES RATE HE HAS TO ALLOW
Railroad wins in motion it prosecutes
unwillingly, fearing to be fined.

The article occupied a full column and still appears in my old scrapbook under dateline June 29, 1915. I quote but a brief portion of it, opining with these words:

"It's an outrageous robbery," declared Circuit
Judge Morrow indignantly, yesterday, supple-
menting "outrageous" by a descriptive adjective
of force when he ruled, against his desire, in favor
of the plaintiff in a suit of the Oregon-
Washington Railroad & Navigation Company to
collect exorbitant freight charges from the
Columbia Milling Company of Portland.

"What in hell did you think you were doing?" sputtered Cotton. "Didn't you know that when the tariff was printed it con-tained a typographical error and named a rate that was monstrous on its face?"

"No, I didn't," I stammered. "I thought the Chief Clerk knew what he was doing when he told me to try the case and I..."

"The Chief Clerk ought to be fired, and so should you, exploded Mr. Cotton. "We have had an application pending before the Interstate Commerce Commission for a long time requesting author-ity to correct the tariff and charge off this unconscionable item. You ought to have known all about it."

With that he turned on his heel, left the office, and closed the door with a bang. All the brilliant colors of my rainbow had faded into a dull gray. But I wasn't fired.

Then came marriage to Lillian, the girl who wished she were a trout so that I would love her more, World War I with a stretch at a field artillery training scamp, and ultimately a law partnership in Baker, Oregon. I never quit thinking about my goal, as suggested by Mr. Jackson. It finally ripened into a firm conviction that some day that miracle too would happen.

Soon came the big George Graham Rice case which took me to New York for almost a year. Rice was a wealthy Jew who had earlier changed his name from Hertzog. He was interested in many mining ventures including the development of an emerald property in Columbia and certain copper mining interests along the Snake River near the now famous Hells Canyon not far from Baker. The fee was a good one.

My experience in the great metropolis, working on the Rice case and living almost a prisoner with Rice and his wife — whose quarters occupied the whole top floor of the Chatham hotel — is a story in itself. I shall not attempt to inject any part of that busy year into this narrative except to mention a little incident disclosing the ready wit with which this remarkable man, Rice, was endowed. Like many city-bred American Jews who had accumulated wealth, he had become quite cosmopolitan.

Returning to the Federal Court House in the big Rolls-Royce one day after lunch, with Rice resplendent in a Russian sable-lined coat and smoking a long black cigar, we were accosted by a ragged hobo as we stepped to the curb who edged up to Rice and said, "Will you give me a dime?"

Rice presented him with a crisp new dollar bill.

"Jesus," said the bum as he examined the bill in his grimy hand. Then he looked up at Rice, again down at the bill, ejaculating, "God Almighty,"

Rice, with his characteristic grin, responded, "Wait a minute fellow, you're promoting me too fast — better call me Abraham."

On the heels of this Rice case came other important legal work, together with a highly successful business venture. And almost before I realized it, my goal had been attained; for though I was not yet fifty I already had both the leisure and the means to take my long-delayed first trip abroad.

Salmon on Nehalem Bay

Faster and more fast
O'er nights brim day boils at last."

Browning

Flaunting its rolling crimson clouds the dawn climbed above the ragged spruces and bathed the many colored slopes of old Neahkahnie Mountain and the long white lines of surf at its base with the ripe mellow tints of an Indian summer morning. It was September. The violets of June which had painted the whole mountain-side and the lower rolling meadows above the sea a delicate lavender, and the myriad purple irises of July, had given way to the brilliant fireweed and Indian paint brush of late summer.

With my brother-in-law Jim Welch, long since departed to the happy fishing grounds, I trudged down the dewy slope, on that quiet morning, bent on a day's angling at the bay some three miles distant, and glanced back at the majestic pile. The sun was just tipping its rocky summit. There it stood, the mountain of Neahkahnie, frowning down upon the wrinkled sea below. And I meditated upon the mystery of the mountain, and of the sea beach stretching to the south.

Jutting out into the restless billows, from an impenetrable forest of spruce, fir, and hemlock, the mountain presents a south slope devoid of trees, save for a few clusters of second growth here and there in the deep ravines, and a bold stand of birches clinging to the sheer walls of the cliff far down the rough incline. The soil is intensely fertile, yet produces only meadow grass, salal, ferns and wild flowers. Did some mighty cataclysm, ages ago, send a once flourishing growth like that of the forests to the north, hurtling down the mountain in a mad landslide to the hungry sea, leaving a bare slope to seed, centuries later, with fern and shrub? Did the Indians, as tradition has it, fire this mountain on the sea side so that green meadows might develop and afford better hunting grounds for the little brown deer which even now come down to the springs for water?

And the mystery of a treasure cove — that wild pocket at the mountain's base where roving pirates are reported to have buried fabulous wealth. Who knows what lawless band adopted as its strong-hold this rockbound cove where sea birds wheel out in widening circles and scream above the incessant pounding of the waves? At least two rock tablets have been found in the vicinity bearing inscriptions in a locked cipher, perhaps the mystic "Open Sesame" to the buccaneer's cache. Many venturesome souls, in search of hidden treasure, have explored the damp and hazardous recesses of the cove, but I know of no more valuable discovery than a battered sea chest, empty and rusted.

There is also the enigma of the Nehalem wax. For a distance of several miles down the beach from the mountain many discoveries of this peculiar substance have been made. These finds are shrouded in doubt. Not only is its source, but also the very substance itself a mystery. It is found in pieces varying in size from a baseball to a wash tub and analyzes more nearly common beeswax than any other known substance. Many people in the neighborhood cling to the belief that it is bits of what was once an ill-fated ship's cargo, wrecked there many years ago, and this theory appears to be pretty well substantiated through investigation by the United States Department of Interior. Some of the pieces bear strange hieroglyphic carvings.

Not the least of the mysteries of Nehalem is the eternal puzzle of the salmon. Year after year, without a pilot, with no charts to aid their navigation, with nothing to guide them but their infallible instinct, countless thousands of Chinook and Silver Salmon thread their certain way along the unmarked paths of the trackless ocean, straight into the shallow and devious channel of Nehalem Bay.

And this brings me back to my fishing.

In those days the quaint, sleepy little town of Nehalem straggled along the margin of the bay on the north, and was seriously threatened by a very obstinate and flourishing growth of trees and brush encroaching from the hills above. The town presented an aspect of uncertainty. It appeared to have approached the bay with some misgivings, establishing itself temporarily up by the old cannery. Then gathering courage, it seemed to ramble, further down, pausing here and there, until it finally settled in the little hollow against the western hills.

At Nehalem, after a forty-minute walk from the mountain, we negotiated the rent of a small skiff, loaded in our miscellaneous assortment of tackle, and were on the point of shoving off when an ancient mariner who had been skeptically eyeing our movements from the wharf above volunteered a bit of advice.

"Ye ain't goin' to try it on this tide, are ye?"

"What's the matter with it?" I inquired.

A broad grin wrinkled his weathered face, "Ye won't catch nothin' but seaweed when she's runnin' like this. You're wastin' your time. Wait for the ebb."

"When is the ebb?" I asked with some misgivings.

He pulled out a little, much-thumbed table, and ran his finger down a column of figures.

"Seventeen minutes after five."

I looked at Jim. We had hurried three miles through the woods because we wanted a full day on the bay, and we had promised them at the cottage we would be back for dinner at six o'clock sharp. It was then eight in the morning.

"And say," spouted a boy who had joined the old man, "better take off that there copper riggin'. These fish wants this kind of a hook. Won't take nothin' else."

He displayed a big red and silver combination which looked

more like a lady's hat ornament than any fish hook I had ever seen.

We were crestfallen. Our kit boasted no such marvelous contraption. This was our first day on the bay and bid fair to be a failure. Rather mechanically Jim began to take down his rod. A little bunch of seaweed drifted by. I noticed for the first time that there were many similar patches floating in on the tide.

The old man had left us, evidently feeling that he had done his full duty and we were worth no further consideration on his part. The boy turned and started away.

"Say, boy," I called, "How much for the hook?"

He looked at it lovingly. "I got five on it yesterday," he volunteered.

"What'll you take for it?"

"And Bob got three Sunday, and the day before that — "

We listened for no more

"I'll give you fifty cents," I shouted, by way of opening a trade.

That boy was fully ten feet from our boat, but he covered the distance — in a bound.

"It's yours," With a face struggling to suppress his glee, he pocketed the coin, grinned at us for a moment, and said, "If you need any more, you can get 'em over there at the store, two for a quarter."

"Jim," I said, "we're a couple of fools."

"So you are," said Jim.

With that we decided to adopt our original plan. Why not fish on a running tide? We were there with the whole day before us. We would fish even though it was a forlorn hope. Rowing a boat was better than sitting on a wharf waiting for the tide to turn.

So we started out. If we caught no fish at least we could enjoy the scenery. The morning was ideal. Over against the west, indistinct in the haze, a long, yellow line marked the sand spit dividing the placid waters of the bay from the billowing sea. We noted the very spot where the ill-fated *Mimi* had ridden the breakers and grounded herself on an even keel high on the beach. This ship, precisely like the *Gleneslyn*, which, a year or two later had wedged itself among the rocks at the base of Neahkahnie Mountain, had come in from the open ocean in broad daylight and fair weather, and had headed straight for the shore. What subsequent investigation respecting these strange wrecks may have developed I do not recall, if I ever did find out, but the hulls of both are grim reminders of these strange voyages of so many years ago. Can it be that somewhere out beyond the Nehalem River as it spills into the sea, a Lorelei lured the mariners shoreward to destruction with dulcet song as did the treacherous nymphs of the ancient Rhine? There would seem to be no reason for a shipwreck in that particular place. To the east the verdant hills closed in about the upper reaches of the bay and quite concealed the river's outlet hid away among the meadows. Monarch spruces on the south shore, with their bare roots twisting into the bay, extended heavy-festooned branches which brushed the surface of the waters.

A half hour's pull up the bay netted us nothing but frequent bunches of seaweed, and some well-meant advice from a passing fisherman that our tackle was all wrong.

"That red thing would scare a shark," he assured us. "What you want is a number six nickel spinner sunk deep with a couple of ounces of lead."

Our suspicions as to the feathered contraption, already having been somewhat aroused, we willingly made the change, started afresh and trolled for nearly an hour before receiving further advice. Then a swarthy young fellow in a heavy boat approached just as we were cleaning seaweed from our hooks for the hundredth time that morning. We didn't see him until we had bumped into his boat.

"In the first place," he snapped, "no fish in the bay would take that. You want a brass tandem and no lead at all. In the second place, fish don't bite on this tide. And in the third place, if you did hook one he'd smash those whips you're usin' first flop. Throw 'em overboard and use a hand line like we do."

We drifted apart.

"I beg your pardon," Jim called after him with an apologetic air. "You see this is our first try and we are a little green," and he added, "I hope we're not in the way here."

I was irked. The thing was getting on my nerves. I began to unstring my rig.

"Going to try the brass?" queried Jim.

"No, I'm not going to try the brass, nor the nickel, nor the feather, nor the lead. I'm going to put on the number five copper, as we originally intended, and I'm going to fish on this running tide in spite of all the seaweed and all the advice in Tillamook County. And I'm going to catch fish. And I'd advise you to do the same."

We got back to our first love, the copper spoons, and out went the hooks. We were under way again.

"See that old bunch of piling," said Jim, catching the spirit. "Before we get there I'll have a..."

He never finished the sentence. I heard the hum of his reel. I saw his rod twice whack the gunwale. I saw him clutch at the grips as his line went out in long spurts. I saw him jump to his feet, with the light of joy in his eyes — that inexplicable joy known only to fishermen. The game was on!

"Owee" he yelled, "look at that!"

Forty yards away a huge, silvery monster cleared the water and hit it again with a mighty splash.

What followed I shall not attempt to describe. To you who have caught salmon, the story is old. And those of you who have not, must have the experience before you will understand. Like all big Chinooks, fresh from the sea, and hooked in salt water on light tackle, this fish of Jim's fought with every ounce of his strength. He rushed and leaped. He circled about the boat. He went deep and "sulked" for many minutes. He was often worked carefully to the boat, only to gush away again, leaving a path of bubbles in his wake.

At last, after a long, hard contest, and to our intense relief, the big fish was led to gaff, and hauled aboard. Our first salmon of the season, caught in our own fashion, on an unprecedented tide, and with a hook which was the subject of local derision!

"Jim," I said, "not so bad. But watch me now. We've drifted way below the piling. I'll hook one before we get back." And I did.

What magic there was about the dolphin, or the water in its vicinity, I shall not pretend to say. But the fact remains that of the many trips we made that memorable day, up and down past the weathered stand of piling, not one failed to reward us with a strike.

How the sun got over into the west and slid into the sea while we thought it was still morning, I do not know. That we, with our beach appetites, should forget all about lunch also remains one of the mysteries of Nehalem. Why the long shadows stretched away from the spruces in midday, and what strange phenomenon painted the placid surface of the bay with evening purple and gold, when by all reason it should have been noon, I cannot understand. But I do know this. We hooked and played that day fourteen Royal Chinooks, and of them we landed seven. We lovingly picked out one fish and left the others at the cannery to be packed. I shall not soon forget that evening trudge through the quiet woods with the tail of a big Chinook strung on a stick across our shoulders, striking Jim's heels at every step.

"What's the joke, Jim?" I asked, for I had heard him softly chuckling.

"I was just thinking," he said, "how we two lubberly amateurs exploded the theory of salmon fishing on a running tide."

The chapter "Salmon on Nehalem Bay" first appeared in The Oregon Sportsman, *Volume III, Number 6, 1915.*

CHAPTER

East is East

L ong ago I saw a perfect model of the great mortuary shrines at Nikko, on the base of which was lettered the famous Japanese proverb, "Never say Magnificent until you have seen Nikko." It was a masterpiece of workmanship as the Japanese possess positive genius for creating the minute. I lingered for hours gazing at every tiny detail, the quiet pools, avenues of cryptomaria trees, great flights of steps, torii, temples, pagodas, lanterns and even people; all flawless, precise, ingenious and beautiful. It glowed with gold, frescoes and lacquer, even the incomparable wood carving complete to the last detail. In fact I believe one could obtain from the miniature a clearer concept of the whole plan than by actually walking in the noble park itself. So when I actually did get to Nikko it was with a feeling of real familiarity that I strolled among the matchless wonders of the shrine. A good Moslem must make his pilgrimage to Mecca and prostrate himself before the animistic Black Stone before he can hope to enter the Pearly Gates, but the Japanese must see Nikko before he dies. It is a solemn but happy place, for the Japanese are a reverent people and they come to worship as well as to admire; to refresh and enjoy themselves.

We found in Nikko an atmosphere of quiet repose. All seemed silent, though birds called as they flitted about in the splashes of sunshine and shade, golden crickets chirruped, and the people laughed and chatted in their soft musical voices. Sunlight sifting down through the great trees fell on little knots and groups of pilgrims, the women dressed in their flowery kimonos, with huge embroidered obis at their backs. The men wore the classic silk robes of the elite or the picturesque faded blue and white kimonos of the simpler peasants. Occasionally an innovator, taken up with occidental ideas, would appear among the throngs and give us cause to wonder whether contact with the western world had been an unmitigated blessing after all. One nut-brown old fellow with a flowing gray mustache wore a pair of knee-length shiny black American gum boots, white linen pantaloons, a long black frock coat and a high silk hat. Another was arrayed in an old-fashioned white cotton union suit with buttons from crotch to neck, many of which, because of the heat of the bright September day had lost companionship with the button-holes across his swarthy chest and belly. This, together with a black derby hat and high-laced American shoes, constituted his entire raiment. Picnic basket and camera in hand he was off for a day of sightseeing, calm and unconcerned, but to us astonished observers he gave the frightful impression of a dream walking. Nearly all wore those outlandish wooden sandals so delightful to behold. They are made of an oblong slab of wood across the bottom of which are wooden cleats an inch or more in height. The sandal is held to the foot by two thongs which separate the big and next toe, so that at best the pedestrian has but a "toe-hold." Yet I have never seen a Japanese cast a shoe either running or walking over any sort of terrain. Upon entering the shrine the worshipers discard their sandals at the entrance, substituting for them soft slippers made of light matting, or entering in stocking feet. So foreign visitors follow the Oriental custom, leave their shoes at the doorway, and come to realize the wisdom and beauty of the old tradition, for the halls are silent and peaceful in spite of the throngs within. The coolness and luxury of treading over the polished floors or thickly padded matting carpets puts one completely in the spirit to gaze with admiration and wonder. These people pass into the glorious golden shrines, their altars adorned with baskets of fruit and flowers arranged as only that nation of perfectionists can, and there they prostrate themselves on the floor, remaining on hands and knees for long intervals of time. Much in their service reminds one of the rituals in the Roman Catholic Church and the worshipers who cross themselves with Holy Water and drop to one knee before entering the pews in their cathedrals. Though the Japanese laugh and chatter as they go about the paths from shrine to shrine, there is nothing boisterous or loud about their conduct. Rather there is a real sense of tranquility and piety.

The village of Nikko is situated high up in the cryptomaria forest. These big trees, somewhat resembling our western cedars, but with foliage far more delicate, cover a substantial area about the town. At some distance from the commodious Americanized hotel along the shaded, mossy stone way stand the Thousand Buddha, powerfully impressive in their passive reverie, and all so venerable that they are covered with lichen. There they have stood since the memory of man runneth not to the contrary. At the foot of the lush green hills just above the inn and flowing toward the town under the ancient and glorious red-lacquered bridge plunges the frothing Daiya River which gouges out a deep green pool directly under the bridge. It may be that since the end of World War II common man is permitted to walk across its high-arched span, but up to the time of my sojourn in Nikko, no profane foot had trod its deck, the Emperor alone being privileged to cross it. Our ex-President, General Grant, when traveling in Japan was extended the great courtesy thus far enjoyed only by Emperors, but he tactfully declined the honor because he did not wish to violate the ancient tradition.

One look at the sparkling river convinced me that I must fish it if humanly possible, although I had learned from the genial Japanese proprietor of the hotel that its waters were not available to the general public. However, yielding to my persistent western importunities he finally agreed that I might fish the pool under the bridge if I deported myself in the orthodox Japanese manner.

My tackle had gone forward to Hong Kong in our trunk so I had to use borrowed native equipment. A Japanese fishing rod is made like a walking stick. It consists of about three feet of bamboo, the knarled, bulky, bulb-shaped root comprising the handle, with a brass collar and plate at the base. When the disc from this collar is unscrewed one may pull out a series of bamboo joints, constructed much like the modern telescoping steel rod. At the end of the tip there is a little loop of strong cord. A line is tied to the loop along, which there are a series of bright-colored feathers spaced at intervals of about three or four feet. When the baited hook is lowered into the water these feathers disclose its depth from the surface. A white feather may indicate four feet, a red one six feet, a blue one eight feet and so on.

In addition to supplying the rod my accommodating host furnished two Japanese guides or gillies, and down the hill we went. One of the attendants carried a small wooden tub. The other had a little pail containing a number of live grampuses which he had evidently secured earlier from the submerged rocks along the edge of the stream. Before we arrived at the deep pool under the bridge I discovered that neither attendant could speak a word of English.

When we came to the stream the man with the tub filled it with water. The other impaled a grampus upon the hook and with many gestures indicated to me that I should lower it into the pool until the blue feather rested upon the surface. This I did, and sure enough, there was soon a vigorous pull on the line, and striking the fish, I discovered that I was fast to a sparkling two-pound trout. The surprise of the gillies was obvious; as it was evident they expected little of me. I wanted to play the fish until it was sufficiently exhausted to be led to the shore and employed such tactics in handling the trout as the unusual character of the rod would permit, but I could see that this was not at all satisfactory to my Japanese assistants. They both uttered piercing yells, jumped about on the rocks and gesticulated with wild antics indicating that I should yank out the trout forthwith. I never saw two human creatures display more excitement than did those Japanese helpers while I was playing the fish and bringing it to shore. The keeper of the tub promptly grabbed it, extracted the hook and placed the startled fish in the tub where it swam about frantically. The same performance was repeated until I had caught three fish, all about the same size. Two of them were eastern brook trout which, of course had been planted in the stream. The other was much like our native rainbow trout, but of a more purplish cast with bluish bands resembling par marks on its sides.

When I had caught the third fish and it had followed the others into the tub, my companions of the Rising Sun indicated by unmistakable gestures that I had caught enough, that the fishing was over, and that we should take our catch up to the hotel. That was all right with me for I had enough for supper. So up the ferny trail we went, with the tub bearer in the lead. At the hotel they set the tub on the floor in the center lobby, and the Japanese guests, as well as the hotel personnel, came out and gazed in rapture. Thereupon my host spoke to the tub man, who stepped forward, promptly hoisted the tub and carried it, fish and all down to the stream where he liberated them without further ceremony! How many times those same fish may have been caught, both before and after my brief acquaintance deponent saith not, but I can imagine that they have given many a tourist the satisfaction of capture.

A visitor to those foreign shores is entranced by the daintiness and beauty of the whole landscape, the mossy paths, and the musical woodlands, the quiet of ages, and the gentle acquired manners of all the people. They work hard, early and late, tilling every inch of available ground, and in their eagerness to catch fish, which is perhaps, except for rice, the most important item of their diet, whole families go far out to sea in little boats. The inbound tourist, looking off across the water from the deck of his ship sees that Japan is indeed a strange country when he watches those frail boats very far out from shore. The fishermen all wear faded blue garments and big sheltering picturesque straw hats. Large straw baskets overflowing with shiny silvery fish fill all available space in the boats except a tiny patch of deck protected by a matting sunshade where the inevitable tea is brewed and served.

In the larger cities such as Yokohama and Tokyo, the fish markets are inviting and artistic with their bright wares in charming baskets and lacquered tubs, while the parks abound in fairy lakes full of exotic gold and silver fish, with always an appreciative audience of dark-eyed children and soft spoken kimono-clad mothers holding their gay parasols against the sun.

Although completely charmed by Japan of those pre-Pearl Harbor days, our itinerary took us south where I was to explore other oriental fishing possibilities and in a few days we were sipping shandy-gaff on the spacious veranda of the exotic old Hotel Raffles in Singapore, the melting pot of the world. On any of its principal thoroughfares, and at any time of the day or night, we could rub elbows with people of every color and clime, race and religion, white, yellow, brown, black, tall and short, rich and poor, princes and paupers, Christians, Moslems, Buddhists, and Jews. It was all a kaleidoscopic jumble of race, color and jargon. The streets were a medley of eastern and western architecture, shops, bazaars, cafes, saloons, limousines, rickshaws, trucks, donkey carts and teeming humanity. In the circular blue bay fronting the town we could see, all jumbled together, every conceivable type of water craft from the great steel dreadnaughts bristling with guns to the lateen-sailed junks and matting-cabined sampans. Sparkling white, sharp-nosed yachts of the rich rode at anchor alongside greasy tankers and clumsy tugs, while great ocean liners, both freight and passenger, carrying flags of every maritime nation on earth, lay in the roadsteads where half naked brown skinned Malayans paddled their long rakish canoes with big staring eyes painted on the bows. Monkeys swung from the trees in parks and near-by jungle forests and with wizened faces and comical grimaces, begged for bananas and tidbits, sometimes even threatening us when we tried to get away before completely disgorging our obvious supply of fruit or candy. The sun beat down upon the rubber plantations and fields of pineapple and upon the hot and dirty streets and byways, but in the breezy old hotel we were more comfortable when content to forget the Occidental custom of bedroom privacy. The doors to the apartments were nothing more than latticed panels extending barely higher than our heads with two feet of open space at the bottom, swinging back and forth on spring hinges, much like the entrances to old-fashioned saloons.

Yes, there was good fishing at Singapore, so my black-skinned guide informed me. When I asked him how I should dress, whether to wear gum boots and what tackle I should bring along, he promptly assured me that I could come just as I was and that the tackle would be supplied. He even suggested that I bring my wife along, expressing the notion that she too might enjoy the fishing, so off we went. Our route took us north of the city toward Jahore, past steaming swamps, through patches of jungle and among rubber plantations where sheets of the noisome white flabby substance hung to dry on acres of bamboo poles, and by fields of pineapple ripening in the sun. We purchased a pineapple for a song and ate it in the car as we rode along. No one who has tasted only canned pineapple, or even those shipped to this country fresh and sold in the grocery stores and fruit markets, can have any idea of the exquisite deliciousness and tender succulent quality of a tropical pineapple wrenched from its protecting bayonet like leaves and eaten on the spot. Next to the heavenly flavor of a fresh ripe mangosteen of Bali, I can think of no more delicious fruit.

When we arrived at a little zoo under the palms near the strait which separates the island of Singapore from the Asiatic mainland, our guide parked the car and took us to see the strange animals and birds. Imagine our surprise when he led us to a pen containing what he said was the most interesting exhibit there — a flock of American turkeys! We had quite forgotten that this bird, after all America's only contribution to the domestic creatures, was quite wild when this continent was discovered and was probably as interesting to the jumbled population of Singapore as would be a cockatoo or a bird of paradise to us here at home. I finally had to remind the guide that we had come on a fishing, not a zoological excursion. With ready assent he walked us out upon a little dock at the edge of the zoo and led us to a space in the center about fifty feet square where some of the planking over the piling had been removed. This left a hole both above and below the water, which was fenced in with chicken wire. Leaving us there for a moment he shortly returned with two long bamboo cane rods equipped with heavy chalk lines and big iron hooks, each baited with a chunk of clam. He explained that the proprietor of the zoo kept this pseudo aquarium well stocked with fish which he periodically seined from the sea, and that all we had to do was to lower the bait over the low chicken wire railing, drag up a captive fish and pay for it at so much per pound. I had some difficulty in explaining to him that this was not quite the type of fishing which I had in mind, where-upon with evident disgust, he returned the tackle and sulked all the way back to the hotel. And that was my fishing in Singapore!

Yellow Tail in Salt Water

S pencer Biddle and I have been fishing companions on many waters for many years. If a man ever lived who could handle a dry fly with more delicacy and skill than Spen, I have never heard of him. It was he who taught me how to drift a tiny bundle of feathers and silk downstream on turbulent water, keeping it as dry as thistle-down; and this, too, long after I had modestly considered myself quite an expert with a dry fly. Spen would spot a lusty feeding trout well over toward the other side of the stream. But instead of casting directly at the fish as one might expect, he would move ahead, study the current, and, by a series of false casts, would whip out an unbelievable length of line and allow the fly to settle on the surface well above the fish, but in the line of flow. Just as the fly touched the water, Spen would check the cast and lower the tip of the rod. As a result of this method, several yards of slack line would follow the fly. Then by slightly waving the rod, and stripping line from the reel, at the same time allowing the slack to straighten out with the current, he would float the fly ever closer to the feeding trout. Thus he was able to avoid cross drifts and that fatal agitation of the surface by leader and line, so sure to put the fish down.

It would be a sullen trout indeed that would refuse the morsel proffered with such perfect technique. I have watched Spen take many fine trout in this way from Silver Creek in Idaho, the Deschutes and the McKenzie rivers in Oregon, the truly glorious Chilko in British Columbia, and from many other big-water streams.

It is said that when the Duke of Windsor, then the dashing Prince of Wales, visited America years ago and was entertained in historic old Philadelphia, he heard the word "biddle" used so often that he finally asked, "What is a biddle"? I do not know what answer he received, but had the question been put to me I could have answered it readily. A biddle is that unhappy result experienced by a dry-fly fisherman when, in his eagerness to hook the trout, he strikes too vigorously and leaves the fly set in the fish's bony jaw. It is an aggravating occurrence, and in Spen's particular case, a little short of a phenomenon, for he is a superb angler. Yet for some inexplicable reason, when he raises a heavy trout, Spen will occasionally strike too hard. We who fish with him never cease to be surprised at the bungle, and, because he mates so few errors in technique, we have come to call it a biddle.

I remember our first trip to Silver Creek. It is a big, placid, crystal-clear, spring-fed stream that flows through miles of high meadow land with only here and there a clump of willows to foul a long back cast. The trout are big, some of them are huge, and because of their size and vigor, to say nothing of the deep beds of aquatic weeds which characterize the stream, many a fish is biddled. In fact, on this occasion, we organized, and became charter members of the "Fooh Club." The name was coined from repeated ejaculations of fellow fishermen strung up and down the stream. One would hook a good trout and yell, "fish on" but when biddling the trout with too vigorous a strike, or when the fish was well hooked but would escape by diving into a tangle of submerged moss and weeds, there would immediately follow, to be borne on the spring breeze, the supplement "Oh, hell." Hence the name "Fooh Club."

The technique used on the Bay of Ensenada down on the coast of Lower California was wholly different. There when we went after yellow tail I had an even chance with this truly remarkable fisherman. We had crossed the border at Texicala in Spen's station wagon, leaving his Palm Springs home one sunny morning. We took along his springer pup, Tuckie, as well as a generous assortment of miscellaneous tackle, and our shotguns, for both the shooting and fishing in this part of Old Mexico are excellent.

The first evening about suppertime we got stuck in the mud on one of the typical Mexican dirt roads through that section of the country where cotton is grown and many of the roads are transformed into bogs from over-enthusiastic irrigation. It was well after dark when a group of friendly Mexicans appeared through the gloom and with the aid of their team of mules, and a couple of fence rails, we got the car pried out. We were well nigh exhausted from our struggles as we went about the task of making camp and preparing supper. Spen suggested that we just open a couple of cans of prepared hash, warm it in the frying pan over our feeble sagebrush fire and call it a day. As chief cook this job fell to me. I fumbled about in the dark found the cans, heated the mixture and we gulped it down with that relish born of hearty out-of-door exercise. But in the morning when cleaning up camp, I found two freshly emptied dog food cans near the fire!

The next day we had lunch on the shore of a slough or backwater of the hardy Colorado River and as we munched avocado sandwiches we noticed several good-sized fish breaking the surface of the water. We hastily rigged our tackle, and put out our flies. But we soon learned that, although the fish would strike readily enough, they were either too quick to be hooked, or were doing what fishermen call "rising short." The fish appeared to weigh a pound or more, their backs were silvery and their bellies snow white. We were much interested in them for they were new to us, but we did not hook a single fish.

About that time I saw a very black Mexican approaching us along the dusty road. He was wearing a big straw sombrero, and as he jogged along on his sleepy-looking mule, his bare feet nearly touched the ground. I hailed him, and in a faltering manner patched together the following inquiry in my inadequate Spanish, "El favor, Signor. Como se llama estos piscados?"

He promptly responded, in excellent English, "Well, down here we call them lisa, but I think up north they are called mullet. They are damn good fish too, but hard to catch."

That night we pitched our camp in the shadow of a massive shattered monolith of basalt rock which rose sheer from the salt grass plain. All day long as we traveled south through the hot sunshine, trying to find a town called San Felipe, we could see this huge landmark. In the glare of day it looked brown and forbidding, but as the evening shadows lengthened, and beckoned us on, its color changed to a rich purple with its shattered top edged in gold. Throughout Northern Mexico, and our great Southwest, these lone shafts stand isolated in the desert while all around the brassy sun beats relentlessly down on the parched earth. To the casual observer, riding comfortably in his air-conditioned Pullman car, they seem but a harsh feature in a harsh landscape. But to him who picks his painful way through dust and heat, they are as beneficent as an oasis to a caravan. We crawled into the grateful shade with a full understanding of the heart of the prophet Isaiah thankfully praising his Maker with the eloquent words, "Thou art like unto the shadow of a great rock in a weary land."

From scattered patches of mesquite, cacti, and thorn brush, coveys of Gamble quail burst with a whirr of wings. Little brown rabbits scurried through the cotton fields and toward evening flights of doves gathered in occasional clumps of willow. This night it was Tuckie who got the canned dog food for his supper, while we ate a big pot of steaming mulligan, containing quail, dove, and rabbit. When the embers of our camp fire faded into the night, a cooling breeze drifted in and we welcomed the warmth of our sleeping bags.

We found the so-called roads impassable south of the rock, as well as from east to west over the ridge of mountains which is the backbone of Lower California, so we had to double back nearly to the border. But we did ultimately find a way through, and arrived at Ensenada at last.

For some distance south of the California line, the coast is edged with gentle-sloping grassland which pitches sharply into the sea, with here and there short stretches of pebbly beach. We fished from the low cliffs and along the beaches, and caught a varied assortment of salt water fish, kelp, rock cod, porgies, and perch on sandworms and tidbits of mussel. No two fish were alike. Their colors ran all the way from white, yellow, green and brown to pink, red and deep purple. A number of them were entirely new to us, but we ate of the many varieties and found most of them delicious. Some were not so good to be sure, but with Tuckie a help, we sampled every one. However we had not come for bottom fish. We were here for Yellow Tail.

We camped the next night on the easy slope of a hill, and made our fire from dead yucca, Joshua tree and manzanita brush while Gamble quail scurried into the thickets at our intrusion. From our vantage point we could look down and see the little town of Ensenada with its flat buildings in soft pastel colors, yellow, blue, pink and green encircling the lovely blue bay like a garland of flowers.

Persistent inquiry, mostly in English, but sometimes in what we at least called Spanish, developed the fact that a swarthy Mexican named Manual could take us out the next day in his boat. Both of us had fished previously in the Gulf of Mexico out from Key West and Miami, so we envisioned a smart launch with green-striped awning and comfortable wicker chairs, but Manuel's boat, the *Tormenta* proved a very different sort of craft. It was a cross between a cabin cruiser and a small tug. The little deck at the rear of the cabin was littered with fragments of rope, chain and miscellaneous impedimenta, and was slippery with an age-old accumulation of grease. The name *Tormenta* was a God-sent inspiration.

Tackle-laden, we were at the dock bright and early the next morning watching Manuel in the tiny cabin tinker with the wheezy motor, surrounded with bilge water. The engine had to be cranked by hand and after many a gasp and gurgle it barked into life, only to die again after few revolutions. Over and over Manuel teased it into brief action, only to have it immediately subside. But at last, like a balky horse who recognizes its master, the motor took hold, coughing and sputtering its protests, and shortly we felt the deep swells of the mighty Pacific as it rolled into the bay across the bar. We trolled without success for several hours and eventually cruised along near the rocky headlands and islands well outside the southern jaw of the bay, now and then catching more of the multi-colored bottom fish. While we were out among the rocks with the rough breakers tossing plumes of white spray up their dripping fronts the temperamental motor died again. We realized at once that our situation was not a happy one, for we were bouncing about on an incoming tide, and each moment we were drifting closer to the jagged rocks which looked very unfriendly indeed. Manuel leaped up in the very shadow of the rocks and set to work with frantic energy to revive the lifeless motor, while we aided him with fervent, heart-felt prayers. Luck was with us, and about the time we were sure that the next swell would send us crashing into the foaming waves at the base of the rocks, the engine sighed, gurgled, sputtered, and took hold. We headed into deeper water without a moment to spare!

When we began to breathe again Spen and I were as weary as the motor. I was squatting on the greasy deck at the stern of the boat, just inside the low bulwark or rail, and he was lying beside me. My Japanese white feathered lure was far out behind, the line cutting above and below the surface at every swell. Suddenly I felt a tremendous pull, and for a moment I thought Spen was having a little fun at my expense by jerking my line, for I was dozing in the sun and was only half awake. But I snapped into consciousness mighty quickly when I realized that because of the drag on the reel had been set much harder than necessary, I was being skidded across the slippery deck straight toward the low rail. Spen saw in an instant what was happening, made a grab for the scruff of my neck and held me as I was being skidded along. But for this timely aid I most certainly would have been pulled overboard for I had no intention of releasing my hold on the rod. Of course, if I had thought of it quickly, I could have released the drag on the reel, but neither of us even considered that possibility. This was the glorious moment for which we had come to Mexico. Here was the pearl without price, our first Yellow Tail, and we held on with grim determination.

The Yellow Tail is not a spectacular fighter, but he is a strong one. Mine never once broke the surface, but pulled like a roped maverick, and explored the depths of the ocean so many times that, try as I would, I never got him to the top until his strength was wholly spent and he was brought to the gaff. Time and again, by straining on the rod, then lowering it sharply, and at the same time reeling in line, I tried to pump him to the surface, but it was strenuous work, and consumed a lot of time and strength. As last he had to yield and I could finally see him through the clear water, a huge torpedo-shaped creature whose bright colors of yellow, blue, green and silver flashed from the crystal depths. He fought until thoroughly exhausted and when gaffed and lifted to the deck, he lay there without a quiver. Never before had I seen such a brilliant fish, nor one more powerful, pound for pound. He appeared to be staring at us through huge liquid eyes, and his markings, particularly the brilliant yellow, were well nigh dazzling in the sun. The fish weighed just twenty-eight pounds, and was the first of its kind that either of us had ever seen.

I rigged up my tackle again and shortly afterwards I had another strike. I hung on desperately and repeated the pumping operation as long as my strength permitted, but I was forced in the end to turn the rod over to Spen, who eventually landed the fish. It was quite as beautiful as the first but was slightly smaller, weighing twenty-six pounds.

I realize now that these fish were caught on my wedding anniversary but, to be quite frank, I had completely forgotten it at the time. On shore we found a fish boy, located a cold storage plant, and I shipped the big fish home on ice. It was so long that I had to cut a hole in the end of the box and let its tail stick out. Anticipating that this portion of the fish might spoil before it arrived at Baker, I telegraphed any wife. She told me afterwards how thrilled she was to receive a telegram on our wedding anniversary, and to realize that, as far away though I was I had not forgotten the date. But when she opened the envelope this was all she read:

> Shipping fish under ice by express
> Keep in cold storage until my return.
> If tail is spoiled have butcher cut it off.
>
> Blaine

8

The High Wallowas

I look on the high Wallowa Mountains of eastern Oregon with the same affection that one feels when gazing on a familiar and well-loved face — a face worn and weathered by the storms of life, a face bearing the proud marks of strength and character, yet mellowed withal by the burden of years. Just so are these peaks softened by the clinging company of shrubs and flowers. I have known the great Wallowas so long and so intimately that I can almost sense their very moods. I find, even in their sternest solitudes, a refuge from the clouding cares of a busy life. It could well be that my familiarity with this splendid range somewhat warps my judgment, but to me it seems the most magnificent sweep of country that I have ever beheld. The Swiss-Italian Alps, lifting their sparkling ice-crowned peaks twelve thousand feet or more into the air, fairly take one's breath away. But they are unlike the Wallowas, many of which are nearly as high, in that one does not see in the Swiss Alps those delightful lake basins, so abundant in the Wallowas, where, among green, flower-studded meadows, the shining blue waters are held against even bluer skies, like turquoise gems in a great diadem. Much of the Wallowa country is drained by innumerable brooks and streams, all combining their waters to form the dashing Minam River which ultimately finds its way into perhaps the greatest natural trench in all outdoors, Hell's Canyon of the Snake River.

Another who is with me in my high regard for these magnificent mountains is my fishing friend, Honorable William O. Douglas, Associate Justice of the Supreme Court of the United States. But for his consuming love of this particular country, so beautifully expressed in his book *Of Men and Mountains*, undoubtedly he would now be sitting in the White House. The historic Democratic convention of 1944 was held in Chicago during the sweltering summer days while "Bill" Douglas, A. T. Hobson, then Secretary of the Reconstruction Finance Corporation, my law partner, Jim Donald, and I were riding the high trails of these glorious mountains and camping at night on the banks of the Minam River, or on the shores of its many lake tributaries. We had a portable radio with us, and while the Convention was in progress we picked up the news of the day, telling how President Roosevelt had selected either Douglas or Truman as his running mate for the forthcoming campaign. Before leaving Washington, Judge Douglas had informed the big-wigs that he would not run under any circumstances, even if nominated, so the lot fell to Truman. As we sprawled about our campfire at night, gazing up at the stars, and listening to the news coming over the air from Chicago, we heard much speculation as to whether the judge was really in earnest in declining the honor. What had become of him? Where had he hidden himself away so successfully? If he were chosen by the convention to run for the Vice-Presidency, would he sill remain adamant? To all of this Bill would chuckle and say, "Let them go at it. My place in public life is on the court. It is an important job over the long pull—and the summers in the mountains are wonderfully diverting from it."

We had spent the first night of our trip at Bill's rambling log cabin, deep in the mountains on the bank of the brawling Lostine River. Early in the morning, mounted on our sturdy mountain ponies, followed by a string of pack mules in charge of our super packer and guide Roy Schaeffer, we headed for the high country. By midafternoon we had pretty well completed the first day's trek, and planned to camp that evening on the shores of Long Lake. We had stopped for a drink and a snack of lunch in a high Alpine meadow drained by an ice-cold snow-fed brook. Upon dismounting we rummaged through the duffle for a knife to cut sandwiches, and made the chilling discovery that all the cooking and eating equipment had been left behind! After some debate Roy turned back, and we pushed on, floundering through snow banks along the north sides of the ridges, and sliding down steep rocky trails on the sunny slopes, arriving at the lake in deepening shadows. The trout rose readily and by dark a heap of shining fish laid on the grass. There was nothing to do but make the best of it until Schaeffer could return with the necessary camp equipment, so we decided to season the fish with salt and cook them on a forked stick held over the glowing coals, but even this was not possible for we could find neither salt nor pepper.

Circumstances like this merely put your true sportsman on his mettle. It is then that he uses his ingenuity. No doubt inventors are often born through just such experiences. We all began to look about and by the sheerest good fortune Bill found a battered quart can and I stumbled on to what remained of an old prospector's shovel. It had no handle, and was heavily encrusted with rust, but by dint of vigorous scouring with pebbles and sand at the edge of the lake, I was able to clean it up after a fashion. With this as a frying pan we cooked generous slices of bacon and in the salty rendered grease we fried our trout, gulping them down loving cup style with drafts of hot black coffee brewed in the can, and ragged chunks of unbuttered bread. Long after we were comfortably settled in our sleeping bags on beds of pine boughs, Schaeffer showed up with the forgotten equipment. He was able, more through instinct than sight, to follow the faint trail in the utter darkness. The next morning while we fished, Schaeffer rode off through the rocks and trees in another direction, heading for one of his numerous grub caches down on the Minam River and returned late in the afternoon with salt and pepper.

Bill Douglas may not possess the longest legs in the world, or maybe even the strongest, but he can certainly set a pace. We made many excursions on foot from our base camps to nearby lakes and streams. Bill usually strode ahead as though equipped with Seven League boots, and at such a gait that a mountain horse would have had to break into a trot to follow him, a pace which left the rest of us panting and gasping far in the rear. Yet, as disclosed by *Of Men and Mountains*, he was stricken with polio when a boy and re-learned to walk through sheer will power.

I have known a few men who could handle a dry fly more expert-ly than Judge Douglas, but I have met none who displayed more native courtesy on stream or lake. Time and again, when we approached a particularly attractive bit of water, he would urge one or the other of us to fish it first, content to drift along behind. Usually he picked up better trout than we of the vanguard were able to coax from the stream. As a camp cook, Bill has no equal. He modestly con-fesses that he learned much of the art from Schaeffer, but I suspect that some of his concoctions, such as potatoes and onions a la prospector, are his own creation. Yet, though he has had much to say in his book about the several ways to cook trout, I have developed one method which neither he nor any other author I have read has ever mentioned.

Take a husky trout weighing one and a half to three pounds. After cleaning the fish in the conventional manner, place it on a smooth log, board, or rock with its head held firmly by a thong, nail or twig. With a sharp knife cut through the skin down the center of the back from head to tail, and also just back of the gills clear around the head. A deep cut on both sides of the dorsal and ventral fins will permit of their being easily pulled out. Cut off the other fins and slit the skin from the vent down to, and clear around, the peduncle or stem of the tail, to join the back cut. Then skin the fish by pulling down from the cut back of the gills. The skin will slip off almost as readily as a glove from the hand. Next split the fish in two by severing the ribs on each side as close to the backbone as possible, discarding the head, back-bone and tail. By inserting a sharp knife beneath the inside film cover-ing the ribs, they can be completely removed, and one has two bone-less, skinless fish filets. These filets should be seasoned with salt, pep-per, a dash of paprika and, if available, a touch of celery salt. Beat up an egg, smear it generously on the filets, roll them in finely crushed cracker crumbs and fry in a kettle of smoking hot deep fat. Perhaps the Greek gods would have preferred ambrosia, but I feel sure that the ordinary mortal will extend the palm to this piping hot delicacy.

The higher our little party climbed, the more beautiful became the scenery. We were among flowery meadows and hanging gardens. But most impressive were the great Wallows themselves towering upward, stern and eternal, draped in lacy sprays of mist from leaping waterfalls, or hidden momentarily by clouds drifting tranquilly across their faces. Somber bands and braids of conifers made their stately progression up the shadowy ravines, and virgin snow-fields clung to the granite pinnacles. Eagles sailed in majestic circles against the azure sky. At night coyotes howled. And all the time mountain breezes refreshed us and cooling waters quenched our thirst.

There is nothing quite so much fun as wandering through the high mountains, making a fresh camp every day or two. Relieved of their saddles and packs, the horses and mules roll in the lush meadow grass and kick up their heels in apparent sheer joy, while we loll in the shade, or flay the waters with our flies, stopping now and then to scoop handfuls of rich purple, luscious huckleberries from the nearby bushes. If we plan to return home with trout, nature is a refrigerator of lingering snow banks furnishing abundant ice, but if we are too far from home, we keep only such trout as we want for food, liberating the others with a parting wish that they may afford as great a thrill to the next angler as they gave to us.

Riding the high ridges one looks back down the trail, or on ahead, if he is bringing up the rear, and sees the surefooted horses clinging to the narrow rocky way, or splashing through the sparkling streams at the many fords. Even atop high passes, one sees on either side, peaks towering to still greater heights, their summits capped in eternal snow. Rock rabbits scurry to their burrows between the masses of jumbled granite, a doe with her fawn looks up as she browses in the leafy brush, turning her great ears to pick up the sound of our approach, and coveys of blue grouse rise from the thickets at our feet and go whirring down the mountainside like feathered cannon balls. Here and there a frowzy brown or black bear, wallowing in a skunk cabbage swamp, or browsing through a huckleberry patch, gazes at us with little pig-like eyes, sniffs the air with sensitive shiny nose, and goes lumbering away over logs and stones to his retreat in the darker forest. Along the trail as it winds through a clump of bull pies, or buck brush, the snapping of twigs and the clatter of stones announce the startled departure of a herd of elk.

As the silent pines cast their lengthening shadows across the purpling waters of the lake, and the last rays of the setting sun paint the further shore in glowing tints of crimson and gold, or sparkle on an open patch of shingly stream bed — just before the scene is swallowed into sable night, we come straggling into camp. The savory odors of another mountain banquet, to which the cook of the day is adding a finishing touch, greets our nostrils. A highball or two all around, chilled from the rime of a nearby snow bank, whet our appetites which need no whetting. We set the table by scattering a few tin plates and cups on the grass, and throw another faggot on the dying fire. We compare notes on the big ones that got away, or tell of the beaver or the fawn that temporarily distracted our attention from the rising trout. Then we all lend a hand with the dishes. Someone pokes up the fire and throws on a big pine knot, sending a banner of sparks leaping into the air, and we slip into our sleeping bags.

True, on a summer night in town some stars may be seen, when one is far enough away from the glow of the street lights, but in the clear air of the high mountains, what a celestial display greets our eyes as we look up beyond the tops of the trees into God's great overspreading canopy of night The Milky Way, glowing as though illuminated with flood lights, spans the whole zenith, spilling its vagrant way across the sky. We watch the brilliant planets drop behind the tree tops to the west, and mark the Great Dipper, with its handle forever pointing out Aroturus, and its cup giving us our direction to the North Star.

Now we learn from the startling discoveries of Hoyle and Lyttleton that scattered throughout our great Galaxy alone are at least a million planets, just as conductive to human life as is the earth, which have been shining in their orbits through countless eons. Whence did they issue? What about the possible billions of souls on these innumerable neighboring worlds? When did they first see the light of their suns? Where are we all going? Contemplation of the stars breeds philosophic speculation.

With advancing years we learn more of the solace that comes from contemplation of God's magnificent universe, displayed so lavishly on every hand — the tiny throbbing organisms seen through the microscope in a drop of water, each pursuing its certain way — the grandeur and stupendous size of the celestial bodies whirling through space at such vast distances from our earth that their light traveling at the prodigious rate of 186,000 miles a second requires hundreds of years to reach us. As Emerson expressed it:

"There is no great end no small
To the Soul that maketh all."

Some believe that on rare occasions God has revealed himself to a few chosen mortals in pillars of flame or shafts of dazzling light and that he has conversed with them in the language of men. The God of my universe reveals himself to us all and speaks to each of us day after day and night after night. To see Him and to hear Him we have but to raise our eyes and open our hearts. The tiny snowflake caught on a black cloth discloses in its lovely symmetrical etchings and infinite interlaced fingers of ice a design and an intelligence no less astounding than of the vast orbits so faithfully followed through space by millions of whirling stars and the mighty comets that streak across the somber night sky. The march of time, so accurately calculated in the observatories throughout the land, is inexorable, infallible, and precise. Those who tell us that in October of 1917 the sun stood still or danced on the horizon while the Virgin Mary revealed herself to three children in Portugal, and that a great Pontiff witnessed the same phenomenon in 1950, must fail to appreciate that should such things actually have happened, every celestial body in the universe including our own sun and this friendly globe which we call earth — with every calculation of time and tide, the advance of the seasons, the hours of the day, and the paths of the spheres — would have been thrown so completely out of balance that the inevitable result would have been utter chaos.

To see a miracle one need but lie down on a grassy meadow any sunny day in spring and with a magnifying glass examine minutely an area no larger than a square foot of ground. Flowers so small that they cannot be seen with the naked eye are pushing up through the warm earth and spreading their tiny petals in colorful bloom. Every stamen, every pistil, every fiber, is perfect — quite as much so as the bloom of the flaming tiger lily that nods in the breeze overhead. The minute grains of soil are built in the same way and from the same material that forms the great monolith which casts its lengthening shadow across the meadow grass. The waters of the meandering brook bubble up and eddy and swirl in precisely the same way, and pursuant to exactly the same law that governs the flow of the mighty Amazon. Little creatures possessing the selfsame physical organs which produce circulation of blood through our veins and enable us to see and hear and sustain our lives move about on tiny legs quite as adequate to their locomotion as those with which we get from place to place, or permit the multi-peddled centipede to follow his accustomed way. Each to his own needs is equipped with everything conducive to existence and to the part, great or humble, which he is destined to play in God's sublime drama of life and death and perpetuation.

To hear God requires only that we listen to the peals of thunder that follow each clap of jagged lightning in the scowling sky or attune our ears to the symphony of the dashing waterfall — the surge of the pounding sea along the crescent beach — the whisper of the spring breeze — the roar of the storm when the needles of the pines sing their wild anthem.

To see and contemplate His glory one need only note the blended tints of pink and purple and gold that mark the sunset, gaze up at the twinkling light of the stars, observe the rifts of moonlight that sparkle on the dimpling lake. As Lowell so inimitably puts it:

"Every clod feels a stir of might,
An instinct within it that reaches and towers,
And, groping blindly above it for light,
Climbs to a soul in grass end in flowers."

Yes, God does reveal himself to man, and does speak to every living creature. Can we question His infinite wisdom? Must we surround our belief in Him with dogma and creed and trappings and ritual? Can we not worship and revere Him with equal sincerity and gratitude when the columns of His tabernacle are none other than the shafts of stalwart pines whose penciled trunks are painted in rich orange by the last rays of the sun? Is not the incense drifting up through the trees from the smoke of our campfire as pleasing to His nostrils as that which permeates our many man-made temples from the swinging censer? Whittier so comfortingly assures us:

"I only know I cannot drift
Beyond his love end care."

Astronomers all agree that our own galaxy has been in existence for about four billion years. Yet many orthodox believers still accept the doctrine announced in Ireland by Archbishop Ussher three hundred years ago that the earth was created on October 26 in the year 4004 B.C. at the hour of 9:00 o'clock A.M.

What of immortality? Did one God send his only be-gotten Son down to earth that our souls alone might be saved, and only so little while ago? Or did each of these many other whirling spheres also receive a Messenger from Heaven? Shall one world be saved and not another? Are those far-off inhabitants of distant worlds peering out into the darkness, questing whether men live and breathe and have their being on this remote end shining planet where we abide? Is there but one Supreme God who counts the hairs of our heads and knows when a sparrow falls, or can we accept the belief of the ancient Greeks — that there are many gods? In that case, would each of the countless distant island universes have its own special god? Does contemplation of infinity leave any substantial basis for orthodox faith? Rather, are we not obliged to put our trust wholly in the unbounded wisdom of one all-wise Creator? Does not such a god know the purpose of our existence, and will it not have its perfect niche in His wondrous scheme? Will He not know whether we are best served by reward or punishment, eternal life or oblivion? And will we not be entirely safe in placing ourselves, with our hopes and fears, under the great protecting shadow of His wing? May we not with confidence rest our case with him?

Alaska Days

W hen I was a small boy, the great Alaska gold rush was on and several friends of our family packed up their pokes and, grubstaked by less adventurous and more prosperous citizenry, took their departure for the Yukon trail. It was all very thrilling. I remember how we waited for letters bringing word that they had found gold in great quantity and were returning to live in ease and luxury and to regale the stay-at-homes with tales of bravery and success. But usually there were no letters at all and after a reasonable length of time, generally during a single bitter winter season in that wild clime, the adventurous ones returned with less fanfare than accompanied them on their departure. They had no gold or at least only a few nuggets for stickpins, as we called them in those days, but they did bring Indian baskets, mukluks, trinkets and good stories of adventure which were quite as satisfying to a youngster as the sight of buckets of gold. They also knew now all about mountains, bears, and fish, and their descriptions of streams choked with salmon, of trout leaping from every lake and stream, made an ineradicable impression upon me. I may thank especially one of these ne'er-do-wells for the graphic recitals which decided me then and there, somehow, sometime, to seek out that paradise.

And indeed, many years later I found that he had not exaggerated. There were fish in abundance for the sportsman, and at the mouth of every bay, a commercial cannery perched high above the water on barnacle-encrusted piling against a backdrop of deep-green forests climbing up from the rugged shore line.

One of our friends of later years was the physicist and mountaineer Dr. Herschel Parker, then an instructor at Columbia University. No man was more intimately acquainted with Alaska, no one better able to describe the grandeur of its scenery. To me it almost seemed as though he owned Mt. McKinley, for he had made many trips in that area. When he recounted to us his experiences on the slopes of the highest peak of our continent, we were spell-bound, and amazed to hear the clock strike two before he had concluded his brave saga.

I should relate some of Dr. Parker's adventures, for his name is intricately interwoven in the history of mountaineering. He had attempted the peak in 1906 with Dr. Frederick Cook, who later claimed discovery of the North Pole. The party had essayed a route from Cook Inlet on the south to the foot of McKinley, but found it too formidable for any hope of success. After incredible hardships they gave up, planning to return another year and seek out a different route. Dr. Cook thereupon took one assistant, declaring that they two would again attempt the ascent. The rest of the party waited for a short time in the wilderness at the mountain's bases. Soon Cook returned jubilant and triumphant. He claimed complete success. Dr. Parker was entirely too conscientious and too competent a scientist to be taken in by those claims, for Cook's trip had been too hasty, and in addition discrepancies in Cook's tale were fatal to his assertions. Parker and his friends stoutly denounced the explorer, but nevertheless Cook was believed for some years and gave many lectures about his great climb.

Eventually it was discovered that a low and insignificant mountain among the foothills checked feature for feature with the photographs Cook displayed and which he asserted were those of the summit of McKinley.

Dr. Parker's last attempt, undertaken in 1912, was the most thrilling and the most heartbreaking of his career. It was unsuccessful and he knew when he descended from the high slopes that he would never set foot on McKinley again. He told us how his party battled its way by a new route to the north face of the peak, step by step, over great glaciers and mighty crevasses, tormented all the way by overwhelming storms and fogs. Wild blizzards broke over them in fury as they climbed higher and higher while they clung to safety ropes and rubbed their benumbed bodies to keep from freezing to death. At every break in the weather they would dash forward a few feet and cut fresh steps in the ice, innumerable steps, every breathless blow taking far too heavy a toll of their strength in that rarefied atmosphere. When they were only three hundred feet from the top, the last blow fell. An appalling blizzard burst upon them and they were thrown back finally and inexorably.

A few days later they were sitting in their camp in the wilderness below when they felt the earth heave and rock. Looking upward in bewilderment and terror they saw the whole north side of the mountain, where they had so lately clung, shudder and hurtle itself in vast tons of ice and debris into the great canyons far below. Later they learned that far to the west, the Katmai volcano had erupted with enormous violence and had shaken the entire Alaskan peninsula.

My daughter Mary, then fifteen, sat through the long narrative with rapt attention. No sooner had the doctor bowed himself out of our home in the wee hours of that summer morning, than Mary was at my side.

"Papa, we must go to Alaska. What fun we could have if you would take me up into that wild country."

"But how about the clients, Mary, and daily bread?"

"The clients can wait, and as to daily bread, we won't need any, we can live on fish."

Well, she was our only child. How could I refuse? And besides, my earlier resolve to see Alaska again had me in its grip. Within a fortnight we were northbound on one of the steamers which ply the picturesque Inside Passage.

Hours on end we sat on deck and imagined ourselves viewing a vast cyclorama as the grand scenery unrolls before us. We craned our necks and gazed at mountain walls, up and up and up, past green forests and bald crags to the very summits where cascades appearing to spring out of the clouds burst forth and plunge in shattering spray far down into the sea. Hundreds of glaciers burden the mountains of the coast and find their way through deep, rugged trenches to the ocean where their ominous glistening fronts split off continually into the innumerable blue icebergs that drift with wind and tide all about those waters. It is a regular tourist attraction for the steamers to approach ice walls as close as possible and blow their horns. Travelers crowd the decks to watch, and often as the sound vibrations strike against the cliffs, they are rewarded by the sight of the grand spectacle of prodigious slabs of ice letting go with a savage roar and toppling into the sea in a great froth of water. Some of these glaciers are enormous. The Muir, for instance, has more than two hundred tributaries and is twenty-five miles wide at its front. All are part of a vast prehistoric ice sheet which in many parts of Alaska still lies very close to the surface of the ground. All move slowly but with irresistible force and one may see enormous scratches made long ago by the grinding ice sheets on the bald granite faces of the huge alps which line the shores. Some of the ice flows seek the streams. The Childs and Miles glaciers, which we viewed on the return trip from Chitna, drain into the great Copper River. They are always spectacular sights with their cold fronts rearing aloft and dazzling the eye with the effulgence of their coloring.

The mountains of Alaska are in a class by themselves. They are among the few on our globe which do not rise from high table lands. Most of these great peaks spring directly upward from sea level, and a mountain climber who attempts to scale them actually struggles up steep inclines for a far greater distance than he would in climbing almost any other mountains on earth. For mile upon mile the white crowned peaks dominate the scene, formidable yet enticing. Indeed one is held spellbound by the wild landscape, for the whole country stands on end and is a mountaineer's paradise. Some of these spires, such as Mt. Logan and Mt. St. Elias, rise nearly twenty thousand feet in the air, but Mt. McKinley is the emperor crest, commanding and overtopping all others. The St. Elias range, further inland, is usually visible, but McKinley, closer to the sea, shrouds itself in clouds and mystery and is seldom beheld in its entirety.

Anyone who has stood at its foot will find himself caught in its spell, and for that reason, I suppose, I purchased a large painting by that artist of Alaska, Eustace Ziegler. The picture not only portrays the scene with beauty and accuracy, but, to my mind, brings the very crispness of the rarefied atmosphere breezing through my library where it now hangs. There in the background, stands lordly McKinley with its banner of clouds flying from the top, while in the foreground, five weary bear hunters sit on a massive boulder, gazing down into the depths of space toward a great canyon where a shadowy river winds through the dark forests of the lower reaches. It appeals greatly to my friends, especially big-game hunters, who like to sit before it smoking, and lost in reverie.

After talking to Mr. Ziegler I felt inspired to try my own skill with palate and brush while I was in Alaska. I can say a good deal for my enthusiasm though I do not claim his talent for myself. Nevertheless the result of my effort, a picture of Russian Lake near Harry Smith's lodge on Russian River, now hangs in the reception room of my office. But even such glorious mountains could not divert my whole attention from fishing. I must cast a fly over those northern waters where fish abound in such countless numbers.

Because the streams of Alaska are mostly glacial, they present a milky appearance, and consequently are not particularly appealing to a dry-fly fisherman. I have swung a rod on many a northern lake and stream, but I have yet to find there any outstanding dry-fly trout water. To the wet-fly or bait fisherman, however, or to one who enjoys trolling for salmon, sea trout, or char, Alaska comes second to none.

In the Russian River out from Moose Pass on the Kenai peninsula, big rainbow trout are plentiful and in the fall, when they are following the salmon up to the high spawning redds, they will strike a wet fly, particularly if it is rigged with a tiny spinner blade at its head. But even so, fly-fishing has its drawbacks for the half-spent salmon, then ascending all the Alaskan streams in such multitudes, are so thick that at times they must literally be kicked out of the way to permit an angler to place his fly properly on riffle or pool. More than once in casting for trout in such streams I have found my fly fast to the dorsal fin or tail of a salmon, only to lose it when the frightened fish made a dash for safer water.

I made my last trip to Alaska in 1938, with my daughter Mary. The Kenai peninsula, which we visited, was then a harsh country, and progress there, in any endeavor, required a vast amount of physical effort. We spent a week at Harry Smith's Rendezvous, a former Russian penal camp, nestled in the hills near the foot of Russian Lake. To reach the remote lodge we had taken the little train from Anchorage to Moose Pass. There Smith met us with his jalopy. The so-called road ended in a clearing where a squat cabin nestled against a background of great conifers. Smith said, "You can put on your outing togs there at the cabin. Leave your surplus duffel. We'll fix up light packs of what you will need at the camp, for our hike in over the trail."

"That's a snug looking little cabin," I said. "Is it yours?"

"No," he said, "Not exactly. I don't know who built it nor when, or who might have the right to claim it now but up here cabins belong to anyone who has occasion to use them."

The door was unlocked and, when we stepped in, we found everything tidy and shipshape, with a quantity of canned goods and staples on a shelf, a lamp filled with kerosene, and a full wood box.

Lying beside it were several short lengths of dry, pitchy wood, partly whittled down all about, so that the shavings stood out from the stick.

"This place looks as though someone lived here," I said. "No," responded Smith with a smile, "as far as I know this cabin hasn't been occupied, except now and then by me or my guests, for a long time."

"How is it then," I inquired, "that it is supplied with groceries, has a full wood box, and is tidy and neat? What are those fuzzy looking little sticks near the stove?"

"I see that you are a tenderfoot in these parts," said Smith, with a grin. "It is one of the unwritten laws of Alaska that cabins are always left unlocked, for everyone is welcome. But, each person is supposed to leave in the cabin about the same quantity of provisions that he consumed. Particularly, he must fill the wood box and whittle several "fuzz sticks" for starting a fire. You see, up here, many people travel by foot, and with old newspapers for starting fires a rarity, the last occupant must leave plenty of "fuzz sticks."

I soon learned that hardships seem only to prove a bond between people isolated in so stern a world. Every man stood ready to help his neighbor.

So we hit the trail with our light packs, and walked three or four miles through deep forests and through shaded gullies until we arrived at the camp. The principal building was a two-story log cabin well furnished and well equipped.

"How in the world did you get all your furniture and supplies up into this wilderness?" I asked. "Well, believe it or not," replied Smith, "everything that you see here, except the logs for building the cabins, had to be carried in manually — food, clothing, furniture — and all that is needed in a place like this."

We shortly discovered that fresh milk was almost an unknown luxury, and that the manufacturers of the condensed substitute must have been doing a flourishing business. Mrs. Smith told us an interesting anecdote about the little fellow who attended school in a primitive school house down on Kenai Lake. He was asked to check the correct answers on a printed questionnaire dealing with various commodities. One of the questions was: "Does milk come in a bottle, basket or box?" He checked the word "box."

We found that the Russian River was literally alive with salmon, lying in the pools below the falls and cascades in such unbelievable numbers that the weaker ones would be pushed out onto the shore as they fought the rapids to attain the lake above. Few trees grew on the great green mountains that lifted their low growth of brush or copse, so that we could view them in any direction for miles. At almost any time, and particularly in the late afternoon or early evening, when we scanned the rolling mountains through field glasses, we could pick out black and brown bears and large numbers of mountain sheep. I still have a bit of hide from one of those sheep in my fly-tying kit, the long rather pinky-white hair of which proves excellent dressing for such flies as the Royal Coachman. A member of the hunting party who killed the sheep told me that in one day moving over the slopes of but two mountains, he saw more than two hundred sheep, ten black bears, four coyotes and one mountain goat.

Brilliant magenta-colored fireweed bloomed all about in the greatest profusion with a liberal sprinkling of wild clarkia of almost identical color, deep blue larkspur, and a northern variety of the delicate white grass-of-Parnassus flower. In the moist places under the trees, deep-red, shiny-topped mushrooms peeked out between the grasses.

"Oh look, Papa" cried Mary, "do you know what those are?"

I bent down in the grass for a minute inspection. I had made some study of mushrooms and had accumulated considerable literature on the subject. Luckily I identified the species, and the Latin name sprang to my lips. I proudly responded: "Yes Mary, these are *Amanita muscaria.*"

"Nothing of the sort," retorted Mary. "They are the homes of fairies and gnomes. I learned all about them from my story books when I was a little girl."

Mary and I spent many happy days on the river and nearby lake. I had taught her to fish and under my tutelage she had developed considerable skill in handling a fly. We wandered along fishing together, enjoying a comradeship not often vouchsafed father and daughter, and having a wonderful time. At least so I thought, but not long ago as I was rummaging through a box of old papers, I was rather taken aback when I ran across the following entry she had made in her little travel diary:

> "Aug. 20. Sometimes F. and his old fishing give me a pain. Yesterday I got my line tangled up in the bushes so many times that he got mad and made me practice half an hour casting at his handkerchief which he put on the grass. I didn't complain as I am going to tell him tomorrow that I want to fly to Juneau with the Earlings instead of going on the boat with him."

The Northern Lights seen from those latitudes are weird, fantastic and awe-inspiring. One quiet night in August we witnessed a truly grand display. The entire horizon to the north was first a brilliant white crescent which shortly turned to green with beams of light shooting into the sky as though controlled by a battery of huge search-lights. Then more and more white beams appeared, all converging at the zenith. This effect, growing more dazzling with each moment, finally spread over the entire northern half of the sky, with the rays intermittently flashing and fading, only to be replaced by masses of color rapidly changing into weird designs that etched the sky directly over our heads. The breathtaking scene lasted for nearly half an hour when the lights faded away as suddenly as they had come.

Ending our pleasant sojourn at the Russian River Lodge, we hiked back to the rough road at Kenai River, and were taken by auto-mobile to the quaint old fishing village of Hope on Turnagain Arm. Here the tides often run as high as forty-five feet, creating a danger-ous bore and savage tide rips so that it is impossible for a small boat to make the passage from Hope to Seward.

A vast section of Alaska north of Mt. McKinley is a great rolling prairie with no cultivation whatever clear to the edge of Fairbanks. It is a relatively flat country covered with stunted spruce, elder, wil-low, aspen, poplar, and birch, with many swamps, much muskeg and sullen-looking streams. Because of the solid prehistoric ice underlying this entire country, only three or four feet under the sod, the trees have no tap roots and consequently adapt themselves to this uncompromising environment as best they can by spreading a thin layer of tendrils around the base of their trunks, thus drawing on as large an area of the barren soil as possible. But the frozen ground does have one advantage. Most of the homes in northern Alaska are one-storey, flat-roofed log cabins with a reinforcing dou-ble wall some three or four feet in height which serves as a bulkhead against the freezing winter winds.

We left Hope for Anchorage and then traveled by rail to Fairbanks where Mary's friends, the Earlings lived. They had a sum-mer cabin on Lake Harding not far from Fairbanks. Although we were far north of the Arctic Circle, the August weather in midday was even hotter than at home. Trailing a spinner behind the canoe, I pad-dled about the lake for several hours catching nothing more than a bad case of sunburn. When I returned to the cabin for lunch, Mrs. Earling said, "How would you like a glass of iced lemonade?" I couldn't image anything more refreshing at that moment. She stepped around to the side of the cabin and returned with the lemon-ade in a glass pitcher heavily coated with frost. I had seen no refrig-erator in the cabin and asked her why she kept it outdoors.

"Come with me," she said with a smile, and led me across the grassy plot at the side of the cabin where she removed a bough-thatched lid from a hole in the earth some two feet in diameter and about three feet deep. To my intense astonishment, I noted that the lower six or eight inches and the floor of the hole were solid ice. On the ice were a bottle of milk bristling with frost particles, fresh vegetables, and a piece of meat frozen as hard as though taken from a deep freeze.

"You see," said Mrs. Earling, "keeping things cool presents no problem here. Every householder provides himself with an excellent refrigerator merely by digging a hole in the backyard down to the prehistoric ice."

I realized then that even in this land where the barest necessities must be brought in and food kept in storage against the long months when no portage is available, even in the country of grim-zero temperatures, there are advantages.

Mr. Earling was Vice-President of the United States Smelting, Refining, and Mining Company and he was in charge of extensive placer mining for his company near Fairbanks. He was then operating six big dredges on Gold Stream Creek and a huge drag line on Cripple Creek. To float the dredges, water had to be piped in over a distance of ninety miles. An outlay in excess of ten million dollars was required before so much as an ounce of gold could be recovered, but, the operations have long since proven immensely profitable. When I was there the dredges were moving more than twenty million yards of earth a year. Because of the ancient ice, the ground to be dredged must first be thawed, and as the bed-rock is from sixty to one hundred and fifty feet below the surface, this barren over-burden must be disposed of, some four or five years being required to complete the dredging in any given area. To thaw the ground preparatory to dredging, pipes are driven into the frozen ground at sixteen-foot intervals all over the area, and cold water is then pumped into them. As the ground thaws in ever-widening circles about the pipes, they are lowered until they finally reach bedrock. Then this enormous accumulation of over-burden must be removed. It is sluiced down the creeks into the great Tanana River, which flows into the mighty Yukon and thence to the Bering Sea. Removing this overburden alone requires some two years. Yet with all of this work, the company could profitably mine ground carrying an average of only twenty-five cents per yard in gold, including the barren overburden. As the ground is thawed and sluiced away to the streams through the employment of hydraulic giants, the bones of prehistoric mastodons and other creatures are exposed, only to be left lying in the litter of mud and debris with now and then some picked up by an occasional paleontologist.

Mary had made friends with the three Earling girls at boarding school in Seattle. One day, after lunch, Mary and the three girls went swimming in the lake while I renewed my activities with the canoe. As I paddled by the little dock where the girls were swimming, Mary suddenly attempted to climb into the canoe. The inevitable result—over we went! For a moment the cold water closed over me. By the time I had come up sputtering to the surface and we were all floundering about, pushing the canoe toward shore and attempting to salvage the fishing tackle—I was thoroughly provoked.

"What in the world did you do that for Mary?" I gasped.

"Well, Papa" she answered, "you surely didn't think I did it on purpose with all of our money on you."

When Mary left Fairbanks by plane for Juneau, I hired an ancient car with chauffeur and drove to the Gulkana River over what was called the Richardson highway, but in whose mud wallows the struggling car often sank to the hubs. The stream supports an astonishing number of grayling. I have never found these fish elsewhere than in Alaska and Montana. They average about one to two pounds in weight, though some are larger. Their color is predominately soft gray. They carry an enormous sail-like dorsal fin, and have a cluster of brilliant purple spots on each side just back of the gills. Grayling were the only fish which I found in Alaska that would readily strike a small dark dry fly, and they were excellent fighters, as well as a good table fish.

On the first day out from Fairbanks I stopped at a low, rambling, one-storey log inn which had been a stage station during the days of the Klondike Gold Rush. Because of the rigors of the climate it had weathered to a soft pearl gray, and was just such a building as one sees in some of the lovely oil paintings by the late Sidney Lawrence who with his palette, made every corner of Alaska his own.

When I asked where I might fish, the portly inn-keeper told me to walk down the highway about a mile to a point where the river flowed against the road's embankment, and to fish there. This I did, but soon decided to work upstream. The fish were rising steadily and I was enjoying the sunny afternoon so hugely that, before I knew it, I had gone a mile or so up the river. The stream had angled away from the highway, but I concluded that I must be about opposite the inn, so I decided to fish up a little farther and then cut across through the brush instead of retracing my steps down the river and back up the highway.

About that time I noticed fresh bear tracks as big as a dinner plate in the moist sands at several places along the bank, and the remains of partially consumed salmon here and there on the edges of the gravel bars. The tracks grew thicker as I ascended the river, and, beginning to feel a little nervous, I started through the brush toward the inn. At first I floundered about in thick shrubbery and shallow swales and sloughs, but soon came upon a series of zigzag trails, and considered myself fortunate to run onto them for the high brush was a jungle. In some places where the trails penetrated the heavy brush, though wide enough, and apparently well trodden, they were over-grown like tunnels. I wondered at the time why pedestrians, wishing to get down to the river, had traveled in such a roundabout way. However, I kept going, following one trail until it forked off into another, heading in my general direction, and ultimately came out upon open tundra and so returned to the inn.

When I clumped across the rough plank floor of the big room, my host had just completed laying a fire on the big stone hearth. Even in late August the nights were chill. He glanced up and greeted me with the conventional fisherman's salute, "What luck?"

Instead of responding I opened my brimming creel and he gazed in admiration at the big fish.

"Well," he said, "I didn't suppose you would make a catch like that in the short stretch of river along the highway grade, for it has been pretty heavily fished."

"I didn't catch them there," I responded, "but worked on up the river, and the further I went, the better was the fishing."

"You worked up the river?"

"Yes, sir," I said, "and it is a beautiful stretch of water. But I had some difficulty in getting back to the hotel until I found the trails and then it was easy going."

He looked at me for a long moment without saying a word He just stood there with his hands on his hips, but his face had lost its sunny expression. Finally he said,

"How were you armed?"

"Armed?" I replied." I had nothing more deadly than my fly rod."

"Do you know what those trails were?" he responded. "They were Kodiak bear trails. That thicket is alive with bears and they are big and vicious. Furthermore, they are near-sighted and, when startled, they promptly attack. Your luck was with you this day."

I caught my breath and shuddered to think of what might have happened had I encountered a bear at any of the innumerable kinks in the trail. Well, since the time of old St. Peter, God has kept his arm around a fisherman.

Grandes Pescados at Loreto

The sturdy DC-3 of Trans Mar de Cortes, which we had boarded at Tijuana, banked to the left and nosed down toward the sparkling blue waters of the Gulf. Over the door to the pilot's quarters an electric sign flashed. No Fuma Abroche su Cinturon. We ground out our cigarettes, buckled safety belts snugly across our laps and peered out of the slanting window. A deep rugged gorge strewn with rocks, cacti, and brush rose to meet us. Just clearing the chasm we felt the rubber-tired wheels strike the pebbly runway as the plane bounced, settled, bounced again, and finally ground to a stop in a cloud of dust at the very edge of another deep gully which marked the southerly end of the short landing strip. Taxiing back to the runway the plane came to rest and we stepped out to get another gulp of clear fresh Mexican ozone as the sea breeze drifted in across the little hamlet of Santa Rosalia. Two hours more and we would be at our destination, the ancient pueblo of Loreto on the east coast of Baja California, scarcely more than a hundred and fifty miles from its tip at Cabo San Lucas.

For years Bill Lorton and I had dreamed of fishing in the Gulf of California, and by five o'clock in the afternoon of a beautiful February day just past, the plane again descended to a makeshift runway and we stepped out among the date palms and ocotoa trees.

"Bill," I had said when our plans were in the making, "you must pick up a little Spanish, at least enough to express your simple wants. In the larger hotels in Mexico it's always possible to find someone who speaks English. But we're going to a very primitive and remote section. It's easy to learn how to say yes, no, please, thanks and a few other simple words like that. If you know how to ask and answer short questions about food and lodging, you will get along all right."

"Nuts," exploded Bill, "everybody speaks English, no matter where you go."

"Have it your way," I said with some irritation, "but if you get stuck, don't come crying to me."

A bevy of brown-skinned, barefoot natives in nondescript clothing unloaded our luggage from the plane, but they overlooked Bill's fishing rod, a fact he discovered just as the ship was about to leave for La Paz.

"Wait! Wait!" he yelled as he rushed toward the plane, gesticulating wildly and helplessly. "My fishing rod, you left it on the plane."

The attendants only stared at Bill with blank expressions and shook their heads. "No comprendo,]no hablo Ingles." Dashing back to the truck which was about to take us to the lodge, Bill repentantly implored me to take a hand. I should have left him in his dilemma, but there was no time to waste.

"I told you so, smart boy," I bantered, when I had hastily

recovered his rod just in time.

Then we were trundled away over a rough sandy road that wound among cactus trees and overhanging brush through the sleepy little dog-infested village and on to a lovely sea beach. There among the palms we found the breezy Sportsmen Flying Club lodge with its big cool living and dining room and its brood of white-washed adobe casas fronting the sea. Our room was fresh and clean with hot and cold shower. The drinking water was pure, the food was excellent, and our American hostess, Mrs. Ed Tabor, was hospitality personified. She and the few American guests were the only ones who spoke English.

The boy who tended the small but well-stocked bar also spoke a little English. But he wasn't there to help us very much for almost immediately upon our arrival, he left to operate a fishing boat out of Guaymas across the Gulf. We were then left in the situation where if Bill wanted to order as simple an item as a fried egg, he was utterly helpless. I enjoyed many a laugh when after unsuccessfully attempting to communicate with the natives, Bill would finally give up in disgust and shout "oui, oui," his sole equipment in any foreign tongue.

The ancient village of Loreto, which we had but glimpsed on our way to the Club, with its frond huts, waving palms, and great splashes of brilliant bougainvillea, lies about a half mile from the lodge. Of its fifteen hundred odd people, not a single soul could speak a word of English. Like all Mexican pueblos, it boasted a central plaza where in the evenings of the numerous fiesta days, young men and women danced to Mexican tunes scraped out on rasping fiddles and battered cornets. As is the custom in every Mexican village that I have seen, the young senors would walk around and around the plaza on the outer edge of the graveled way and the bright-eyed senoritas, would circle the little park in the opposite direction. As the discordant music started, the youths selected partners from the circling parade of girls and the dance got under way.

All the cooking in Loreto is done out of doors on little stone braziers; the bread is baked in dome-shaped stone ovens which, though out of doors, are protected by palm shelters. On the floor of the so-called oven, a good fire is constructed of native fuel, largely of the hardwood type. This produces a fine bed of coals. Then the little lumps of bread are shoved onto a rack above the coals with a wooden paddle. The oven is sealed and the baking is accomplished by means of the heat thus accumulated. The little buns or loaves which are the product of this baking method are really quite delicious, possessing a rich nutty flavor. Fish are filleted and dried in the sun on a bamboo rack, and life in general in rude villages like Loreto is simple in the extreme.

The mission of San Gabriel had been our objective one day when we were trundled some twenty-five miles over the rugged range which constitutes the backbone of the peninsula, over a scar which the natives call a road. It was undoubtedly the roughest trip by vehicle that I have ever made. The ancient mission stands in a desolate, remote desert section of the mountains, looming against a shadowy black cliff and bordered on one side by a tiny oasis of palms, fruit trees, and little vegetable patches from which the natives have to eke out an existence. Although over two hundred years old, the mission is in a remarkable state of preservation.

Clusters of little palm frond huts mark isolated habitations here and there among the rocks. Many of these huts are no larger than a big doghouse, but most of them are overrun with flowering trees and vines of multi-colored bloom in beautiful profusion. Along story trails came ragged, barefoot boys leading sturdy little burros so laden with fagots that only their sharp hooves were visible under the huge loads.

As far below the border as Ensenada on the Pacific side and in the more level valleys still further to the south, there is some cultivated land on the peninsula, particularly at the big Hamilton ranch, a well-known landmark to air travelers and by far the largest agricultural venture in Lower California. From the air it was a vivid spot of emerald green. But beyond this, clear to the cape, the country is one vast expanse of rugged, broken, rocky mountains, some over ten thousand feet in height, and deep gullies, sand, cacti, Joshua trees, Yucca, scrub, and thicket. One would not expect to find much evidence of cultivation in such a parched desert, but it is astonishing that so little attempt has been made to reclaim even the broad expanses of sandy loam that border the Gulf. The water table is only a few feet below the surface of the ground and a little ingenuity and labor in removing stones, bruth, cactus, and in sinking wells, could make of these lands a veritable garden. Here and there where tiny trickles of water appear, the Mexican farmers have with a minimum of effort built ditches and developed oases of date palms, orange and lemon trees, bamboo, grapes, corn, and vegetables. Such of the few pumping plants as we found consisted of a shallow well, a circular stone vat, and a burro-operated treadmill which dragged a chain equipped with rubber flanges up through a pipe whereby the water was precipitated into the tank, and from thence carried in buckets back to a few trees and little garden patches. Possibly the local laws against foreign land holdings and the general communal plan of breaking up the old ranchos may account for this noticeable lack of cultivation. But one is immediately struck with the thought that American capital and energy could soon change the face of much of this forbidding desert. As it is today, myriads of Gamble quail, rabbits, bobcats, cougar, and deer haunt the thickets and scurry away at one's approach. Mountain sheep still abound in the rugged highlands and clouds of ducks rise from the swamps and bayous.

We spent the first two days inspecting the village, wandering about the countryside, hunting quail, and walking up and down the deserted beach. Naturally enough, one would expect to find seashells on the shore, but the sight that rewarded our lonely marches along the strand is well nigh indescribable.

Every conceivable type of seashell, great and small, spiny, smooth, scalloped, twisted, with colors ranging through the whole spectrum, were strewn on the beach in unbelievable profusion. Some were twisted cornucopias, lacquered soft-glowing pink within and armed on the outside with a formidable array of spikes. Others, like the nautilus, displayed pearl-gray linings which sparkled in the light. There were little ones and big ones, shell-like retreats, spirals and conches, all interlaced with vivid multi-colored seaweed and odd-shaped coral fragments. The water of the Gulf is crystal clear, and as we gazed into the shallows we were astonished to discover that what we had at first thought to be colorful pebbles and stones were in fact living creatures, all on the move, with each preying upon his neighbor.

Gulls, cormorants, great grotesque gray pelicans, and many other sea birds bounced upon the sparkling waves or dove into the sea for fish in a continuous round of feasting. Flocks of fifty or more pelicans sailing majestically, some thirty feet or so above the water, would suddenly stand on their heads and with tightly folded wings, long necks, and wedge-shaped bills pointing to the water, drop into the sea with a resounding splash and bob up to the surface holding in his bill a shiny fish. We marveled that these big birds did not collide with each other when half the flock would suddenly dive into a school of fish. Each had apparently marked his prey from the air, and though so close as actually to touch wings, would emerge with his own particular finny morsel. Authentic literature on the subject which we consulted disclosed that in the Gulf there are not less than six hundred and twenty-five known species of fish, as that term is generally understood. This does not include the infinite multitude of mollusks, clams, snails, and other crustaceans.

But it was the fishing not the scenery that had brought us to Mexico. The countryside, the beauty of the painted hills at sunrise, the varied colors of the sea ranging from deep purple in the depths to pink, emerald, and yellow in the shallows, the rocky islands rising from the depths, the flying spume dashed from the rugged headlands when the wind blew, the rhythmical sway of the palm fronds, the native costumes and customs, the musical note of soft Spanish talk and infectious laughter were but incidental.

We were assigned to the *Bonita*, a comfortable, green, twenty-six-foot cabin cruiser, equipped with a powerful Evinrude motor and manned by el capitan Ricardo and his assistant Alfredo.

Just as the first faint light of dawn touched the shattered top of old Mount Gigantia, a vigorous rap on the door and a cheery "Buenos dias senores, ahore nosotros vamos a pescar," brought us to our feet from comfortable, clean-sheeted beds, and Bill murmured sleepily, "What is he talking about now?"

"Never mind," I said. "Get dressed, this is the day."

A hearty breakfast of Papaya, bacon, eggs, hot cakes, and coffee, devoured to the accompaniment of speculation on what lures we should use and what fish we might catch, put us in a proper state of expectancy. I had done some deep-sea fishing and had always felt well rewarded if lucky enough to get several strikes and to land a fish or two in a day's cruise, so I was wholly unprepared for what was soon to follow. With lunch, water bottle, and fishing tackle, we climbed aboard and were soon gliding out across the sparkling waters of the Gulf, leaving a train of white bubbles to mark our course. The pelicans and sea birds were still gorging on schools of herring and small fish. A great whitish-gray osprey held himself aloft with fluttering wings, then like a thunderbolt crashed into the sea and came up carrying a fish in his talons quite as large as himself.

Soon we were churning through countless acres of shiny red shrimp that stretched mile upon mile across the sea. They were three or four inches in length and the color of boiled lobster. The busy little fellows would rise through the clear water in countless billions, painting the whole ocean as far as we could see a brilliant vermillion, turn at the surface like red bubbles, and return tail first to the limpid depths. Schools of iridescent silvery-blue bonita thrashed about gorging on the shrimps, while off to the right or left as we approached the rocks we could see vast numbers of yellowtail whipping the water into a froth as they dashed about in pursuit of smaller fish.

"Look at that — look at that!" yelled Bill, pointing to the south. Not a quarter of a mile away a huge gray whale broke the surface, poking her dark cone-shaped head ten feet into the air. Beside her floundered her calf, and in a moment we saw that it was being attacked by an enormous manta ray with flippers at least thirty feet across. The mother was evidently attempting to protect her offspring. For a full half hour we watched the battle rage, not daring to approach any closer, for an angry whale can be dangerous. The sea was churned to a mighty froth as whale and manta floundered and struggled before our fascinated gaze. Finally all three disappeared into the depths and we pursued our way towards Carmen Island looming pink and inviting in the morning light, some ten or twelve miles out from the lodge — regretful that we would never know the outcome of the struggle, but mindful that the creatures of the deep are forever battling for their existence.

A company of sharks with sharp triangular fins cutting the surface of the sea sailed majestically by. As we approached the shattered headlands of the island, sea lions wallowed among the swirling fish, and from the rock ledges seals barked, basked in the sun, or slid into the breakers which pounded the rocks. Statuesque pelicans and cormorants gazed sadly at us from the crags, and great turtles three feet or more in length floated about in the sunny swells, all wholly indifferent to our approach.

The rocky walls of Carmen Island, through centuries of incessant pounding by the surf, have been cut into caves, recesses, and caverns from which the receding waves boomed their doubtful welcome. Some hundred yards from the shore Ricardo slowed down the motor saying, "Pescar shore."

"Now what?" inquired Bill.

"Fish, you rascal, fish!" I told him, "he says fish now."

We lowered our big Martin plugs onto the water, paying out the lines from the singing reels. The lures should be cut about one hundred and fifty feet from the boat, but they didn't get that far. At the precise instant each rod was yanked to the thwart with a resounding whack. In spite of the heavy drag which we had set on the reels, they whirred with an angry buzz, and we frantically pressed the butts of the rods into our stomachs and hung on. The lines cut through the water and we yelled like wild Indians. Bill was the first to recover his senses, and with all of his strength he gave his rod a mighty yank and frantically reeled in nothing but what was left of his line! "Damn!" he ejaculated, when realizing that he had lost fish, plug, wire leader, and a good section of stout line.

But my fish hung on. Either because I was too excited to strike, or because the hook had become firmly imbedded in his bony jaw, the fish was still there and the real work began. After running with all the line that I was disposed to yield, he went down and sulked. Then it was a case of lowering the rod, recovering what line I could, raising it again, and continuing this pumping process until the fish tired before I did. 'Mucho trabajo." grinned Ricardo, and he was right — it was real work. There were more vigorous runs, each a little shorter than the last, and finally when the line pointed almost straight down from the side of the boat where the fish sulked, Alfredo peered into the clear water and shouted, "Me veo! Me veo!"

Still pumping, reeling in, and lifting on the rod, I staggered to my feet and peered into the depths. Down through the clear water I too could see a huge, lithe, torpedo-shaped fish, flashing blue, white, and yellow as he wallowed in an expiring effort to dislodge the hook. But his struggles were in vain and at last with a triumphant shout, Ricardo gaffed and lifted aboard a prime sparkling yellowtail. When we got back to the lodge that evening we found that the fish tipped the scale at precisely thirty-six pounds. "Grandes pescado," grinned Ricardo, displaying two rows of magnificent white teeth. The first fish of the day, and we had only started!

Around the headlands and in and out among the projecting rocks we went, catching fish and losing others, while the seals yapped their protest from the ledges and the sea birds sailed about us against the azure sky. Schools of big mottled sullen-looking cabrilla infested the deeps near the dripping rocks and struck as vigorously as did the yellowtails. Now and then we would haul in trim, streamlined, iridescent blue-green bonita, or long rakish vividly speckled sierra mackerel. Further offshore we got into a school of rooster fish, "papagallo" as the boatman called them, displaying their spectacular dorsal roach, a waving purple mantilla. Huge ugly groupers of the sea bass type which the boatman called "ropa" weighing up to two hundred pounds, inhabited the submarine caves and caverns of the rocky shores. Every now and then when we had about finished off a bonita, cabrilla, or yellowtail as large as fifteen or twenty pounds and were prepared to raise it to the gaff, the line would begin to run out in a steady pull, for all the world as though dragged by a donkey engine, straight for some shadowy cavern in the submerged cliffs. We could do nothing to check the even, steady, pull, and finally in desperation would hand the rod to the boatmen. With apprehensive shakes of the head and scowls born of many similar experiences, they would haul on the line hand over hand until it parted.

Time and again this happened during our many days of fishing. The grouper, whose open mouth is wider than the largest part of his body and who could swallow a basketball with as much ease as we might take an aspirin tablet, would simply gulp our fish, and with irresistible and deliberate force, take it to his rocky cavern. Once there, wedged among the rocks, he could digest it, plug, hooks, wire leader, line and all at his leisure. But one day a couple of our fishing companions who had thoroughly wearied of feeding Martin plugs at $2.75 each to the groupers, conceived and executed a successful assault upon these monsters of the sea. They fished further out from the rocks where they would catch a ten- or fifteen-pound fish of one type or another. They then impaled the fish on a big hook weighted with a chunk of lead, and sank it to the bottom. When the grouper ventured out from his cave and took the fish, they never gave him a chance to get back. They hauled on the heavy line, hand over hand, and the fish simply had to come in. These men brought in seven groupers that day averaging one hundred and fifty pounds each. The groupers were too large to be hauled into the boat, so as they were caught the boatman strung them on a rope behind the launch, and they were towed in, not unlike a raft of logs. The largest we were able to land, fishing close to the rocks with our light tackle, weighed only fifty-seven pounds.

As our intended ten-day vacation stretched into three weeks, the fishing continued and improved as the sunny days followed one another in delightful succession. We caught yellowtail up to forty-one pounds and huge cabrilla almost as large as the groupers. The work was strenuous, and because relentless years had taxed our strength and stamina, we adopted a plan of fishing one day and loafing the next.

Though taken in unbelievable quantities, the fish were not wasted. All were edible, in fact quite delicious, cooked as they were in Mexican style — barbecued — filleted — boiled in deep fat. A sufficient quantity was kept in the cold room at the lodge; but at the close of each day when the last boat had come in, the surplus was loaded into a truck, trundled up to the village, and distributed among the eager villagers who, like all rural Mexicans, were ever hungry.

We were too early for the sailfish, marlins, and broadbills, but we were assured they would be in the Gulf in fabulous quantities in late April and early May. The fishing at Loreto is a year-round activity. Our dream had indeed come true.

One day a graceful, white, sixty-foot yawl, the *Mischievous*, dropped anchor at the lodge. Its genial owner, Mr. Joseph Reynes of Los Angeles, took us for a sail down the Gulf and urged us to join him in a trip to Peru. His crew from Los Angeles around the cape and up to Loreto had consisted of an American skin-diver and a husky Mexican lad, both of whom had to leave the yawl there. The skin-diver was spearing and photographing fish under water, and Reynes was taking pictures for television.

Reynes offered us a share of the profits from the venture with all expenses paid if we would join him in his prospective trip down along the west coast of South America. But clients and patients could be put off no longer, and with much regret we had to decline the invitation. The Mexican bar boy who had left to operate the fishing boat out of Guayamas was a pearl diver. We learned from him when looking over a collection of some of the pearls he had gathered, that the oysters of the Gulf produced magnificent, iridescent gray and black opaque gems, some of astonishing size.

The gray whales produce their calves in the bayous and lagoons along the Pacific side of the peninsula. While we were at Loreto a group of scientists, some representing universities of California and others coming from Washington, D.C., flew in and established headquarters at Loreto. These scientists were not only counting the whales from the air, but were actually studying them at close contact in the shallow waters of the bays. They reported hundreds of females with their calves in Magdalena Bay and elsewhere along the coast. One party was stranded in a little rubber boat on a lagoon on the Pacific side of the peninsula and had to subsist for about forty-eight hours on a bottle of Tequila, bean soup, and cormorant eggs. They pronounced the eggs not only edible, but even better than the product of the barnyard hen.

Toward the end our stay, Ed Tabor, our hostess' husband, returned by plane from the mainland. The story of his jaunt, as he related it to us, seemed almost incredible. Tabor operates his own plane. Just before we arrived at the lodge, he had flown a party of sportsmen across the Gulf over to the mainland to a point in the rugged mountains about 150 miles south of Guaymas, where they hunted wild turkeys. The country there is extremely primitive and they employed a Mexican guide. In tramping about through the brush over the rocks, up one hill and down the other, the guide stopped short and declared they were in a territory where a tribe of aborigines lived. They wore no clothes, said the guide, lived in caves, and ate raw meat, to secure which they would periodically raid the cattle herds of the Mexican villagers. Their method of obtaining this meat was to kill the animal with a crude stone knife, gouge out a chunk of the flesh, and beat a hasty retreat, leaving the remains of the carcass on the ground. The guide said the aborigines spoke a jargon which only they understood. The villagers treated them as though they were wild animals and would shoot them on sight, for the villagers were constantly losing cattle and were greatly embittered toward the aborigines. Ultimately Tabor and his party had the good fortune to stumble onto a series of caves at the base of a frowning cliff high in the mountains which clearly bore evidence of human habitation. Beef bones were scattered about, but nothing resembling furniture or domestic implements was found. Clearly the aborigines had hid in the brush.

This is the story as I got it from Tabor who, in turn, got the best part of it from the guide. If the anthropologists and the ethnologists have not as yet had wind of this unexplored path to knowledge of a branch of our curious humanity — and almost in our midst — they had better make haste to do so. It would take a lot of explaining to satisfy me for no fictional mystery can so enthrall as the mystery of man's development or lack of it. If no one is interested, I shall either go to that spot some day to see for myself; or, if I choose to go fishing that day, I shall label the story as another very good, possible fish story.

But all good things must come to an end. So, with an astonishing fund of unusual facts and real fish stories, and with a last look at the blue Gulf, the palm-girt shore, and the rugged mountains, we bade farewell to our host and hostess, the Tabors, and were soon winging back to desks and duties.

Behold the Fisherman

Men angled for fish in the prehistoric seas and inland waters, long before they were able to record their achievements, even in the simplest of hieroglyphics. The Prophet Amos mentions fishing, and in the Book of Job, written nearly 3500 years ago, one finds reference to fishing with hooks. The tombs of the ancient Pharaohs, and various cave remains of western Europe, contained evidence of the use of many different kinds of fishing gear, including hooks made of stone, shell, or bronze, and lines constructed of fiber, wool, or hide. The capture of fish as food for man has been carried on from the very earliest time.

On a quiet Sabbath morning, nearly two thousand years ago, as Jesus trod the pebbly shore of the Sea of Galilee, he came upon Simon and Andrew, casting their nets. He told them that if they would follow him, he would "make them become fishers of men," but he never suggested that they should discontinue fishing for fish. Some of the apostles, after deciding to follow Jesus, and to preach the gospel of peace on earth and good will toward men, likewise became fishermen. Remember that when Jesus was transfigured on the mount he had taken with him as witnesses only those disciples who were fishermen. He never criticized any of them for their humble calling, though he often reproached the scribes and the money changers. He must have found, in the hearts of these simple fishermen, the qualities of gentleness, love of peace, and a disposition toward quiet contemplation. On one occasion the Master even went so far as to inform the Pharisees that it was entirely proper for men to procure food on the Sabbath, saying, "The Sabbath was made for man, not man for the Sabbath."

And so, down through the centuries more and more people fished for trout, and for the finny denizens of ocean, lake, and stream. Today, most sport fishing is done on Sunday, and, because of deep-rooted religious convictions, most of the fish are eaten on Friday.

I will venture the assertion that fishermen, as a rule, are men of mild temperament, of generous disposition — men who respect the rights of their fellows, and revere their Creator. They make their periodic pilgrimages in ever-increasing numbers. They constitute an important segment of society. But no one has yet been able to account for the irresistible urge which sends so many anglers forth throughout each fishing season. It must be something far more compelling than a mere desire to eat fish, for the nearby markets afford every known variety, and at modest cost. Can it be something that men inherited from their cave-dwelling ancestors, something that was bred into them with the first stir of life? Is it something in the bloodstream, or has it been acquired? May it not even be a disease?

I recently found a printed notice on a tree in the Whitman Forest of Eastern Oregon. It read:

"WAR N I N G!
Fishing-Pox
Very contagious to adult males
Symptoms - Continual complaint as to need for
fresh air, sunshine and relaxation. Patient has
blank expression, sometimes deaf to wife and
kids. Has no taste for work of any kind.
Frequent checking of tackle catalogues. Hangs out
in sporting goods stores longer than usual. Secret
night phone calls to fishing pals.
Mumbles to self, lies to everyone. No known cure.
Treatment - Medication is useless. Disease not fatal.
Victim should go fishing as often as possible."

The symptoms are well stated, and the malady is correctly described. However, the notice contains one statement which clearly discloses that its author is not a dyed-in-the-wool fisherman, for he says that the ailment is not fatal. I know from abundant experience, and from years of observation, that this is far from true. When fishing-pox has once attested a man, he will have the disease for the rest of his natural life. There is absolutely no cure. While the victim goes fishing, the germ merely hibernates, and for the time being he seems to improve, but he is not cured. Sooner or later the germ again becomes virulent and the same old symptoms again manifest themselves, whereupon another fishing trip is necessary in order that the patient may secure even partial relief.

Victims of fishing-pox should be very careful, during winter months not to read resort propaganda, particularly that which emphasizes fishing. When the weather is so inclement that even the thought of fishing is out of the question, the victim may appear almost normal, because his thoughts are on other subjects. But the reading of such literature will promptly reactivate the germ, even during the winter period, causing the patient to suffer throughout the balance of the closed fishing season.

The fraternity of fishermen is a huge organization. Its members, except when they go fishing, are normal enough. They possess the same attributes, and are actuated by the same motives and impulses as other human beings. Even when suffering from fishing-pox their actions do not render them particularly conspicuous. But get them out on a trout stream and you will find them to be very different creatures. Most of them are superstitious and many become pig-headed. They have their many ways of taking fish, their various and sundry items of tackle, and their favorite fishing waters. Most fishermen are selfish about revealing where they took their last heavy basket of trout, and are stubborn about what they believe to be the correct way of fishing, and about the proper tackle to use. They have their many idiosyncrasies, but for generosity, loyalty and simple delight in innocent pleasure, they cannot be excelled. "Who steals their purse, steals trash," but the man who usurps any of their sacred angling prerogatives is a scoundrel indeed.

> "Oh the gallant fisherman's life!
> It is the best of any.
> 'Tis full of pleasure, void of strife,
> And 'tis beloved by many."

A fisherman is a living exemplification of the old adage that anticipation is greater than realization. He goes fishing with high hopes. He conjures up scenes of magnificent pools full of great fish eager to take his fly. He plans another trip, and another, ever confident that the next will prove the fulfillment. He is never wholly discouraged, even when he has to admit, as so often he does, that the fishing wasn't quite what he had expected; for behind it all, far back in his primordial self, there lurks still the hope, nay the conviction, that some time, somewhere, he will find the fishing of his dreams.

Family background, social position, wealth and business interests, all so important in the city, count for nothing in the woods. There, a spirit of comradery, of good fellowship and of common interest brings together the rich and the poor, the expert and the novice. When one fisherman encounters another on the stream, self-introductions are spontaneous. Each hails the other with the salutation "what luck?," a bond of mutual respect and friendship is immediately established, and when they sit down together on a mossy log, admire one another's catch, and talk about the state of the weather, the state of the stream, and the habits of fish. An acquaintance is established which lasts for a lifetime.

Observe that old fellow setting up his rod on the bank of the stream, and actually trembling with the excitement of anticipation. You can guess rightly that he has been a fisherman for more than half a century, but that he is now experiencing the same thrill that he did when he caught his first trout, so many years ago. And look at his hat. He may be a steel tycoon, a railroad magnate, or the president of a big bank. But that old hat, punctured with several holes, and garnished with a collection of frayed flies, is the most precious article of his possession. It has accompanied him on fishing trips throughout many summers. Time and again he has used it as a cup when drinking from the cold stream. The binding has long since left the brim, for it was beaten off years ago by repeated use in fanning the embers of his campfire. It is smudged with soot and wrinkled with age, but it has brought him good luck so often, and has accompanied him on so many happy excursions, that he would not part with it for all of the wealth of King Midas.

One of the subjects of frequent disagreement among fishermen is tobacco. They will all agree that cigarettes, of most any brand, are good enough for city smoking, and may even be carried to the stream, when the angler intends to be out for only a few hours. But the confirmed fisherman will not pack his duffel for an extended trip into the wilderness without storing away his pipe, and can or pack of smoking tobacco. He may even surreptitiously tuck in a small chewing plug, to be enjoyed in solitude. A fellow angler on stream or lake, who offers another a pinch of smoking tobacco, must be sure that he proffers the right brand; else his generosity will probably be met with a shake of the head, or even with a scowl.

More than once, in the evening around the campfire, as the anglers chatted pleasantly of the events of the day, I have seen the happy atmosphere changed to one of discord and gloom by a chance statement, to be followed by a violent argument over tobacco. On such occasions the party breaks up in a huff, each angler sulks to his sleeping bag, and the gloom is not dispelled until the next morning over a cup of steaming coffee.

A fisherman, particularly one who smokes but little at home, and would not dream of chewing tobacco there, is quite unable to say why he needs these stronger comforts when he is fishing. But without attempting to analyze it, he knows that they are the very balm of Gilead to his soul. If he loses fish they console him, if he hooks one, he puffs away more vigorously, or bites off another bit from his ragged plug, while bending to his task. They are as essential to his equipment as his wool socks or his waders.

Why a pipe is so indispensable to a fisherman, no one can rightly say. I have known anglers to forget their reels, flies, baskets, and even their rods, but I have yet to learn of one that forgot his pipe. Yet a pipe on a fishing trip is probably as useless a bit of equipment as could be imagined. When fishing a mountain brook, how many times has the stubborn thicket torn the pipe from the angler's mouth? And on the open river, how often does the fisherman hiss curses, between set teeth, when the stripped line, on a long cast, whips itself around the bowl of his briar? What earthly good is a pipe to a fisherman who must pick his way down the roaring course of a swollen stream, where hands and feet are all too few? It is out most of the time, and is often upside down, but the angler only bites it the harder, and loves it the more. A stout pipe it is that can withstand the grind of a good set of teeth through a full season of fly fishing on rough water. But there is something about the feel of a pipe between set jaws that is intimately associated with the caress of rushing water about one's knees, and the pull of a good fish, out where the riffles break. They are all a part of the inexplicable joy of fishing.

I remember an incident of some years ago. We had waded out upon a long, triangular sand bar that lay in the elbow of a big green pool, with white water on the far side. Perhaps three feet in depth, the bar pitched abruptly into deep water, and thus we were standing waist deep in the choppy edge of an eddy. It was a long cast, but we were getting our flies out where the fish were rising. Any one of these rainbow more than compensated for cold legs and aching wrists. It was the kind of fishing one pictures to himself on winter nights, when musing over a volume of Henry Van Dyke; the kind one looks forward to with such eagerness, but so seldom experiences. We knew that it couldn't last. Fishing like that never does. It is common knowledge to every trout fisherman that there are times when, for some unaccountable reason, and usually for but a brief period, the big fish of a pool will suddenly, and of one accord, become violently attracted to the fly. At such times a confirmed angler gives little thought to wet legs.

In an effort to make a longer cast my companion moved a little further out and, leaning forward with the swing of his rod, lost his balance. The pitch of the sand bar sent him into deep water, and the twist of the eddy swept him off his feet, and spun him half way around, directly in front of me. All was submerged in an instant—that is, all but the periscope. The water closed over his face, but not over his pipe. For a fleeting second he bobbed along, completely under the water, except for that pipe. The next instant I had him by the collar, and we were in shallow water. The pipe had gotten upside down, and he was blowing sparks like a Mississippi steamboat, but true to tradition, he had hung on to that pipe, and what is more, he had kept it alight.

Schopenhauer pronounces pipe smoking a substitute for thought. There may be grounds for the statement, but I find no application for it in the case of an angler. It doesn't account for his smoking proclivity, because, on a fishing excursion, there is precious little thought to be substituted. A fisherman, when he gets down to business, isn't doing much thinking; he doesn't go fishing to think. He goes fishing to fish and to smoke. His whole concern is that little bundle of feathers and yarn, bobbing along the riffle in such a tantalizing fashion. To him, during those hours on the stream, with spring in the air, and out in the pools, there is but one idea dominating his mind, the taking of fish. It is true he notes the glory of the sunshine, the fragrance of fresh growing things along the shore, the infinite depth of blue, where sky meets the tree tops, and the farther rim of the hill. With languid interest he watches the startled duck wing out from the weedy bank. He sees the deep hung nest of an oriole stitched to the highest branch of a flowering hawthorn and he experiences a mild sense of virtue in the absence of his boyhood desire to rob it. But these things are borne in upon him without effort and without thought. He is a part of what he sees and feels. He is revolving in his mind, to the complete exclusion of everything else, such mighty questions as: "What will that riffle yield? Can I reach that little patch of water under the willow? How much of a strain will the leader stand?"

All about him is the throbbing life of June. Nature is at her loveliest, and he is a part of the great cosmic scheme. He is dumbly grateful, and consciously happy, but he doesn't have to think about it. There's thinking aplenty back in town. He just puffs on his pipe and soaks up the scene and the situation as he goes. He knows it will live in his mind. He needs a lot of just such material for winter reflection.

The North Beckons

High, faint, and far, the melancholy call of the Canadian honkers headed for the southland, announced to us in unmistakable terms, that white frost would be glistening on the grass in the mornings throughout northern British Columbia, and that vine maple and quaking aspen leaves would already be turning to crimson and gold. We knew then that the summer days of sluggish inactivity among the big Kamloops trout of the Dominion were at an end, and that the fish would be cruising about again ready to leap at the hapless insects dropping to the surface of the many lakes.

So once more Spen Biddle and I got our duffle together in the station wagon, with Tuckie, his Springer spaniel, plenty of grub, fishing tackle, and firearms. This excursion was to last a whole month, and on a bright, late-September morning we left Spen's stately grounds on the Washington shore of the Columbia River not far from Vancouver, and headed for the border. For many miles our route took us through fragrant orchards, innumerable melon fields, and acres of big, red, ripe tomatoes, some of which we bought and added to our supply of consumables.

The first night we camped on a sagebrush flat just south of the Canadian line, and the next day, and through the days that followed, we were in the big rolling open country of our British cousins. As we worked farther north the evenings became crisper and our sleeping bags, downy and warm, were truly welcome. At night we often heard the whistle and whisper of beating wings as great flocks of ducks rose from their summer marshes and pursued their certain way toward Texas, the Rio Grande, and old Mexico. Yet many of the ducks, seemingly reluctant to essay the long journey south, still lingered on the thousand lakes, pools, and marshes that characterize this vast territory. The thickets were alive with ruffed grouse, and the flash of leaping trout broke the placid surface of many a sparkling lake. The country is a medley of grassy meadowlands, knolls, and low hills, broken here and there along the ridges and in the gullies by patches of dark green pines. At first the aspens and maples wore their mantles of summer green, but as the days shortened and the miles lengthened behind us, the frosty nights painted them lemon yellow, then orange, and finally brilliant russet.

We came one evening to a quaint little inn at Spence's Bridge on the Thompson Fork of the Fraser River where we decided to spend the night and inquire about the fishing. The proprietor was civil but not too chummy, having a goodly quantity of British reserve in his makeup. We were used to that however, and after a reasonable time we asked him to join us in a highball. When he had imbibed a couple of drinks he was ready to talk, so we asked him about the fishing, for we were wholly unacquainted with the country and not certain even of our destination. After sizing us up for a moment he said:

"Well, I don't know whether either of you fellows can handle a fly, but I do know this; if you take that dog with you out on a raft in Surrey Lake and tie a rod to his tail rigged with two flies, he'll catch two trout every time he wags it, and they'll be good ones too."

He told us that if we would follow an old road up a particular meadow and look about through a willow thicket at its dead end, we could find the beginning of a trail. He said it would lead us to Sussex Lake, some seven miles back in the hills, where it was not unusual to catch Kamloops trout weighing ten pounds or more, and that Surrey Lake, where Tuckie could catch our fish, was only about a half mile beyond Sussex.

It was while we were thrashing about in the willow thicket, trying to find the trail, that Tuckie flushed a fool hen. I had heard many stories about these stupid birds, but I was reluctant to believe them until I picked up first-hand information by actual experience. This bird hopped into a jack pine tree, some fifteen feet above the ground, almost directly over our heads. We pelted away at it with rocks and sticks, but our aim was bad. Once or twice we struck the branch upon which it perched, only to see the foolish creature teeter a bit, regain its balance, and continue to crane its inquisitive neck at us. Occasionally a missile even grazed its feathers, but the bird only shook itself and settled down again on the limb. At last with a lucky shot for us, if not for the bird, I knocked it out of the tree, and we broiled it over the coals for our supper. It was tender and delicious.

We did finally locate the dim trail, loaded ourselves down with duffle, and, leaving the car in the meadow, headed for Sussex Lake. We ran across coveys of fool hens here and there in the grassy patches under the trees, or perched in the low branches of the jack pines. They appeared to be utterly fearless, and we could walk to within eight or ten feet of them before they would hop from the ground into the trees or move from a low branch to a slightly higher one.

Spen said, "When I was a boy I snared a fool hen with a fish line. Maybe I could do it again." The thing sounded fantastic to me, but we agreed that it was worth a try, so we struggled from beneath our packs, got out our fishing tackle, and set up a fly rod with reel, running the line through the guides to the tip. Spen tied a slip noose two or three inches in diameter at the end of the line. He quietly approached one of the birds, which merely stood and looked at him, and with trembling hands tried to slip the noose over its head. In his excitement he nicked the creature's bill with the tip of the rod and fluffed up its feathers with the noose, but the ninny only shook its head, moved a step or two, and continued to gaze at us. At last, with a deft flip he snared one and then another. As the captured birds fluttered about, the others remained wholly indifferent. They did not fly away, but just sat gawking at their turn at the noose. Two apiece were enough for an excellent supper, so he stopped with four, but during all our days in Canada we could, and did, snare fool hens whenever we wanted them and in any desired number. How those dull fowls have survived the numerous predators such as coyotes, bobcats and foxes, I do not know, but they were overwhelmingly abundant.

We pitched our little pup tent on the shore of the lake and lived on a royal diet of fried trout and broiled grouse. My very first cast in

Sussex Lake raised a fighting, six-pound Kamloops trout, and though we did not tie a fly rod to Tuckie's tail, we did learn that the innkeeper was telling the literal truth about the number, size, and fighting qualities of the trout in Surrey Lake.

A remote section of the country, which I had traced from a forest map, disclosed another lake not far away labeled "Bob's," and we determined to find it. Following a faint, almost obliterated trail in the general direction indicated by the map, we located this lovely little sheet of water nestled in a basin among the pines, where we were fortunate enough to find an old Indian raft hidden in the brush at the shore. We pushed out on the lake and paddled about as best we could with the clumsy contraption, and we soon discovered that the water was full of great trout averaging three to six pounds. The instant a big Royal Coachman Bucktail fly hit the water, one of the husky fellows would have it, and the fight was on! Often when we caught too many trout we would release them after the fun of netting such warriors, but on this occasion we wanted to bring home some smoked trout so we kept what we were able to land and anticipated a weary trek back to camp burdened with a heavy catch.

But a series of untoward circumstances soon put an end to our fishing for that day. In an idle moment, as I paddled along, I let my fly dangle out behind as the rod lay on the raft. With a mighty surge a big trout grabbed the fly and in a twinkling my entire outfit — rod, reel, line, leader, and fly — was overboard. As the fish dragged my gear about the lake, the rod would bob up toward the surface for a moment, and I would paddle frantically in that direction, only to see it disappear the next instant and reappear some fifty feet on the opposite side. Then it sank, and as the blue waters of the lake closed above it, I charged an investment of about eighty dollars to profit and loss although I did later arrange with a friendly Indian to try to recover the rods, and offered him a reward of ten dollars for his effort. If he ever did find the tackle he was probably smart enough to keep it for himself.

The other circumstance which might easily have spelled *finis* to both of us was the wholly unanticipated and really terrific thunderstorm that hit the lake without a moment's warning. Suddenly the sky was almost as black as night, the wind howled, and the lake rolled up in great churning waves. The spume flew like ribbons at the whim of the crazy winds. Huge hailstones battered us as we struggled against the mounting waves, and we had difficulty in making headway against the savage gale. At last we stepped on shore with considerable enthusiasm though thoroughly drenched and beaten. Shivering in our wet clothes, and assisted by the Indian, we salvaged at least one rod and a generous quantity of fish.

One of the daintiest and most succulent *hors d'oeuvres* I have ever tasted is smoked Kamloops trout, and because nearly everyone seems to agree with me, I have described in detail elsewhere in this volume the method both for making a smokehouse and for curing the fish.

For some time we thought that the wilderness where we camped was our own exclusive property, but much to our surprise, one day we saw a man and his young wife with their fishing tackle and camping outfit coming up the trail. After we had struck up the customary western acquaintance, we found that the lady was so captivated by our little smokehouse that I yielded to the male impulse of courtesy (for she was really very good looking) and suggested that, while we were away on our next day's excursion, she might tend the smoking operation, including, with our many pounds of fish, any caught by her husband and herself. She was delighted.

As we neared camp that evening, we saw a curl of smoke among the pines, and upon arrival, found the pretty young woman sitting in tears beside the smoldering remains of our smokehouse and our last batch of trout. She had gotten the fire too hot and burned the whole thing to the ground, fish and all!

The next day we broke camp, followed the historic old Caribou Trail which extends for nearly a thousand miles through western British Columbia, and got into the more rugged timbered country, less frequented by those from the outside. While the trail was still in good condition as Canadian highways go, the branch roads and little byways serving the back country, much of which we explored, were often well nigh impassable. Soon we were traveling across a high plateau, and though much of it was comparatively level, there were many low, rolling hills cut up by little timbered ridges and flaming islands of aspen and vine maple. The whole area was distinguished by innumerable large and small lakes, all of them containing fish. In spite of our experience at Sussex Lake with the loss of our smokehouse and its contents, we were able to improvise another and our accumulation of smoked trout was soon replenished. With Tuckie's help we consumed unbelievable quantities of fish, grouse, fool hens, and ducks. The evidences of moose were abundant, but at that season of the year they kept well out of sight. Sometimes we camped in the rain, and often we had to break through a film of new ice on our water buckets in the morning when the grass was white and stiff with hoar frost. We had heard of Chilko River, and upon making inquiry at the little town of Williams Lake well up in northern British Columbia, we learned that it could be reached by a rough, stony road some seventy-five miles to the southwest. After scraping over many a high center and detouring around many a downed tree across the road, we located this primitive wilderness.

Chilko Lake is a vast sheet of sparkling water some sixty miles in length, hidden away among the weather-beaten crags and peaks of the coast range. Its brimming waters are carried away by the Chilko River which has it source at the east end of the lake where it becomes one of the important tributaries of the mighty Fraser River. In late summer and fall, sockeye salmon in unbelievable multitudes ascend the stream to spawn in the lake. As the season advances their bodies take on a deep tomato red color but their heads remain olive green. We found salmon everywhere in the river and in the lower reaches of the lake. Although they do not feed during their spawning migration, some of them seemed to resent our big wet flies and would strike at them so savagely that often while we fished the river, we found ourselves fast to a big salmon. To land one on light fly tackle was out of the question, so it was a matter of hanging on with a tight line until the fish broke loose, carrying with him the fly and often the whole leader.

But trout were there too, in astonishing numbers, and had vigorous appetites. We used an outboard motor attached to the stern of our rowboat in order to get back up the river at the end of the day, and would allow the boat to drift with the current until we reached a likely looking spot. There we would anchor the boat and cast our flies upon the fast rolling waters, permitting them to quarter in with the current. It was the exception rather than the rule, when we did not strike a good trout before the drift of the fly was completed and retrieved for another cast. While the trout, on average, were not so large as those in Sussex Lake, and in some of the other landlocked waters which we had fished, they ran from two to four pounds, were in fine condition, and were as brilliant and vigorous as any fish I have ever taken.

I will not soon forget our last day on the Chilko River, for it was one of those rare occasions when I took more and better fish than Spen. We had planned to leave at noon, and we were enjoying our last morning on the river. I was fishing with a number six wet Hallock Killer, drifting the fly a foot or so under the surface of the water, getting vigorous strikes, and landing heavy trout at almost every cast. Spen, who ties his own flies, and consequently does not take too kindly to the idea of using one of my patterns, kept experimenting with various types. I repeatedly urged him to use one of the Killers, but he persistently declined. Every time I landed a trout, Spen would haul in his line and feverishly re-rig, tying on another and another of his own flies. But he failed to get so much as a single strike. Noon approached, and time was short. Spen gave up at last and grudgingly accepted one of my flies, which he sent sailing out over a likely patch of water. In a flash a big fish struck it, but broke away just as the doleful toll of the dinner triangle floated out from the lodge across the water. Fishing was over. Vacation time had ended. We pulled up anchor, cranked the little motor, and headed for the resort and the long trip home. We did not talk about the Hallock Killer.

CHAPTER

Princely Waters

A book which even mentioned fishing in the Northwest, and did not describe Oregon's two famous trout rivers, the MacKenzie and the Deschutes, would be like hotcakes without maple syrup or, more aptly, like poetry without song. Known far and wide to anglers everywhere, these two rivers are transcendent among fishing streams in any clime, and though they have suffered from the inroads of civilization, are still princely waters. The days when they "knew no sound save their own dashing" were not long past when I first cast a fly upon their sparkling riffles. I have seen their wildness violated by axe and plow, railroad and highway. I have even witnessed, with dismay, the advent of the auto-court along their banks. But I remember and love them best as I think of old times when roads were hardly more than trails, and one met only the shy forest denizens when fishing from their shores.

The Cascade Mountains are the wild and free source of many crystal streams, and these two glorious children of a glorious mother rise no great distance apart in the heights of that proud range, where the air is clearest and the setting most magnificent. But they part company forthwith.

"The waters know their own, and draw
The brook that springs in yonder height."

John Burroughs

In spite of their kindred place of birth, they possess little more in common, other than that each carries an abundance of fine rainbow trout; but when that has been said almost nothing of similarity remains.

The Cascade range, extending north and south through the State of Oregon, roughly "divides the desert from the sown." The Deschutes drains a big arid and semi-arid section on the eastern side of the mountains, while the MacKenzie, finally making a confluence with the Willamette, gathers its waters from a vast verdant area on the western slope.

The Deschutes is a man's stream, strong and vital. Through its higher elevations it glides for some distance among quiet meadows, including that altogether lovely spot, Crane Prairie. Then it flows through silent forests of pine and tamarack, splashed with patches of white-trunked aspens and clumps of silvery cottonwoods, until it tumbles and roars between the towering ramparts of its basalt cliffs. There it grinds and churns its way through deep canyons, bordered by massive slabs of shattered lava rock, hot on summer days, to the very edge of the water. From the point where the stream enters this steep and rugged canyon, clear to its confluence with the mighty Columbia, the country is harsh and arid, a living is hard to come by, and the few homesteads along the benches are bleak and dreary. The steep hillsides are burned and sere, and fuel, even for our campfires, is scarce. This stretch is a land of sagebrush, greasewood, and rattlesnakes; but nonetheless, especially at dawn and sunset, it is impressive with its solitude and grandeur. The days are stern, winter and summer alike, but the night are blessed with such a canopy of bursting stars as is seldom seen elsewhere, all glittering in a somber velvet sky.

By contrast, the MacKenzie sings its way in white cataracts down the western slope of the mountains, dashing over rocks through heavy stands of fir and hemlock, between lush, ferny banks and among moss-covered boulders, kept moist and green by rills and sprays from splashing waterfalls. Then it loses some of its youthful vigor and glides placidly past fields and meadows between banks shaded with staunch oaks and far reaching maples. What a glorious sight it is in the autumn when frosts have turned all the foliage to crimson and gold!

Along the MacKenzie an occasional scorpion, with its sharp, stinger tail arched high above its segmented body, may crawl from beneath a mossy log and impel the angler to gather up his lunch and move a little further away. The fisherman on the Deschutes, more than once hears the startling hum of a rattlesnake, or sees one gliding through the dry grass just in time to avert a fatal step. Yet neither pest holds terror sufficient to discourage the angler or to deter him from repeated excursions to both rivers. Much like a mountain brook many times enlarged, the MacKenzie is a series of riffles, eddies and pools, with caldrons of white water churning between great rocks. It presents few long, relatively smooth strips of water until well down toward its confluence with the Willamette. The Deschutes, on the other hand is just a big, mad river almost from the start. True, high up in the mountain meadows, stretches of the river are quite placid, as though it were flowing along in contemplation of what lies ahead, but then it finally does make up its mind to hurry away from its childhood haunts, attain maturity, and dash for the sea where it whips itself into mad, whitecap fury. Woe to the angler who ventures any distance from shore along this part of its wild course, for at one moment the water may be but knee deep, while in the next a whirling eddy may surge about his legs and spin him off balance in a twinkling.

In the earlier days of boating these restless rivers presented hazards, and more than one fisherman forfeited his life for a wild ride through the foaming rapids. Since the development of the light, wide, plywood boat, with an exceptionally high stern, now used on both streams, each can be navigated with much less danger. However, boating is no longer permitted on the MacKenzie above its confluence with Blue River, or on the Deschutes below a strip through the high meadows south of the city of Bend. In times past both rivers yielded more lusty rainbow trout than any others that I know, but, like so much of the fishing water of the Northwest, the prolific yields of fine fish year after year, have generally reduced both their size and number. When I first knew the MacKenzie one could travel many miles of its wild course without seeing a human habitation, but today its banks are crowded with fishing lodges, cottages and great country estates, many of the latter owned by Californians, and it is spanned by numerous bridges. In spite of the high cost of floating the river, its shores are lined with automobiles, fishing parties, and camp litter on the opening day of each season and over weekends. From one to a half dozen anglers are to be seen at every good pool and riffle, and many trout are caught by those weekend bank fishermen.

The Deschutes River, too, is fished more heavily each year. Many Portland people now own cottages and cabins on the stream, and a substantial strip of the best water, some twenty miles in length, is controlled by the Portland-Deschutes River Club. As a final blow, power companies are about to construct two big dams on the river which will convert a vast section of this restless stream into two placid ponds.

So I prefer to think of these grand rivers as I first knew them in the old days. The two chapters that immediately follow, one about the MacKenzie and the other about the Deschutes, are not written for the purpose of implying that the fishing on these streams now is comparable to what it used to be, but rather with the thought that those who knew these waters when I did, so many years ago, may find their earlier recollections pleasantly revived, and that those who did not, will get some idea of what these streams meant to us more than a third of a century past.

Supreme Court of the United States
Washington 13, D. C.

CHAMBERS OF
JUSTICE WILLIAM O. DOUGLAS

October 26, 1953.

Dear Blaine:

It was nice to get your letter of October 15th,
as well as your earlier epistle about the fishing on the
Lostine. I think Sam Clark's memory must be failing him a
bit because I have caught some wonderful trout in the Lostine.
Once I made a bet of $5 that I could catch three legal-size
rainbow trout on a dry fly from the pool in front of my cabin
on the Lostine in five minutes. I naturally used a Hallock
Killer. On the first cast I hooked but lost the trout -- a
nice one -- and figured that I had disturbed the pool and
lost the bet. On the next cast I got an eight-inch trout,
on the next one a six-inch trout and on the next a ten-incher --
all from the one little pool. With the $5 I bought a chair
and named it after the man who was foolish enough to bet
against me and that man's name is Saul Haas at Station KIRO
in Seattle.

I would like to get to Nova Scotia and try
the kind of fishing you had there. I went down the Mackenzie
River 1400 miles to the Arctic Ocean this summer. I did very
little fishing. They have up there great big northern pike,
about as big as that table in your office. I did hook on to
one of them. But if I told you what I used, I would get thrown
out of the Dry Fly and Wet Drinking Club of which you are, I
hope, still president.

I am glad you liked the piece I did in the American
Law Journal, which was my speech before the American Law Institute.
What you said about it touched me deeply.

Yours faithfully,

Bill

Blaine Hallock, Esq.,
Sommer Building, 2nd Floor,
Baker, Oregon.

E. C. POWELL, *Angler*

FLIES • • FLY RODS • • SPINNERS • • LANDING NETS AND LEADERS   ROD REPAIRING

MAKER OF **Powell's** HAND MADE
TROUT TACKLE

TELEPHONE 3-3260
624 C STREET
MARYSVILLE, CALIFORNIA
Nov. 4 1953

Mr Blaine Hallock
2nd. Floor Sommer Bldg
Baker, Oregon

Dear Mr. Hallock:

        I have not contacted any one to repair your rod.
If you wish to send it to me I will look it over and tell you what
I think of repairing it .   I do not like to repair Hardy rods
and do not take in any other make but my own as I am plenty busy
with my own rods. However I do not like to turn you down so
will do my best to serve you with this rod.

                    Sincerely,

                  E C Powell

November 25th, 1953

Mr. E. C. Powell
Manufacturer of Fishing Tackle
624 C Street
Marysville, California

Dear Mr. Powell:

It is indeed kind of you, as disclosed by your
letter of the 4th inst., to accomplish the repairs
to the Hardy rods. I am forwarding to you under separate
cover by express three Hardy rod tips, with accompanying
broken parts.

I will say that the man responsible for all of
this breakage (not myself) was extremely careless and
that the damage is quite inexcusable. What he did was
to ride along through the brush in an automobile with the
rods carried on the sides of the car. As was to be expected, the overhanging brush fouled these rods and broke
them. You will note that the tip to the two piece rod
broke off several inches from the end, and was subjected
to a terrific strain before breaking. In other words this
tip is dreadfully bowed. Is it at all possible that by
steaming, imposing weights on the rod or otherwise, any
of this strain could be removed? Whether or not that is
possible I realize that some five inches of the tip are
permanently gone with the result that the rod will necess-
arily be that much shorter after repair.

You will note that the tips to the lighter rod
have also been subjected to the same terrific strain.
Apparently the rods were almost bent double before breaking. About all I can say for the man responsible for this
breakage is that he ought to be locked up in jail for
awhile.

Anyway, the rods are forwarded to you with the hope
that you can do something with the wreckage.

Thanking you in advance, I am,

Yours very truly,

BH:b

photographs.....................................

The Mackenzie River in the Long Ago

I t is nearly thirty-five years since my first trip to the MacKenzie, yet so vividly etched in memory are the recollections of that far-away weekend that I can tell the story as though it happened only yesterday.

It was July. Henry Isaacs, Bill Umbdenstock, and I were smoking our pipes on the spacious porch of Trotter's cozy home, watching the lovely river slip along the pebbled shores and gather speed for the leaping rapids below.

Back of the house were green woods, quiet and cool. No irritating noises, stifling heat, or crowds marred the peace and simplicity of our sylvan retreat. A little garden patch of corn, pumpkin, and some kitchen stuff spanned the narrow stretch between the house and the silent firs. A stalwart company of tall sunflowers flanked the garden as if holding the threatening woods at bay. At the front of the house, mid-way between the porch and the split rail fence, a bed of dainty poppies, red, pink, and white, caught the last afterglow of sunset, their heavy heads nodding on fuzzy, slender stems. Here was Arcadia.

The shadows gathered as we sat talking little but thinking much of the day coming so peacefully to a close, a day which I think none of us will ever quite forget. Memory will keep it green long after those that followed, and perhaps those yet to come, fade away and are forgotten. A day on the South Fork! Even now my pulse quickens at the recollection.

First the brisk pull across the hurrying river. We could see the clean pebbles at the bottom despite the depth and the current. Then the walk through the woods, I won't pretend to say how far we walked for it was not measurable in miles. There, in the morning, with the dew on the grass, distance wasn't a factor, nor was time. I don't even know for how long we walked. I know only what we saw and felt on that journey of impressions, not of minutes or miles. Hans Christian Anderson must have known just such woods as those that lie between the majestic MacKenzie and its sparkling tributary to the south. He filled them with fairies and giants and strange shifting shadows which children fear yet love. We too knew as we walked beneath the quiet trees that these woods were enchanted. The birds sang it. The flowers proclaimed it. The needles of the great firs whispered it among themselves. And we felt it and were children again. The trail wound among big moss-covered rocks and under the reaching branches of hoary trees. Into the deep shadows it led us, then out again where the sun had sucked the dew from the white and blue anemones. Here a log lay full across the uncertain path and we vaulted the mossy hurdle with Bill, who was somewhat broad of girth, the last man over. Pushing through a fragrant hedge we came unexpectedly upon a tiny

sunlit meadow dotted with flowers. Pausing there to admire its loveliness, we heard the tinkle of a bell and looking back saw coming up
the trail a forest ranger mounted on a sturdy pinto, leading a string of
pack mules. When he overtook us as we loitered in the flowery glade,
the caravan stopped. As the animals nibbled the lush green grass, the
ranger, long, lean, and sunburned, threw a leg over the pommel of his
saddle and displaying a set of magnificent shiny white teeth
addressed us in a quiet drawl.

"How's the fishin', boys?"

"We really haven't started yet," responded Bill. "We just came
across the river from Trotters and are headed for the South Fork. The
country is so green and refreshing, we're just loafing along, admiring
its beauty."

"Yes, it's fine now," said the ranger, "But if you had been here last
week I would have had to muster you in as fire fighters. We had an
awful burn about two miles up the creek which took out a lot of fine
timber."

"What started the fire?" I asked.

"Fishermen. If you build a fire, be mighty careful, and be sure
that it's out when you leave. I'm heading for a camp well up the fork
where we are building access trails to the big stands of timber so
important to this country. A forest fire in the big trees where there are
no roads or trails can be really tragic. So do watch your fire."

With that he got his foot in the stirrup, gave the pack string rope
a yank and started up the trail, calling back, "Good luck."

We had almost forgotten the purpose of our expedition, so fascinated were we with the scene, when a sudden turn brought us full
upon the river. I have fished a lot of streams and have splashed along
the margins or stemmed the springtime force of many a rushing river
and many a babbling brook, but there is only one South Fork. We
came upon it there curving in friendly fashion about the little point of
hill where we stood. It was just the right size, neither too big nor too
small, exactly deep enough and precisely the right width. Here and
there clumps of sword fern and brake overhung clear pools. Each riffle was just where it belonged, and the logs and half-submerged rocks
lay as though placed by an all-wise Providence at the special request
of some ardent angler.

Bill stayed right where we had first encountered the little river. Bill
was a bait-caster. He had learned it back in the Minnesota lake country
where the whole art of angling may be summed up in one's ability to
drop a shackled frog or a bass plug into a patch of water between lily
pads no bigger than your hat. He swooped down upon a stretch of comparatively quiet water which slid deep and dark beneath a jam of logs.

"I'll stay right here," said Bill, after a brief survey of the sparkling green pool. "This is ideal bait-casting water."

"O.K.," said Henry. "Blaine and I will stay with the fly."

To Henry and me that stream invited fly-casting if ever a stream did, so we pushed on, eager to accept the invitation.

At noon we sprawled on a little sand bar in the elbow of the stream. A wild raspberry bush nodded from the bank. We had eaten of its fruit, along with our snack of lunch, and were soaking up the sunshine.

"Henry," I bantered, lazily scanning the stream, "I'll bet you my biggest trout I can cast across to the other bank."

Henry squinted across the sparkling water and after a moment's hesitation responded, "It's a bet."

I got to my feet and cleared for action. Out went the fly, farther and farther at each swing. There was just the suggestion of a breeze and I was casting practically all the line I could handle, but the fly still lacked some ten feet of reaching the opposite bank. One more swing would do it if I could get a clean back cast. The line should shoot that distance of its own weight. Back came the fly, the line straightened, and the rod bent against the forward strain. It was a clean cast, and it was my limit. The line rolled out ahead, took up the slack at the reel and fell straight and true — a foot short.

We saw the fly light, and we saw it there on the water for a moment as it floated almost under the bank. And then we saw that which has gladdened the hearts of fishermen even before the days of good Saint Peter. We saw the "lump" on the water, the flash of silver and crimson, the tightened line, which so surely bespeak a big fish.

To you who have taken big trout on delicate tackle, who have felt the quiver and thrill of fighting rainbow in wild water, the rest need not be told; to you who have not, my words will be meaningless. Nobody has yet succeeded in describing even remotely the inexplicable joy experienced by a true lover of the art when he plays and lends a heavy and vigorous trout. The creek wasn't wide but it was plenty long, and the trout knew it. He started for the big river and I after him.

"Owee!" yelled Henry. "Hang on. Take up that slack — quit floundering about — act like a fisherman, not like a scared moose — no, no, look out."

As I again stumbled over the slippery rocks and saved myself from sprawling into the icy water by executing a vigorous serpentine twist.

"What a sight," roared Henry, shouting with glee.

For me it was mighty serious business. There was no humor about it. If I could land that fish I would die happy. I floundered on over the rocks with my line running out all the time. Just when I thought he had it all and must gain his freedom, the fish suddenly turned and rushed back up the stream with such speed that I found myself reeling frantically at a great quantity of loose line floating about my legs. But this lasted only long enough for the fish to take up the slack, which he did with a jerk. And I was again splashing after my rapidly going line. Contrary to all precedent, the fish remained hooked. I uttered another prayer.

The home run was not so long. The fish regained the pool where he had taken the fly and rushed toward the overhanging rooty bank; but by this time I had recovered my breath and some of my equilibrium and he was checked. Then he sulked and jigged and see-sawed and performed all of those tricks so familiar to the angler. But with each show of fight his resistance was less stubborn and I knew then that he was mine. He was game, every inch of him, from his blunt nose to his broad, speckled tail, and many times we listened to the reel sing wondering if in the end he would prove to be a reality or only an addition to our already large stock of fish stories. But I landed him at last and a big fish he was, even for the MacKenzie.

"Isn't he a beauty?" I said for the twentieth time that day. Every fish taken in the South Fork is a beauty, be it eight inches or eighteen. "And the biggest by far?"

"Yes," said Henry, "Quite the biggest, and therefore he's my fish. You didn't cast quite across the stream." Then he added perfunctorily as he assumed possession, "A bet is a bet, and it was a pretty cast."

We splashed back down the stream, taking good trout as we went. The next we knew it was late afternoon and we were at the big hole with Bill. We had a goodly catch and very wet legs all around. Bill, his brand-new pair of waders notwithstanding, was the wettest of us all. He had fallen into the big pool, filling his waders. But it had been such a job getting out of them that after several unsuccessful attempts to stand on his head and drain, he had just left the water in.

The day was all too short. When the sun dipped low and disappeared behind the ragged firs leaving the trail in deep shadow, we had to pick our way with caution through the darkening woods.

Supper late but steaming hot, and the homely bustle of evening chores. Night settled upon the little farm, the home of a good man and a good woman living close to nature and to God. We enjoyed another pipe on the porch by the poppies, all of us there in the dark. Henry related the story of the wager and they laughed at my expense. Our pipe bowls glowed red and died. Then goodnights all around, and bed — and blessed sleep.

At breakfast the next morning, with a generous bite of home-cured ham suspended on his fork midway between plate and mouth, Bill abruptly announced: "By George, I forgot my bait. A spinner isn't much good without it."

Trotter's boy, Jeff, a gangly, tow-headed youngster whose face was generously splattered with big round freckles, looked up from his plate. "What kind of bait?"

"Oh, angleworms, periwinkles, hellgrammites, grasshoppers, most any kind of worm or insect," responded Bill.

"Grasshoppers," murmured Jeff half to himself. Then with emphasis: "You come with me, we'll get grasshoppers all right."

With breakfast well stowed away, the boy led us to a particular sunny clearing near the house. "There are plenty of grasshoppers here, and in the morning when they are cold we can catch lots of them."

Now that boy of Trotter's was a nice boy. And I think he meant to tell the truth. I prefer to believe, rather, that we got there too late. But those grasshoppers were about as sluggish as a cat on a hot stove. Henry and I, being confirmed fly fishermen, were quite disdainful. But Bill needed bait. He kept hammering away with hat, sticks, and rocks until he had beaten down and captured some dozen grasshoppers or so.

After all, there's something to be said for the bait fisherman. "I caught my last trout with a worm," confessed the great Izaak himself. And Bliss Perry observes in his charming little treatise *Fishing With a Worm*, "If he be, so to speak, but a worm fisherman, a follower of humble occupations and pledged to unromantic duties, let him still thrill with the pleasure of the true sportsman. To make the most of dull hours, to make the best of dull people, to like a poor jest better than none, to wear the threadbare coat like a gentleman, to be out-voted with a smile, to hitch your wagon to the old horse, if no star is handy; this is the wholesome philosophy taught by fishing with a worm."

With this defense for the lowly worm, may not Bill dream his dreams while fishing with grasshoppers? In his behalf, may it also be remembered that it was July, that in the big river many of the trout had sought the recesses of the deeper water and might not be so easily lured to the surface with a fly as those of the smaller South Fork. Nor should it be thought that Bill intended to impale these luscious creatures on a plain hook to be sunk into the deep pools. Bait to be sure, but bait as a garnish to bright copper or brass spoon hooks which, if they are to lure fish in that roaring stream, must be handled with skill.

Returning to the house, Trotter met us at the gate. "The boats are here," he announced, "I just heard the Thompsons come in with them."

Grabbing our tackle and lunch box we hurried to the river, and sure enough there were the boats, two of them. They had been hauled up the road some twenty miles by team on specially constructed trucks. Big, flat-bottomed, substantial-looking craft they were, with just enough deck in the stern to permit a man to sit cross-legged like a Turk and swing a rod. Bill and I occupied one boat. It was piloted by that veteran boatman, Cary Thompson, long since gone to his reward. Henry took the other, handled by Thompson's son, Milo, both experts as they had to be to navigate the MacKenzie.

The boats shoved off. We waved goodbye to the Trotters, and the hurrying waters caught and sped us on toward the white rapids. The current does the work. The boats are piloted stern first and it is the boatman's serious duty to keep them in the channel and to avoid the rocks. What pulling must be done, and there is much of it, is against the current, not with it. The purpose is not to retard our progress, but to prevent being dashed into one of the too numerous rocks or logs. The effect is apparently that of being swept madly on at the mercy of the stream, while the oarsman tries to row against the pull of the current. And often the uninitiated angler, squatting in the stern of the boat or crouched amidships with gripping hand on either gunwale, feels that he is hopelessly in the cruel power of those roaring, whirling, splashing waters.

The river rushes up to meet him. It splatters him with spray, and often sends a goodly measure of white water up into his apprehensive face, or down the back of his neck. He may be assured that he will be ducked more than once ere that twenty miles of wild water is negotiated.

There ahead, but well to one side, loomed a menacing jagged rock. Around it the troubled waters thundered. They piled against its staunch front, and curled in spinning eddies on either side, throwing white spray high into the air. It was well for us that we were not bearing down upon that angry maelstrom. The boat swept on. We were bewitched and spellbound by the noise, the flying spray and the wild speed. Suddenly the boat veered and was borne down directly toward the rocks faster and faster! What of the man at the oars? Bill and I cast a frightened look at Thompson. Had he lost control of the boat? His great hands were knotted to the oars and he was pulling — pulling — not away from the rock, but squarely at it! Could the man be mad? Was he courting suicide, and murder too?

The great rock rushed at the boat; scarce ten feet of wild water separated us from that death trap. And yet the boat-man, firm, confident, completely unafraid, added yet another pull to the stout oars. Our boat, caught by the piling water, was lifted, partly turned, and slid easily and gracefully upon the curling lip so roughly repelled by the boulder and shot through a boiling caldron, just missing on the other side an almost submerged rock that had quite escaped our notice and against which, but for his skillful maneuver, we would have been dashed.

Thompson looked as though nothing out of the ordinary had happened. To a boatman like him who had spent a lifetime on the big river, nothing had. We realized then what we already knew, that Cary Thompson understood his business, and that he knew the MacKenzie River. He had merely executed a little trick, old to him but startlingly new to us, whereby he kept the boat in the channel and us in the boat. We breathed again, and our hearts beat a wild tattoo. Looking back we saw Henry and Milo taking the same chute — and in precisely the same way, even to the scared expression on Henry's face. Again our blood began to circulate, and with that altogether satisfactory assurance that we were still alive came the wild desire to yell. And yell we did.

We took no note of time, but when a sudden turn carried the boat into a deep green pool shaded by ancient cedars and far-reaching mossy oaks, with one accord we thought of the inner man.

"How about stopping here for lunch?" inquired Thompson.

"Lunch," said Bill.

"Lunch," I agreed.

At that moment, Milo's boat swung around the big rock and slid into the pool.

"Isn't it about time for lunch?" called Henry.

"Lunch," agreed Milo.

Mooring the boats on the sandy crescent beach at the edge of a friendly green slope which extended from a tangle of ferns and scrub to the shingly shore, we built a little fire without thinking why. Mrs. Trotter's cold fried chicken and generous slices of wild blackberry pie needed no further touch of cookery, but we all wanted a fire. It seemed a natural and quite indispensable thing. A fire spans the whole distance between a wilderness and a camp. Even after a leisurely lunch and a post-prandial pipe, we were reluctant to leave and prolonged our noonday siesta until the urge to fish again sent us forth upon the river.

This, I think, would be a good place to end the chapter, but I must tell the rest. The pleasant day waned to its close. Many good rainbows lay in the little fern-lined boxes under the decks as we approached the last and wildest part of the trip, Martin's Rapid. Since the advent of the light plywood, high-sterned, wide-beamed MacKenzie River boats, this rapid is run scores of times each season, though still with some fatalities. Even the Thompsons ran it in the old days, but not in the dark. Here we were to make the usual portage. But just before reaching the fierce broken water, Bill made one last mighty cast with his spinner. I heard the swish of the rod, a stifled exclamation, the clank of his weighted spoon hook striking something in the boat. It all happened in an instant. A slip, a back lash, Bill didn't know quite how, but there was Thompson bending to the oars, with Bill's hook dangling from his nose! We were at his side in a leap, which threatened to upset the boat. The hook was buried in his nostril, above the barb, and we could not get it out. But we had precious little time to try. It suddenly dawned on us all that the rapids were just below, and that we had already passed the customary landing. The current swept us onward and darkness was falling fast.

"The willows!" yelled Thompson. "Grab the willows as we swing in." His face now showed genuine concern.

Decorated like a Zulu chief, he urged the boat toward the shore with a few powerful strokes, and we grabbed with all our strength. It was a mighty comfortable sensation to feel the boat slide in under the willows and come to rest. Thompson soon had it back at the place of portage.

When we could draw a quiet breath, we got out a flashlight and looked at Thompson's bleeding nose. He told us afterwards that it was not the first time he had been hooked by some wild flying barb, and he directed the operation like a veteran. With Bill's small wire clippers we cut the hook to pieces, bit by bit, worked it through, and finally were able to get it out. We didn't like it, but we were sure that Thompson liked it even less. We settled down in silence then for the last quiet mile of smooth water.

Thompson, who had much cause to complain, uttered not a word as he brushed a drop of blood from his lacerated nose. We were all tired, we were all at peace. The velvet sky was powdered with stars, a night bird called from the dark woods, a cowbell tinkled. We saw the lights of the cottage gleaming on the shore and knew that we — especially Thompson — had earned the benefit of tranquil sleep.

Big Rainbows on the Upper Deschutes

It was nearly forty years ago that I walked out upon a crude log footbridge, the only crossing of the Deschutes for many miles up or down the river. Above the bridge the water threaded its placid serpentine way through the widening prairie, stretching to the far, blue, and jagged summits of the Cascades. Below the pines advanced to touch branches in some places across the quiet flow. Farther down, the river became more turbulent, until it finally tumbled, a mad white cataract, into the rocky gorge through which it flows for nearly two hundred miles to join the Columbia.

The stream was very clear, and from the middle of the bridge I could see, here and there along the yellow sand, the backs of big spotted trout lazily maintaining their position in the current with slowly fanning fins. My hopes were high as I sent the flies out over the water, but repeated casts proved that the fish were not feeding. Nevertheless I hopefully whipped the stream for another fifty yards which brought me out of the timber. There was nothing to impede a long cast.

Now the fish were breaking the surface here and there. I could see the peculiar lumps and swirls made by big trout sucking in tiny insects, and up and down the river an occasional flop announced that some over-eager fellow had cleared the waters. The sky had been overcast all day, with intermittent drizzles, and it began to sprinkle again. A hundred feet above, beyond a partially submerged log, several trout rose almost together, and my hopes rose with them. I waded as close to the log as my boots would permit, and put the flies out to the water along its shore side, where I hooked a one-pound trout. It promptly dove into the tangle of aquatic weeds at the bottom of the stream, but I was not to be eluded after so long a wait. I played the fish patiently with as much skill as I could, and finally landed it. Though not large, the fish was remarkably heavy, and so deep of belly and broad of back that it looked almost deformed. But it was beautifully colored, and far more brilliant than the fish of the lower river. I remember what a distinct impression this fish made upon me at the time, though I have since noted that many of the Crane Prairie trout are like that.

By this time the trout began feeding on insects so small that I could not see them, though my fish had taken a number ten Kamloops. (This was in the days before the Hallock Killer). So I changed to a duet of small dry flies, Red Upright and March Brown, and no sooner had they touched the surface of the water than they were taken — literally taken. A splash! The feel of my leader tightening over the log, and then that maddening realization that I was hauling in only the line! Another cast, this time with but one fly, another strike! The fish kept the deep water for a few moments, then darted under the log, and another fly vanished.

My third cast with the dry fly raised a heavy trout. I reasoned that with the fish on the other side of the log, the odds were a hundred to one in his favor, and my flies were disappearing at an alarming rate. So, before the fish had time to follow the example set by his fellows, I gave him such a long and strong pull that he came flopping over the log, and into the tangle of weeds on the inside. But matters were not greatly improved. A little submarine maneuvering on his part so laced my line in and out through the weeds that I was shortly pulling on what greatly resembled a bale of hay.

"This must stop," thought I, "at any hazard." So I backed away across the prairie, dragging a liberal section of the bottom the river, but from which I would catch, now and then, the gleam of an exceptionally big trout, thrashing in the litter at the end of my leader. How the tiny fly held, I do not know, though it did. But alas, my rod! I snapped the tip end of the middle joint with the last heavy tug which brought the fish and its garnish of weeds almost to the shore. Like most youthful fishermen when they hook a big trout, I had been too vigorous, and too excited. The fish darted back to its element, and my rod was broken. I was cold, disheartened, and all for quitting. To add to the general gloom, it began to rain in earnest, and the rain shortly changed to a heavy fall of big, wet snow flakes.

Jack Morrow, the long legged member of our party, was taking fish from a point some fifty yards above me and he urged me to join him there. I was downcast and consented only half-heartedly. I had repaired the rod after a fashion, by scraping down the broken end of the joint and forcing it into the ferrule.

The submerged log lay just at the mouth of a small backwater which joined the river at that point, and Jack had leaped it without difficulty. I sized it up. The channel was about six feet wide and four feet deep. I soon learned that it was also very cold. You already suspect what is to follow, but you must not suppose that I failed to leap across to the little hummock which I had selected. It extended rather beyond the common margin of the stream, and I made a successful running jump, landing squarely upon it. But, ah, it was but an illusion, a phantom, an *ignis fatuus*, for it had no foundation whatever. It was a clump of floating weeds upon the surface of the deep water. I sank to the bottom, and rose, grimly realizing, even then, that I had reenacted, quite unintentionally, one of those preposterous episodes from a Mack Sennett comedy of the Nickelodeon days.

That ended my fishing for the day. Returning to camp I shivered in the rain and tried to dry out at our feeble, steaming fire. My three companions were painfully sympathetic. I noted more than one covert wink, and could hear, now and then, a half suppressed chuckle. Even the incomparable savor of fried trout, so fresh from the water, did not altogether revive my drooping spirits. When supper was over, we presented weird figures as we groped about our sputtering fire, performing the last offices of the night. They were brief, with just a touch of sadness. Discarding as much clothing as he dared, (I recall wearing my hat to bed), each fisherman, with a solemn "Good-night," crawled under his particular tree, rolled himself up in his particular damp blanket, and began the long vigil.

I have read a lot about beds of fir boughs under the stars. I have slept on many of them too, and capital beds they were. Often have I sprawled on such fragrant heaps under August skies, fascinated by the mountain stillness, and have watched the stars file across the velvet curtain of the night, and disappear behind the tree tops to the west. On such a bed I have been lulled to sleep by the murmur of a mountain brook, and hours later, long after any self-respecting fisherman should be up and away to the purple waters, I have been awakened by the warmth of sunshine sifting down through interlaced branches.

But there was no poetry about those beds on Crane Prairie. They were hard, lumpy, and wet. I will not dwell upon the details of that night. I think I slept a little, just a little, before dawn. At any rate, after what seemed an eternity of cold, cramped twisting and turning, I was aroused by a colder splash of big wet snowflakes on my face. It was morning. That is, the east showed gray through the trees. It was morning for the woods. In the city, it was still the middle of the night.

Hot coffee, with bacon and trout, helped somewhat to dispel our disappointment at the weather, and proved a marvelous remedy for cold backs and cramped limbs. The flurry of snow continued while we ate. Big, feathery flakes came twisting down through the trees, and sizzled with the bacon, but the snow melted almost as it fell, so that the prairie soon beckoned fresh and green, though damp, in the morning light.

We had planned to leave by noon, and wanted to have full creels so we scattered up and down the stream and began the serious work of the day. But it seemed that we were to be disappointed again. Though we fished for hours not a trout would rise. About ten o'clock I found myself back in the vicinity of camp. I was tired, disheartened, and fully determined to give it up. But I didn't of course. You who fish for trout know that I didn't, because you too have experienced that stubborn persistence, that indefinable something which so often grips the fisherman in his hour of discouragement, and carries him on to success. Gamblers call it a hunch. Fishermen don't bother to call it anything. They just feel it. They can't resist it, and they fish on. That urge sent me up the prairie again, casting as I went. The sky was still overcast, and the trout were just as unresponsive as before, but there was an indescribable atmosphere of promise, and I quickened my pace.

Suddenly for no apparent reason at all, since the air and the water were quite clear of insects, a big rainbow broke the surface not more than ten feet from me. Several hurried casts into the widening rings failed to incite the fish to further action, but I sensed the change. I felt it. I saw it. A breeze came hurrying from out of the pines off to the west, and the long prairie grass nodded and swept in graceful response. The wind danced along the bosom of the shining river, and whipped little choppy wavelets about the reeds against the shore. It scattered the gray mists, and rolled up ruffs of white cloud. It let the sunshine through, and showed great patches of blue sky. And it stirred to life hundreds of gauzy-winged insects. They had been clinging to the shore grasses, but the lapping water, the breeze and the sunshine put them to the air.

Already the water, well out from the bank, showed signs of life. It lumped and twisted here and there in a most surprising manner, and I knew what it meant. I sent two Blue Uprights whisking out on the next favoring breeze, but they were caught by a cross gust, and doubled back, falling into the water twenty feet short. I would try again. Hauling in the line in swinging loops, I was on the point of retrieving the flies, when a mighty tug, accompanied by a swirl of the surface, quite upset my plan.

That was more than a generation ago. Often since then have I felt it, yet I want to feel it all over again — and I want you to feel it; that tingling thrill, that intense excitement, that quickening of the muscles, of the eye, of the senses. After hours of disappointment after so long and patient an effort this big fish, taking the fly almost at my feet, and the dozens of others rolling and leaping out there where the water flashed, told me that the moment had arrived!

I could have waved my arms and yelled with sheer joy but for the delicate business in hand. I struck firm and hard. The little bamboo curved to the work and quivered as the hook went home. A splash, a spurt, and a lordly leap, a gleam of red and silver against the blue! I can see him now in the sun. I have seen him a hundred times since that epoch marking day on the prairie. And as often have I seen the many others, which followed him out of the cold, sparkling water onto the green prairie grass at my feet.

That day on Crane Prairie, I was realized the fishing of my dreams. Literally every cast brought a strike. But every strike did not bring a fish. Sometimes it was the fly that would go, sometimes the whole leader; more often the tiny flies would tear out of the fishes' mouths. And the trout were big, many of them weighed over two pounds. They fought as I had never known rainbows to fight before.

Often I was compelled to run up or down the bank for a hundred feet or more before I could check and finally land the fish.

How long this lasted I do not accurately remember, probably about two hours. At any rate, when Jack found me and pulled me away, urging that it was then past the hour for our departure, and that I had eaten no lunch, I discovered that my wrist was played out, that my legs were wobbly and that I had more fish than I could conveniently carry. But remember, that was almost forty years ago.

Now here is a strange thing. I was sitting with my friend Spencer Biddle at one of our camps in Canada more than twenty five years later when he suddenly broke in with, "Well, I'll be damned." He was obviously thunderstruck. "I'll be damned," he repeated, peering sharply into my face. Then he continued. "Do you remember two fellows you talked to at the railway station at Bend many years ago while you waited for the night train to Portland"?

I recalled then that two men, a father and son, had come up eagerly to view my catch, had inquired where I had caught such magnificent trout, and what fly I had used. We had stood talking until the train pulled in and I had left them to follow my directions.

"I just now realize," he said, "that you were the fellow with the fish. My father and I often spoke of him and wondered who he was. I am beginning to think you have been one jump ahead of me on the fishing all my life, you and your Hallock Killer."

CHAPTER

He Restoreth
my Soul

Fishermen possess a secret and personal retreat where no others may follow. They sort their tackle, rewind their rods, think their thoughts, and thus escape both from the discords that arise in their households, and from those that confront them in the outside world, which then assume no greater importance than echoes on a faraway shore. The only realities to a fisherman are his flies, leaders, reels, and lithe rods. He is rich with enthusiasm, plans and pleasant dreams; rich because he has a hobby.

How poor by comparison is the opulent Croesus who makes money and its hoarding his god! His imagination will starve with nothing to feed upon, and youthful friends will pity his senility and leave him to his empty treasure. Hs will outlive his capacity to enjoy wealth, and be compelled in the end to yield his bursting coffers to the vandalism of his heirs.

What a blessing a hobby is, and what magic it holds! It not only makes the enthusiast feel that he is young, but it actually keeps him so. It is the key to eternal spring. It is warmth, interest and enthusiasm. And hobbies are so easily come by. It has long been acknowledged that without them, life can be very dull; yet how strange it is that before reaching middle age scarcely more than one person in a hundred has a passion for anything at all. The gleam has faded and only the elect of God cling to that heady elixir of youth. These fortunate few may bore the whole world with their enthusiasms, but they possess an inner glow of undiluted happiness, and life will never seem dull to them. One hobby is a joy, two are a benediction.

On many a day in early spring, when the trees are pushing forth their first delicate green leaves, and the sky is a far blue banner, mottled with fleecy white clouds, or in mid-October when the earth is full of ripeness and the landscape is splashed with great patches of russet and gold, I have set forth with my paint box and easel. When the nights are long and the winter winds howl about the chimney, I have devoted countless hours to the fascinating occupation of tying flies.

Of course hobbies are a matter of temperament. The man who excuses himself for not developing one, by claiming that he does not have the time, may sound a bit silly when he is faced with the example of numerous successful men. Indeed, men of accomplishment seem to be the very ones who invariably ride their hobbies. Ford with his antiques - Morgan with his art collecting - Roosevelt and his stamps - Churchill and his painting. Undoubtedly as Mr. Churchill himself states, he was able to bear the weight of his burden during the war days by retiring periodically to the solace of his paint box. As I walked the picturesque streets of the ancient village of St. Paul in southern France, I thought of him squatting at his work, sheltered by his wide-brimmed hat. There he painted so often as to become a familiar friend to the simple villagers, and there several of his paintings now hang.

A paint box is a romantic thing. The smooth tubes of pigment are delightful to handle, and their very names conjure up a thousand thoughts for pleasant reverie; Burnt Sienna, that reddish brown, the color of the wonderful Italian hill towns, and its sister, Raw Umber, the duller shade of the Umbrian earth; Crimson Lake, a color made from the dried bodies of female insects; Sepia, brown from the ink of cuttle fish; Yellow Ochre, with its base of iron. I squeeze the paint in little blobs on my palette, and the old painters and saints and peasants come crowding upon the mind. For now the brocaded world of Dante lives again. Yes, the simplest paint box represents a rich trove, gathered from the whole world, for even the brushes of camel's hair and pig bristle have crossed the Seven Seas to aid our craft.

But oh, the base use to which we put these treasures in the beginning! The first painting is shocking, the second and the third are dismal failures, but if one keeps pegging away a picture does finally develop. What started out to be a flowered meadow may wind up as a seascape; a picturesque barn or tumble-down cabin against a background of somber trees may shortly assume the proportions of a mountain range or a ship at sea. Perspective, which refuses to develop in spite of one's best efforts, may suddenly ripen into a subject where perspective is of little account. If he paints in oils as distinguished from water color, the would-be artist finds that, by scraping off some of the paint with a palette knife, and adding generous quantities of different color, he can arrive at something in the nature of a picture, even though it may prove wholly foreign to his original intention or subject. In fact these unexpected results in my own case have caused me to ponder, and come to believe that those prize-winning modernist paintings, frequently hung upside down in perfect innocence, are the result of just such accidents rather than genius in the artist who depicts what to me seems a cockeyed world.

A painter's workshop is the whole outdoors. How delightful it is to set up one's easel in a broad field, with a view of distant hills and drifting clouds, and to turn a farm building, wholly devoid of paint and care, into a thing of beauty on his canvas. And what double pleasure one enjoys when the simple farmer comes to gaze and praise. Farmers are an inflexible lot whom resent any liberties an artist may take with their property. If a window looks out upon a cluttered chicken yard, he wants the window painted exactly that way. He wants to see the hens pecking around in the rubbish, and if his tractor stands at his front gate, obscuring the rose arbor, he wants it painted that way, red wheels, yellow body and all. Sometimes he leans against the fence chewing a straw, and asks about his water rights, and so I gain a client. Or sometimes his wife comes out and invites me into the kitchen to eat cold fried chicken and homemade bread.

While most of my feeble paintings adorn only the walls of my garage, I can still look them over and conjure up not only many a scene which would otherwise he forgotten, but a garland of friendships as well.

When the weather thickens, and it is no longer possible to set up my easel in the blustering winds, I know that the season for fly tying is at hand. The fun of tying flies is by no means confined to the mere mechanics of pattern or technique. The really observant angler is continually finding a new insect on his favorite trout water, and when he is unable to locate in his collection a single fly that resembles it, he may duplicate the bug in silk floss, feathers, and deer hair. What a satisfaction is his when, on his next excursion to the stream, he finds his lure so perfect an imitation of nature that he lands a generous basket of trout!

Down through the years of studying insect life on streams and lakes, and in experimenting with various patterns, I finally developed the Hallock Killer referred to in such glowing terms in Judge Douglas' book *Of Men and Mountains*. It may be tied in any desired size, both for wet and dry-fly fishing. In all of my long experience with a fly I have never used one seeming to possess as great an attraction for the fish, nor have I found any other so uniformly successful throughout spring, summer, or fall. If the fly is to be fished wet, the deer-hair dressing should be used sparingly, and should be tied closer to the body. If it is to be fished dry, the hair should be short and generously employed.

With this modest introduction to the merits of the Hallock Killer let us proceed to make one. It is assumed that the reader has never tied a fly in his life.

Place a number ten or number twelve eyed hook in the vise. With beeswax dress the shank of the hook and fifteen or eighteen inches of number fifty black silk thread. Hold one end of the thread between the thumb and index finger of the left hand, draw it across the shank of the hook and make four or five tight twists, overlapping the end of the thread as it is carried toward the curve of the hook. With small scissors snip off the short end of the thread, and with the long end bind in a tail consisting of a wisp of bright red feather.

Then in the left hand hold together a strand of corn yellow silk floss and a bit of thin gold ribbing and bind those in with three or four rounds of thread. Twist the binding thread about the shank carrying it up near the eye of the hook and fasten it with a half hitch. Snip off the stub ends of the floss and ribbing, and twist the floss up toward the head of the hook to form a body. Fasten it with another half hitch of the binding thread and cut off the surplus floss. Now bring the gold ribbing up along the body, barber-pole style, binding and cutting it off near the eye of the hook. From a piece of deer hide pinch a little wisp of hair between the thumb and index finger of the left hand, trim the heavy or hide end of the hair at a slight angle and, holding this down on the shank of the hook, bind it in just back of the eye with four or five deft and snug twists of the thread. Again tie off with a half hitch and dress the head of the hook with a thin brown hackle feather. The heavy end of the feather should be tied in just behind the eye. By grasping the other end of the feather with hackle pliers, it can be twisted three or four times about the shank just back of the eye of the hook, tied in and made fast. The balance of the binding thread is used to tie on the head which is completed with a jam knot. A touch of transparent fingernail polish will give the bead a shiny appearance and prevent unraveling. When you have finished you will possess a fly which, if properly handled, will take trout in almost any water at almost any time.

Then too, there is the intense gratification of tying, right on the bank of the stream, a fly which will finally capture that bane of the angler's life, a fastidious or "choosy" feeding trout. I was fishing Silver Creek one bright June day when the trout were rising all about me. Many of them were big, as the "lumps" on the surface of the placid stream clearly indicated. But I could not seem to find just what they were taking, though I changed flies at least a dozen times. As I walked down the stream I located an unusually fine trout rising steadily, well toward the opposite bank, In the course of five or ten minutes I floated every pattern in my fly box over him, but to no avail. The fish was not frightened, for he often rose within a few inches of my fly to take a bug which I could not identify from that distance. I was determined to capture that fish, and I went down the stream well below him, crossed, at a point where the water all but lapped over the tops of my waders, and sneaked back up the opposite side. There, beyond a patch of tules, this great trout was still rising, and when I peered through the tall rushes down into the clear water I could see him busily engaged in his feeding. As an insect floated down to him, he moved leisurely to right or left, rose toward the bug, looked it over and then dropped back to his customary lie. There was a heavy hatch on the water that day, and I saw the trout decline any number of little bugs, big bugs, brown bugs, yellow bugs, gray bugs, black bugs. Finally a spent blue dragonfly floated by and, without hesitation, the trout moved over and gulped it, the first of such insects I had seen him take. I was willing to wait patiently and watch for his next rise. He touched nothing more until another dragonfly drifted his way. In an instant the insect was gone, meeting the same fate as the first, so I knew then what fly I should use, but I had no such pattern in my box. I hastily returned to camp and tied up a couple of blue dragonflies. Then I hurried back to the rising fish, and placed my cast carefully and well. The trout took the fly and he was mine. I am sure I got more satisfaction out of that experience than if I had taken a dozen equally good fish on flies selected at random.

It is a real pleasure to start a boy out tying his own flies and to watch his development of taste and skill. At first he chooses the gaudy impractical materials, but as he advances he selects the more somber feathers and muted silk, and finally makes patterns which will really catch fish.

Hobbies pay enormous dividends, but best of all they provide food for the soul. Perplexed and oppressed though I may be with the problems of the day, when evening comes I can dismiss them all from my mind and meditate such pleasant questions as, "Will I be able to get that distant hill in the picture to look just as I want it to?," or "Had I not better make up a few more flies to give to the fellows on Chrismas?"

Down to the Sea in Ships

In January, 1939, I was recuperating from a severe illness and the doctor recommended a sea voyage. Little did we suspect then that before another year was born that the world would be plunged into bloody conflict. Although we finally did get under way, we lay fogbound in the harbor at Portland for several days on a clean white Norwegian freighter expecting the mists to rise any moment, then we would be off for the Panama Canal. I can never forget how those strangely still days dropped over me like a balm. We read and rested and ate and had the run of the ship, being the only passengers from Portland, though a half dozen more boarded our vessel at San Francisco. The crew liked us and we liked them, and the good-looking Norwegian steward came every morning with an apologetic grin to show us his menu for the day and be praised for his work in its preparation. The food was delicious but occasionally we had a hard time to keep from smiling at his composition which we never dreamed of correcting, for we read with delight such items as "posted eggs," "ox soup," "crimp salad," "veal whith oyster branket."

When the fog dissolved at last we heard the rattle of the winches as the heavy anchor chains came in, the clanging of bells, the deep-throated boom of the whistle, and soon we were gliding down the great river to the sea. Time lost all significance and the luxury of unbounded leisure enfolded us in its magic robe, while all about "old ocean's gray and melancholy waste" stretched to the horizon with no sight of land in any direction for days on end — old ocean, tireless, ceaseless, eternal since the spirit of God first moved upon the face of the waters. The duties and problems which had seemed so important, the responsibilities which had appeared so heavy were forgotten, or if remembered, at all, rested but lightly upon us as we gazed out upon the rolling sea and contemplated its infinite grandeur and repose.

When we entered the Golden Gate at San Francisco, the steward brought us a formidable looking document. "Sign here, please," he said in his halting English. When we spread it out on the table before us we found it to be in the form of an affidavit, with many blank columns, each carrying a caption. He had filled it out as far as he could go, Port of Embarkation, Sex, Nationality, Cabin Number, etc. We signed in the column "Name," and he requested us to fill in the next column. It read "Age, if child under eight." Without too much difficulty we convinced him that we were over eight years of age and left that space blank. The next blank, "Piece of Luggage" was easy. When he directed us to write in the last column, we read the caption "Date of Death." This was a shock indeed, and catching our breath we suggested to him that it depended upon the captain's success in navigating the ship. Perplexed and with some reluctance he took the form away, the last column blank, leaving us to speculate as to when we were supposed to die. Later we learned that customs officials had supplied the forms, one to be used to cover deaths at sea, and that having no other and being required to report certain information with respect to his passengers, he had picked out this form — rather a novel procedure — this thing of signing your death statement and allowing someone else to fill in the date.

There was abundant time for listless meditation, and we were refreshed in both body and soul. The same poetic muse still pursues me which prompted the rhymes about the people of Pendleton so long ago, and I find jotted down in my old notebook this little jingle written when crossing the Pacific:

"Sprawling on a deck chair,
Gazing out to Sea.
Neither cares nor worries,
That's the life for me.

Puffs of briny sea breeze,
White flecked wake astern.
Pushing ever westward,
No thought of return.

Stomach full of lobster,
Fancy food and beer,
Time and space forgotten,
Life is now and here.

Seagulls wheel about us,
Now and then a whale,
Spurts his plume of vapor,
Showing fin and tail.

Shuffle board and dancing,
Idle talk and wine
Speed the languid hours.
Bless me, this is fine.

Loafing's such a pleasure.
Time was made for slaves.
Let the land-bound struggle,
And dig their six foot graves.

Office tasks and clients,
They can wait for me.
Nothing's quite so pleasant
As summer days at sea.

A freighter isn't in any hurry. Though its ports of call do sometimes include the larger coastal cities, it makes many stops at unfrequented and remote bays, harbors, and islands. Out go the anchors to the rumble of heavy chains, the great hatches are opened, the winches whine, booms swing from ship to dock, and the yawning hold belches forth or receives within its dark recesses an indescribable jumble of crates, drums, bales, cases, barrels, bundles, and heaps of cargo. How a ship, even a large one, can carry such a huge quantity of goods baffles the imagination.

In the Orient the ship may pick up a consignment of sharks' fins, furs, rice, rugs or silk. In Mexico it may deliver a fleet of new automobiles or tons of machinery and tools. Throughout the South Pacific islands the principal export is copra, while in the Dutch East Indies and at Jamaica it may be coffee, citronella, rubber or pineapple — an endless array of things to use and to eat, but our clean, new freighter carried lumber. Surely this old world of ours is bountiful! Although many people have little and others have much, the fault lies not in God's generous program of production, but rather in man's confused fumbling with the processes of distribution. It was wintertime, so the northern ocean was stormy and gray, but we felt very snug in our comfortable double cabin with port holes looking forward to the wild waste ahead. There we sat reading in inviting chintz-covered chairs, or strolled down to the little dining and sitting room to play bridge with the captain and first mate. Before this program had become monotonous a few other passengers boarded the ship, and shortly thereafter came the great morning when the captain appeared in white linens and we knew that we were in the tropics. Then we spent all of our time on deck and as the ship carried so few passengers, we were privileged to wander about it at will. We soon discovered a little patch of decking at the over-reaching bow of the ship and there my wife and I would sprawl, craning our necks over the low rail and gaze into the translucent sea water ahead. One who has never done this would be astonished to learn of the sights that reward the patient sea gazer. Sometimes right under the very nose of the ship we saw great schools of wide-flanked, flat-bodied fish of deep lavender marked with large purple spots and festooned on both sides with cordlike fibers such as one sees on the ends of Oriental rugs. At other times we would note white plumes and spurts of water out toward the horizon indicating a school of porpoises. In no time they would head directly for our vessel and would play about its bow for hours at a time. These ocean mammals seemed to be attracted by the ship and loved to leap, roll and sport in the swell rolled up at its very bow. Often a calf porpoise would swim beside its mother, imitating her every movement perfectly. When the cow leaped, so would the little one, precisely as though fastened to her side by invisible wires. What wondrous unseen signal governs these wild creatures? Who has not marveled at the same precision displayed by a flock of birds in flight? All of them will turn together in an instant, wheeling in as perfect unison as if controlled by an electric current.

In the South Pacific as well as in the Gulf of Mexico and the Caribbean Sea, flying-fish are everywhere. They leap from the billows and go sailing off across the water on a favoring breeze until with their momentum spent, they plunge into the crest of a rising swell. We watched them hour after hour.

One day we saw a great hammerhead shark swimming along only a few feet below the surface of the water at the very bow of the ship, unconcerned and ominous looking and we involuntarily drew back. Here and there we saw huge multi-colored jelly fish shaped like enormous iridescent parachutes, vast schools of floating Portuguese-men-of-war flying their brilliant purple and magenta standards, or off to the right or left, big sleeping turtles basking in the sunshine. Now and then a whale would rise to the surface spurting a plume of spray high into the air. Most of these marine creatures gamboled about so close to the ship that with paint box and paper at hand, we could make quite accurate sketches of the different types. We saw again, as we had previously seen in the Indian Ocean, numerous sea snakes with their banded black, purple and yellow backs, poisonous evil creatures which swam along rapidly with their heads held high in search of prey. When we told the captain what we were seeing from our little observation perch, he was polite enough not to appear too skeptical, though we felt that he was not convinced. But when we returned for luncheon one day with fairly accurate paintings of these strange creatures, he displayed real interest in spite of himself. When he thought we were not looking we saw him go forth privately and assume the undignified posture which we had held for so long on the little deck. Presently he returned shaking his head, and informed us that he had seen a sea snake, the first he had ever beheld in all his years of navigation. From that time on we noticed members of the crew slipping quietly forward to view the wonders. It is obvious, of course, that they had failed to see this strange and abundant ocean life only because if they watched from too far back it would all be lost in the jumble of waters and the "whiskers" of the ship.

The day came too soon when we arrived at the lovely Bay of Panama where, because of the hook-shaped configuration of the Isthmus one saw the sun apparently traveling in the wrong direction, sinking in the east instead of the west. Of course one looking out across the bay is actually facing more nearly toward the Atlantic Ocean than the Pacific, but it is a confusing experience in spite of maps and charts.

We had sent our trunks containing my fishing tackle to Colon on the Caribbean side of the Isthmus where I intended to pick them up, but no sooner had we landed in Panama than I learned that fishing was excellent, and there I was without equipment, a situation which often seems to confront me. My wife was horrified, but not surprised to learn of my plan to hang around the Boat Club on the Bay of Panama and invite myself along with any fishing party that might show up. So acting upon an impulse born of earlier like experiences, in which I had successfully talked myself into fishing trips as a self-invited guest, that is exactly what I did. A young man owning a small launch soon appeared with his best girl, his sister, and an ample supply of lunch. While my sad story did not exactly bring tears to their eyes, they did consent to take me along cheerfully enough, and even went back to their house near the bay to pick up additional fishing tackle for my use. I shall never forget those good people, Stanley Whaler, his sister Bobbie, and Ruth Bain.

We went out some three or four miles to a series of channels between rocky islands where we fished with big nickel wobblers which carried a heavy hook at the end. The lure was about six inches long, fastened to the line by a wire leader and held down with some ten ounces of lead. I got the first strike. There was a firm tug at my line but very little action thereafter. I thought I must have hooked a sluggish bottom fish. Stanley slowed down his boat. I reeled in the line and soon to my astonished gaze appeared a complete fishing outfit with rod, reel, line, hook and sinker, ready to my hand! Here was a miracle, I thought my wishes granted, my needs supplied, exactly as if I had been the fisherman in the Arabian Nights who pulled the cask from the sea and the genie came to gratify his every desire!

The scenery was magnificent. The rocks and small islands were covered with pelicans, gulls, boobies, frigate birds, and other saltwater fowl. We could often approach as close as ten feet before they arose and went screaming off on the breeze that rumpled the surface of the bay into little wavelets on which the sea birds bounced, splashed, and dined while we fished.

Late in the afternoon someone noticed out beyond the mouth of the bay what at first appeared to be a long wavy mist or film of smoke, extending from south to north as far as we could see. A closer look disclosed that it was the most enormous flock of birds that I have ever seen. It is difficult to imagine one kind of bird in such fabulous numbers anywhere in the world. We could not identify them, but they appeared to be about the size of small pigeons, of dark color resembling, what they may have been, the stormy petrel. At any rate they diverted us so completely that for a time we even forgot about our fishing and were fascinated with the sight. The flight kept up for hour upon endless hour and appeared to have no beginning or end. When the day waned and we had to turn back and head for shore, the birds were still moving in an infinite procession across the evening sky. It was February and it may be that we were watching a northern migration which would take the birds over thousands of miles to their summer habitat far away among the mist-shrouded islands, rocks and headlands of the Bering Sea.

About dusk we got into a school of big fish. How they did strike! Twice all four of us had a fish on at the same time. We trolled deep, letting the lead strike the bottom, and then pulled our lines up so that the lure just cleared the sand. We caught cobina and pompano weighing from ten to twenty five pounds. The cobina has a very tender mouth and we lost many of them, getting only four into the boat. When Ruth landed her first fish she was so excited, so delighted that she picked the flopping monster up onto her lap, threw her arms around it and kept murmuring, "Oh, my darling, Oh, mamma's baby, Oh, my lovely fish."

I think of the run back to the dock as a beautiful dream. The deep velvet tropical sky was studded with stars. Splashes of warm sea water struck us in the face as the launch churned through the waves, and we were treated to the most dazzling display of phosphorous that I have ever seen. It was so bright that both the bow and stern of the little craft appeared to be illuminated with soft bluish-yellow light. A shower and change of clothes at the Whaler's home, several rounds of Planter's Punch and a big lobster dinner prepared by Bobbie finished the eventful day.

We enjoyed more tranquil days at sea when, just before World War II, we made a trip to the enchanting island of Bali in the Dutch East Indies, often referred to as the "Last Paradise." We boarded the immaculate Dutch ship *Tjisadane* at Manila and made our first acquaintance with a "Dutch Wife," so popular everywhere throughout the East Indies. "She" is a hard, round bolster placed in the netting screened bed, over which the perspiring occupant throws a leg and an arm to take advantage of every breeze and so cools himself off as best he can. At first it seemed to us a poor substitute for an electric fan but any stranger ultimately learns that those who live in the tropics have discovered the best way to be comfortable in the never-ending heat and we came to be enthusiastic users of our pleasant bedtime companion. From Manila we sailed south through the Sulu and Flores seas, glided past the shores of Borneo with its little grass huts on stilts, touched at the ancient spice port of Macassar on Celebes and finally arrived opposite the town of Boeleleng on the island of Bali. There are no facilities in that shallow bay which will enable a vessel of any substantial tonnage to berth, so our ship merely slowed down and while still making slight headway, lowered the companionway from which we stepped into a native canoe and were paddled to shore.

The sharks of these waters may be harmless enough. I do not know nor do I care to find out. I do know, however, that the bay was cut here and there by their huge, triangular, dorsal fins as they milled around the canoe and accompanied us from ship to shore. In another canoe, likewise meeting the ship as it glided slowly through the waters of the bay, rode a Balinese princess. She had been squatting on the deck all morning selling curios, a large woman, somewhat past middle age, robust and happy looking. She had been one of the wives of the last Rajah of Bali, and was still numbered among the quick only because when he died, she had refused to follow the ancient Malayan custom of dying with him on the cremation pyre, or of submitting to the usual torture in such cases. She ran away, hid out successfully, later married an Armenian and returned to Bali where she joined him in his flourishing curio business.

One evening when we were crossing the Java Sea in the little Dutch cattle ship *Tobelo* after one of those sudden tropical rains when all the water in the sky seems to be dumped out in a solid stream, we saw far ahead the loom of a palm-girthed island, and the twinkling lights of a village. Soon, to the accompaniment of rattling anchor chains, the ship came to rest opposite the village of Tanjan Pundon on the tiny island of Billiton. By that time it was as dark as a tropical night can be, though with our binoculars to pierce the shadows, we could discern the village. At the equator, the sun, with hardly a suggestion of dawn pops up out of the sea and it is broad daylight. At six of clock in the evening, with but a brief glimmer of twilight it sinks behind the western horizon and it is suddenly dark. I never witnessed this phenomenon without thinking of the Ancient Mariner, when he so mournfully described evening in the tropics.

"The sun's rim dips, the stars rush out:
With one stride comes the dark."

And that is exactly the way it is. All through the night and far into the next day a swarm of natives carried tons of copra on their backs from the lighter, and stowed it into the hungry hold of the ship.

In the morning while the ship lay at anchor in the quiet bay I looked over the rail, and through the clear blue waters I could see a school of strange brilliant fish. They were about eight to fourteen or fifteen inches long, were deep green on their backs and blue on their sides: their heads terminating in a long bright red spear or sword. I had no fishing tackle at hand, but as I had picked up a few words of Malayan while on the islands of Bali and Java, I was finally able to talk one of the deck hands out of a spool of black thread, a pin and a little piece of mata sapi or fried egg, for bait. Shaping the pin into a barbless hook and baiting it with a bit of the egg I dropped it over the rail. The fish acted in a most peculiar manner. One would rush for the bait, but would appear to stop when it rested directly on top of his head just at the base of the spear-like bill. I could see no movement of what I supposed to be the fish's mouth, but to my surprise, upon pulling in the line I found that the fish was hooked. It was a delicate operation to lift a fish up over the rail to the deck on the light thread and barbless bent pin, and I lost several in the attempt. When I finally got a good look at the first one to be caught, I was astonished to find that the bill was not a mouth at all, it was more like the horn springing from the head of the fabled Unicorn. Apparently it is a weapon for attack or defense as the fish's mouth is but a tiny slit underlying a small lip of gristle at the top of its head just in front of its eyes at the base of the shaft.

Its mouth was so small that when the fish took the bait it appeared to have been absorbed through its head. I could see that the native passengers sitting and lying about the deck beside their bundles of luggage took very little interest in me or my project, but when I actually caught a fish they came running and jabbering and crowding so closely around me that I had difficulty in handling my line.

I finally landed four of those strange fish which the natives call Ikan puput. The pectoral fin was clear back of the middle of the gill covering. The fish had a wide, thin, forked tail of deep purple and enormous yellow eyes. The bill, or spear, was a rich turkey red. The body was about the same size and shape almost from head to tail, a cross section disclosing it to be almost square. The natives indicated that these fish were good to eat so we had them cooked and served, and, as my notebook recites, found them "quite delicious."

All through the Java Sea, far from the sight of any land, from time to time we saw more of the strange-colored serpents, or sea snakes slipping through the water. Some, running four to seven feet in length, were marked with alternating bands of brilliant purple and deep black. Others, not quite so long and of a slightly different shape, were scalloped with black and orange. We learned that both types were poisonous. The natives who swam about the innumerable islands feared them and often died after being bitten.

The airplane has come to stay, of course, and flying across the ocean is an everyday affair, but I believe that I shall never change my opinion that the most delightful, the most serene, the most soul-satisfying way to span the sea is to sail it. I have great understanding of a Dutchman whom we met vacationing with his wife in the Indian Ocean. He said without apology that he had navigated those very waters as captain of a vessel for twenty-five years, and although retired, he returned to the same run every year. "There is a real vacation for you," he exclaimed, and I quite agreed with him.

Land of the Palm Trees

To paraphrase Izaak Walton, doubtless God could have made a more delightful place than the island of Jamaica, but doubtless He never did.

It was a half generation ago that the luxurious Grace liner glided slowly into the quiet bay at Kingston, just at dawn, on a soft February day, as the changing light tinged the tops of the many wooded hills. I thought of the apt description which Columbus, the island's first tourist, had given to Queen Isabella upon his return to Spain from its discovery. History has it that he crushed a piece of paper in his hand, placed it on a table, and said "That is San Jago," as the land was first called. However, the native name Xayamaca, "Land of Water" persisted, and in English it became Jamaica.

My wife and I spent several days in Kingston at the exotic Myrtle Bank Hotel, embowered in flowers, and musical with the songs of a tropical bird. We had ample leisure to poke about the city and its environs. A surprisingly large proportion of the population is black, their ancestors having been imported as slaves from Africa when the British took the island from Spain in the mid-seventeenth century. Their speech is soft and musical, their accent is decidedly British, and their utterances are liberally punctuated with such phrases as "righto," "Cheerio" and "bloomin."

A lean, weather-beaten old Negro with a thatch of white hair talked us into a tour of the city in his victoria. Because it would go slowly, and we like time to look about when traveling, we got in the ancient vehicle and swayed over the stony roads, with the driver perched on a high seat in front, and his lazy horse sauntering along, thinking its own thoughts. We had no more than started, when our host, who proved to be a garrulous old codger, opened the conversation.

"My name is Rufus," he said, as he turned an ebony face toward us over a thin, faded shoulder, his black eyes shining expectantly. But before I had time to participate in this exchange of confidences, he added, "That's the name of my horse too."

We were somewhat taken aback, but my wife, sensing an opportunity for cordial response interjected: "That's also the name of one of your passengers."

Alas, it was true, for I was christened Rufus Blaine, though I do not often admit it. Thereupon he became chummy indeed and went out of his way to show us a good time. We drove through pleasant streets shaded by luxuriant trees, and edged with an unbelievable profusion of flowers, but wound up in a sort of compound where a vast number of desperately poor Negroes lived in little huts and shacks constructed of odds and ends of boards, corrugated iron, scraps of canvas and the like. When I attempted to take some pictures I could see that these people deeply resented our presence. They scowled and gathered in little knots where they muttered and gesticulated angrily, clearly indicating to us that we were exceedingly unwelcome visitors, whereupon we beat a hasty retreat. This was a curious and rather alarming experience, for in all our travels I believe it is the only time we have ever been received in an unfriendly fashion.

The bay fronting the town is studded with picturesque islands, but the back country on the south shore is not particularly attractive, as much of it is rather dry and desolate. After we had spent a few days in Kingston we were driven across the island to the north shore. Oh, what a contrast it afforded!

We rode through forests of mahogany, ebony, balata, coconut, and other tropical trees, with here and there a coffee, pineapple or orange plantation carved out of the jungle. All of this slope was covered with a dense growth of forest, giant ferns, lianas and blooming shrubs. Leafy vines, studded with bloom, dropped like mantles from the tall trees, multi-colored orchids hung clustered in the branches and woodland waters threaded their errant way through ferns and bowers, while in the open glades we glimpsed plunging waterfalls and sparkling streams. Thick moss carpeted the ground, and age-old leaf mold furnished nourishment for a bewilderment of small, bright blossoms where bees and butterflies darted and drifted through the long shafts of sunlight which filtered through the leaves. Stillness, deep and enveloping, covered all like a garment, so that we trod the springy turf as silently as moccasined Indians. Shiny big beetles scuttled into the shelter of damp, crumbling logs. Leaf-bearing ants walked with businesslike precision along their forest paths, carrying their tiny round, green banners, and overhead bright birds flitted high among the branches. Now and again a sharp-eyed mongoose scurried through the tangle. Each moment as we descended the road to the sea, the woodland became more entrancing. Interlacing branches met in archways above us and we traveled in a gloom of greenery, shadowy and cool, as we came upon Fern Gully, a scene of surpassing beauty. Not only was the jungle growth of ferns and moss exquisite to behold, but the very breeze bore along the deep cool earthy smell of intense vegetation, spice laden and romantic.

The island abounds in deserted sugar and coconut plantations, ruins of ancient buildings, cattle compounds, walls and grave-stones. In the dryer sections we found "catchments," used for the purpose of collecting rain water. A catchment is a big sloping stone or cement slab, shaped like a huge slice of pie, at the point of which, on the downhill side, is a basin or tank where the water accumulates, and later is carried on the backs of Negroes to irrigate the land.

Suddenly the jungle gave way and before us the rolling

Caribbean Sea was spread to the distant horizon. The shore is dotted with coral reefs and islands, and is scalloped into many tiny bays, so that on quiet days the force of the billows is broken and the sea leaves the shore in soft creamy swells. The water is crystal clear, and the underlying coral sands impart to it myriad hues of blue, green, yellow, pink, soft brown, and rich purple, all woven into a shifting pattern of color. One may look into the clear water above the bright sands and see, gliding in the depths, schools of silvery fish, including the rakish gar, with its long, thin body, about one-third mouth. Coconut palms lift their curved trunks out over the surf at the very edge of the sea, and at dusk, myriad fireflies dart here and there like sparks or white flame.

We found accommodations in a quaint little inn at St. Ann's, and whiled away many pleasant days exploring the countryside, and watching the people as they went about their daily tasks. On weekdays they come out of the jungle-clad hills, wearing loose white cotton garments, somewhat resembling old-fashioned "Mother Hubbards". They walked barefoot down the rough roads, talking and laughing in their soft musical voices, and leading or driving little donkeys laden with brilliantly colored baskets, coconuts, and produce, but on Sundays they presented a very different picture. Then they would string along on their way to church, both men and women dressed in very clean clothes, but still walking in their bare feet, carrying their stockings and shiny new shoes under their arms. Upon reaching the church they would sit about on the grassy knolls, and just before the service began, would pull on stockings and shoes and file soberly through the great arched door. But as soon as the service was over, off would come their precious shoes. It was an interesting, and to my wife, a shattering experience to watch the women put on their stockings. They did not go about it as do our American ladies, by rolling the hose down from the top, inserting the toe and working the stocking up to position. Their method was to stand on one broad brown splayed foot like a stork, hold up the stocking like a sack, lift leg, shove foot vigorously down and pull stocking relentlessly up, never pausing until the last trace of slack had disappeared. What about runners, we thought? Perhaps they didn't show on those chocolate-colored skins, or maybe, because their wearers were bent on good deeds, or through the influence of Voodoo, their hose just didn't rip.

The Landovery River, a small stream rising in the jungle heights, tumbles in a cataract down the face of a mossy cliff, tearing itself into thin strands of mist, and stirring the bordering ferns into billows of waving green. These falls are justly famous, and it was the proud claim of the Jamaicans that they were the only falls in the world depicted on a postage stamp. While the falls are not impressive as to height or volume, they are among the loveliest of all cascades. Against the waving green of their background the silvery strands leap in veils of mist, drift on the ever-present breeze, and gathering again, froth and sparkle in a deep pool at the base. When the fragmented waters again unite the stream meanders through coconut groves and finally debouches into the sea. While my wife sat in the shade or the palms on the green turf at the edge of the sand beach, one day being almost struck by a falling coconut, I fished the lower reaches of this river.

While experimenting with various types of streamers and other wet flies, I tied on an outlandishly big white buck hair and tinsel contraption, of a pattern which I had made and used in fishing for cohoe or silver salmon, in the Straits of Georgia near Campbell River on Vancouver Island. The first cast with this monstrosity produced startling results. A fish with huge silver scales, and a rakish undershot jaw, weighing perhaps five or six pounds, which I recognized as a tarpon, struck the fly with a vicious lunge, turning upon it so suddenly that I was left to retrieve but part of my leader. I had in my kit only two or three of these lures, and I promptly lost another in the same fashion; but before the last one had disappeared, I was able to hook and land a husky snook, with its big head and two dorsal fins. These fish frequented the freshwater pools, just above the reaching wash of the breakers. Whether they run in and out between the fresh and salt water, I did not learn, but they were plentiful in the estuaries of the several streams flowing into the sea along the north shore of the island.

This assault on my big, outlandish, Christmas tree flies necessitated my canvassing the neighborhood for material with which to construct more. It was a lot of fun to scour the village in search of hooks, yarn, tinsel and feathers, for the dialect of the shopkeepers was quaint and pleasing. But the real problem was to find something which I could substitute for white buck hair. In my rambles over the island I had seen a great many goats, so I conceived the idea of employing one of the Negro boys at the inn to get me some white goat hair if he could.

"Wha you wan boss?" he inquired.

"I want some white hair for tying fish flies. Can't you get me some from goat tails?" I inquired.

"Sho boss," came his quick response, as he pocketed a shiny new shilling. Armed with this fortune, and a pair of my wife's scissors, he fared him forth. In no time at all he was back wearing a grin which, for all the world, resembled a slice of ripe watermelon with white instead of black seeds. Greatly to my surprise he presented me with eight complete goat tails intact! Just what the owners of these animals may have thought or said when they discovered that their goats had lost their tails has never been reported, but I was thus supplied with enough material to make a great many flies.

Some of the higher-class natives, and by that term I mean the descendents of the first imported Negro slaves, were extremely courteous and cultured. We were entertained by several of them, and found that they were deeply interested in the Oxford Peace Movement. They abhorred war, though they appeared intensely loyal to their mother country, England. Our newfound friends were a bit too well informed to give credence to Voodoo, but they made no secret of the fact that it still has a powerful hold on many of the natives, and is far more prevalent than we had supposed.

Devastating hurricanes occasionally break over the island in the late summer, and cause much damage, with considerable loss of life. These appalling storms have left graphic impressions on all who have survived them, because they contrast so violently with the usual balmy climate. Marks of flood and fury are to be seen in many places. The natives have an expression "July, stand by; August, you must; September, remember; October, all over."

We returned to the continent via Cuba, and on the boat trip we encountered an unusually rough sea. I have never experienced the distress of seasickness, but my wife is a poor sailor, and knew enough to take to her cabin at once. It was amusing to watch the gay passengers that morning as we left port, lolling on their deck chairs in the bright sunshine on the calm sea which preceded the storm, and to hear them make their eager arrangements for tables at lunch. Just before noon big swells began to roll, but undaunted, the happy passengers hurried to the dining salon. The force of the storm struck suddenly before the meal was over, and one by one, with white faces and set lips, they would gaze at their food for a moment, clap their hands over their mouths, make a run for the door, and dash toward the potted palms, or any other nearby refuge. But before they could make it, two officers in natty uniform would grab them by the arms, shout "Not there, not there," and would boost them upstairs in an undignified lump to the deck rail and the open sea.

In many respects, sections of the beautiful city of Havana compare very favorably with parts of Paris. There is much similarity in some of the magnificently ornate buildings, wide tree-shaded avenues and brilliant promenades. The Malecon, a wide drive between the sea amid the buildings that front it, is as fine a thoroughfare as one may find anywhere in the world. It curves along the edge of the bay, and is heavily bulwarked against the wild waters which, during a storm, beat at its base, and send showers of spray against the windows of the buildings along its course. It reminded me too of the Blind in Shanghai, though in many respects it is more beautiful. But on this particular day the storm had so churned up the sea that great stretches of the boulevard were awash with a flood against which the occupants of the buildings had barricaded doors and closed shutters. We rolled up the windows of our car, for the water flew in great showers as we drove along, and the sea spume flung itself against the panes.

Havana has a novel way of disposing of the city's daily accumulation of garbage. It is carried out to sea on a string of barges drawn by tugs, and the sharks, which infest these waters, having by long experience anticipated a feast at each trip, literally swarm about the boats, where their triangular fins cut the surface of the sea as they move in for the banquet, and observers look and shudder and look again, drawn, yet repelled by the sight.

Key West in those days, was a quaint weather-beaten little town, spread out over the flat palm-shaded island. People moved about in leisurely fashion. No one seemed to be in a hurry. Everyone was friendly and cordial, and the town invited lazy restful days. There I made good use of those flies which I had improvised from the goat tails and tinsel, although I was not successful in landing any of the fish which struck them.

One hot afternoon we were wandering about a park at the edge of the key where a lagoon, communicating with the sea, twisted among the trees. It was spanned by several foot-bridges, and from the center of one of them I saw, through the limpid depths, schools of fish, some deep parrot green and others silvery white. This was an irresistible invitation! I hailed a taxicab and hurried back to the hotel, got my light fly rod, returned to the lagoon, and cast one of the big flies out onto the quiet water. The very instant it struck the surface a tarpon, two feet or more in length, gulped the fly, throwing himself high into the air. With a whoop of delight I struck firm and hard. The big, evil-looking fish thrashed about on the surface, and walked on his tail in various zigzag patterns. Here was wonderful and wholly unexpected sport, for he was a warrior and far from ready to give up the fight. To my delight he dashed and hurled himself about, and then plunged violently to the bottom. Then the tragedy. I could actually feel the leader being sawed against the sharp coral, and in the next instant the fish was free. I was greatly excited, and immediately cast another of the big flies on the lagoon. Again a big tarpon, again a fight and again the leader was sawed through. I kept on until I had not one of the flies left in my tackle box. I had no more time and no more flies, so I gave up the battle, but someday I am going back. Then, I will use a light wire leader instead of the conventional gut. Maybe in that way I can drag one of those fighting silver-scaled brutes out onto the grass.

It seems astonishing to me that, with this lagoon so full of fighting fish, right in the city limits of Key West, not a single angler put in an appearance during our several days in that sleepy old town. But it was not that there were few fishermen, for the launch operators were doing a flourishing business. Each day the entire fleet of trim, white boats, with striped awnings, and comfortable wicker chairs, put out on the rolling Gulf of Mexico, where saltwater fishermen, including myself, had no difficulty in catching large numbers of barracuda, amber jack, groupers, pompano, and an occasional sailfish. Sometimes a shark would follow a hooked fish and bite off a goodly chunk before it could be landed. The barracuda too are bold and vicious. Their huge mouths are equipped with rows of sharp tiger-like teeth, and they will strike at anything. Behind our launch there dangled what our boat captain called a "teaser." It skipped about some twenty feet from the stern, on the crest of the churning white water, stirred up by the propeller. It was a round stick of wood, twelve or fourteen inches long, painted half white and half red, and dangled from a cotton rope such as is used for clothes lines. As we ran through a school of barracuda, each of the two rods received a strike, and at the same instant another of the vicious creatures seized the teaser. It was snapped from the rope as though fastened by a mere thread. I have often wondered how palatable it was, and whether the gastric juices in the stomach of that savage creature were sufficient to digest it.

CHAPTER

Old-World Wanderings

Most of my life has been spent in the great arid West, where vistas are broad and empty, and distances are vast. So, when another miracle came true, and I actually found myself in Switzerland, it seemed a land of remarkable contrasts. All about, range on range, majestic and awe-inspiring, towered the mighty Alps, each pinnacle and crag glittering with eternal snow. I delighted in the villages perched here and there on the mountainsides, or nestling at the feet of snow-crowned peaks, and I was fascinated with the innumerable waterfalls that leaped from rugged heights and tumbled into the green vales below. The atmosphere was so clear that distances were deceptive and made everything appear diminutive. It took some effort of imagination to remain convinced that I was not a giant wandering in fairyland. Story-book chalets, ornamented and trimmed in quaint fashion by the Swiss woodcarvers, clung precariously to the steeps. Each bore a name and became a personality. On broad verandas, under embellished eaves, hung the prototypes of Tyltyl's bird cage, each with its beloved tenant sitting contentedly behind friendly bars. The countryside was a miracle of orderliness. Even the woodpiles were stacked in neat precision. The comely housewives literally swept their green lawns with switch blooms. In the forests not a branch or twig littered the ground. Goats, sheep and cows roamed the flowery meadows, their melodious bells ringing gently as they walked. The lead cow of each herd wore the greatest bell of all, a huge affair not less than a foot in diameter hung on her neck from a loose leather collar. In the spring when the cows are taken up the mountainsides to the summer ranges, the young people make a festival of the event. They weave garlands of flowers for the lead cow and crown her with a great bouquet, then the procession wends its way upward to the grassy meadows where the cows remain all summer in the charge of a herder who makes cheese in his lonely hut, to be brought back to the village in the fall.

Rosy-cheeked little boys and girls would stop their play in the dooryard to watch our tiny mountain train jog by. It moved so slowly that we had ample time to observe and enjoy, and to wave a return to their grave greetings. The children looked for all the world like little Hansels and Gretels, dressed in heavy boots, and snug woolen clothing. The girls wore their flaxen hair in thick braids and stood soberly at the mountain stations with baskets of strawberries, while the boys offered for sale bouquets of wild narcissi. I could never quite forget that this really might be fairyland, for always in the background were the black and mysterious forests where gnomes and witches must certainly abound.

The rural people are experts in carving wood and in making fascinating toys. In Geneva, and in all of the larger cities of Switzerland, one sees shops utterly filled with ingenious treasures, probably intended for children in the first place, but irresistible to grown folks. There we saw merry-go-rounds, music boxes, dancing dolls, quaint frogs, gnomes, weather vanes, sewing boxes and every conceivable animal and bird, each done in lifelike miniature or Puckish caricature. We were wholly unable to resist them, burdening our ever-expanding luggage and excusing ourselves by assuring each other that we were buying them for little friends at home.

At Geneva we stayed at the Hotel De la Paix, overlooking the lake which is the source of the Rhone River, and I never tired of gazing into its depths from the many bridges. Always there were huge trout cruising about through its clear waters. Izaac Walton reports that at one time most of the trout which found their way to the tables of European epicures came from this lake, then known as Lake Leman.

One day as I was looking across the lower end of the lake from the magnificent promenade that fronts the hotel, saw a small shop with the words "Articles de Peche" above the doorway. I wandered over the bridge and down the cobble stone street until I came to the unpretentious little establishment, where a bewildering array of fishing tackle crowded every corner of the cramped display window. Within the tiny bazaar sat the portly proprietor, spectacles hanging on the end of his nose, his flaxen mustache curving stiffly over his mouth, in which he held a long carved pipe. He bent over a tray of wobblers and, looking on with exactly as much interest and scrutiny, his gray cat peered over his shoulder. When my shadow fell across the doorway he looked up and greeted me in thick French which I did not comprehend, but because of my eagerness to understand and be understood, we managed to patch up a sort of jargon. With this babel, and that psychic rapport which always exists between anglers everywhere, we got along comfortably enough, and I was able to purchase a good supply of leaders and flies, plenty for myself and more for fishing friends in America.

By pointing and nodding and going through a lively pantomime, I indicated that I was eager to fish, but that I had no tackle. This was another of those annoying occasions when our trunks, including my tackle, had been sent on ahead, this time to Paris. The shopkeeper was sympathetic and interested, and he offered to lend me a rod, reel and line. By this time his smiling spouse had appeared and my wife sauntered in to the shop just in time to hear me making arrangements for borrowing equipment. She covered up her disapproval of this transaction by making friends with old Graimalkin, and before leaving the shop gave the proprietress a gay cat collar which she had purchased earlier, so that we all parted in the happiest and friendliest of spirits.

I made my arrangements to fish a nearby stream, but when I called the next morning for the tackle, I found that, instead of getting what I thought I had bargained for, a three- or four-ounce fly rod, the proprietor had selected a huge three-joint salmon rod, weighing not less than five or six pounds. But beggars cannot be choosers, so away I went to try my luck with the Swiss trout. On the previous evening, when purchasing my fishing ticket, I learned from the manager of the hotel that the season would not open for a couple of days. I made no attempt to conceal my disappointment. The host was sympathetic and obliging. Elaborate negotiations were started at once, and soon produced a special dispensation. So I looked forward to fishing a foreign stream in advance of the opening season, when I could be the first for that year to lay a fly upon its riffles and pools. But what was my astonishment, when I arrived at the stream, to find it literally lined with fishermen, I could not discover a single one of the many anglers who could understand my French, nor could I understand their English, so I was left to surmise either that dispensations were cheap and plentiful, or that the other anglers were poachers. Be that as it may, I joined the throng. I thought a bit sadly of my good boots and waders now locked up in Paris, as I stepped into the water, waist deep, in my second-best pair of trousers and my business shoes, but once in the stream all was forgotten in the business of angling.

By a man who uses a dry fly on light tackle, my struggles with the salmon rod and size sixteen flies will be understood, To him who does not, further expatiation would make no difference. Anyway, because of these handicaps and the overwhelming competition, I did not catch a single fish.

In the late afternoon while I waited for the car that was to take me to Geneva, I sat on a sunny boulder, smoking a cigarette and trying to dry out my wet legs, when along came another angler. In my best French I inquired if he had caught any fish, but his response was such a blizzard of ejaculations and characteristic gestures so that I could not understand a word of what he said. Nevertheless I did get the story as completely as though he had told it in English, for, sitting there on the stone with me and smoking my American cigarettes, (which he appeared to relish), he told me in pantomime of the very pool where he had cast his fly, the huge fish that had taken it, the terrific fight that had ensued, the size and strength of the monster, the many runs it had made, its spectacular leaps, and its ultimate escape by taking both fly and leader. With sparkling eyes and eloquent waving of his arms, in unmistakable gestures, he related the whole tragic tale. Then, with a shrug of his shoulders, he displayed his empty basket. I offered another cigarette. He accepted it with a bow and went off up the stream, evidently in search of another leviathan.

One day we drove out from Rome to have a look at Lake Trasimene where, more than two hundred years before Jesus saw the light of day, Flaminius with his Roman legions fought the hordes of Hannibal, and was so disastrously defeated. It was impossible not to be lost in one's thoughts while standing in such a place, and we felt all the despair of those weary overwhelmed soldiers as they fought their losing battle, desperately realizing that nothing was left to stand between the great Carthaginian and their beloved Rome itself. It is all so quiet and peaceful now, but in our reverie we could see the banners of the opposing forces rising and dipping across the plain, the flash of shield and spear in the Umbrian sunshine, the wild fright of the Romans at sight of Hannibal's African elephants with their flaying trunks and trampling feet, the first of those awesome creatures the Romans had ever seen. We could almost hear the drums and tramplings of conquest, the clash of arms, the neighing of plunging steeds, the trumpeting of the elephants, the shouts of the victors and cries of the vanquished. We thought of the blood that had been spilled on those quiet meadows, and of the pathetic young men of so long ago who would never return home, but had lain down and died there on the very sod where we stood.

Crimson is inalienably associated with battlefields. The red poppies of Flanders, and, on the shores of that great lake, count-less wild red strawberries dotting the plain in unbelievable numbers. We wondered if those scarlet fruits had sprung from the life blood of the fallen heroes of so long ago. We are of that romantic generation given to quoting Omar, so long gone out of fashion, and here, beside the lake, the pertinence of the old Persian's thoughts struck us simultaneously.

> "I sometimes think that never grows so red
> The Rose as where some buried Caesar bled;
> That every hyacinth the Garden wears
> Dropt in her Lap from some once lovely Head."

The world's cycles are so short, warriors perish and flowers spring up in endless routine, the fate of one apparently not more important than that of the other.

We were recalled to reality by the sight of fishermen in the little, dilapidated, weather-beaten village on the north shore of the lake. They were gnarled and worn, revealing that life had been a struggle, and that they had sailed the lake in all weathers to garner in their nets of fish. The fish of the lake are called tinka, weigh about a pound, and constitute an important item of diet in many Italian families.

But the strawberries charmed us, and as we paused to gather them we recalled how, as children, we had picked our native varieties on the sunny hillsides of the New World so far away. It was a real labor then to gather as much as a cupful, for the berries were small and easily crushed, but the heavenly flavor was reward enough for the work of picking. It seemed wonderful to find these wild strawberries served in restaurants all over Italy, delicious little fragoli a bit larger than the wild variety at home, but still very tiny. They make a most delicious desert, The Italians stir them into a frothy whipped cream and one is served an entrancing mound of pink polka dotted delight, topped with a generous powdering of pulverized sugar.

I was told by a friend in Rome that some fishing was to be had near the mouth of the ancient Tiber, where it flows into the Mediterranean Sea, so off we went. Our route took us past the Capitoline Hill where, in that night so long ago, the clacking of geese warned that enemy spies were attempting to scale the cliff in the dark, and the aroused garrison beat them off with boulders and boiling oil. The old story had a particular meaning for me. I remembered, while I stood on those very heights, and peered over the parapet, that I had sat spellbound beside my father as we ate our lunch one day on the mossy banks on Herman Creek, and he explained why the Romans considered geese sacred. He had told me too about the Forum and the Coliseum where the wild beasts fought, and where gladiators slew each other while Roman sailors held the great roof of canvas overhead to shelter the thousands of spectators from the sun. How he would have loved every stone of eternal Rome, and perhaps how grateful he would be if he could know of the impression left by his heroic tales on the mind of a little boy so many years ago! The consciousness of his presence never left me while I was in that immemorial city.

Just before we came to the sea a magnificent spread of weathered ruins caught our eye, and we learned that here, some twenty six hundred years ago, had stood the city of Ostia, housing a population of more than a hundred thousand people. The ravages of war, repeatedly waged by pirates and buccaneers, and the ebb and flow of violent human struggle, finally resulted in the complete abandonment of the city. Nothing now remains but acres and acres of deserted streets, paved with great slabs of stone, into which the clattering wheels of the chariots have cut their telltale grooves. Theatres, baths, shops, temples, columns, statues, pavilions, homes, spread out in the sunshine, with no living creature in all that vast expanse, save the little green lizards sleeping on the rocks or scurrying into the cracks between. Red poppies flame in every chink and crevice, but all else is desolation and decay.

A branch of the Tiber flows into the sea not far from Ostia. I flayed it persistently with a fly rod, following it down to the

Mediterranean and casting in the eddying waters behind the green water-worn jetty. But no fish of any kind responded to my efforts. My companion had brought along a good can of worms for bait, and, with high hopes he dangled his lure into the deep water at the mouth of the stream; but before he could so much as make a second cast, a group of youngsters, walking along the jetty, gave the can a playful kick, and if his bait attracted any fish, they consumed the contents of the can without fear of encountering a hook. There were no fish for us that day, but we did see some fish taken, if such they may be called. A short distance above where we were fishing, a group of men and boys had rigged up a huge purse net. It was suspended between two long poles which were hinged at the bank of the stream. By means of ropes and tackle they lowered it into the stream, and allowed it to remain there for some fifteen or twenty minutes. When they hauled it up, it contained a substantial number of tiny little flashing and wiggling minnows much like what are termed whitebait, the largest not over two inches long. That type of fishing did not particularly appeal to me, but the net operators seemed well pleased, for they capered about with joy every time they lifted the net and gathered in a handful of the tiny squirming creatures. I have seen almost the same device employed on the rocky headlands of southern Korea, but there the nets were larger, and were lifted by a hand winch. The Korean fish were more varied in color and shape and were fairly large.

While in Europe I was frequently impressed with the thought that fishing is a serious business there. Comparatively few sportsmen were in evidence, and generally the people who cast out nets, or angled from their boats were those who fished to eat, and who worked as hard at their task as they would at any other labor. Commercial fishermen drifted on the Adriatic, the Mediterranean and on nearly all available waters. They used seines and nets and caught many varieties of fish that I had never seen before. But weather beaten and gnarled as those men were, and marked with the blight of penury, they had a robust and wholesome look about them, a look that spoke of long contact with fresh winds and sunshine.

The greatest array of big and little fish of every conceivable kind and color that I ever saw, or ever hope to see again, was in the shady stone-floored fish market in Venice. We had wandered down one of the many narrow crooked streets leading away from the great square of St. Mark's, had crossed innumerable arched stone bridges, and finally stood by the Grand Canal at the foot of the famous bridge of the Rialto. Like all the streets, and every bridge in Venice, it is designed solely for pedestrians. In that great city of nearly four hundred thousand people, there is not a single truck, bus, automobile, carriage, wagon, cart, horse, mule, or even a bicycle. One travels by gondola, launch, on foot, or stays at home.

Like the famous Ponte Vecchio across the Arno River at Florence, the Rialto Bridge is bordered on both sides with shops and bazaars, full of the strange and interesting merchandise of the east. We ambled across the bridge and down another street, rounded a bend and found ourselves at the entrance to what I am sure must be the most exotic fish market in all the world. It stretched away in every direction through unbelievable lengths of booths and counters, littered with hampers, baskets, tubs, and tanks, and all the time more barges and small boats drew up at the pier bringing fresh cargoes. Here were tables and trays of little squid as black as ink, with slimy opaque fluid dripping from their dangling tentacles. Other trays held great banks of little fish resembling smelt, but as blue as indigo. Huge flounders, with the smaller halibut and turbot, gazed at us with sad, glazed eyes. Fish with big roseate scales and vermillion fins vied with others great and small, of every color in the rainbow. Some had huge heads with vicious mouths equipped with rows of sharp teeth, while others carried little chisel-like snouts. Some had swords and spears. Huge sharks, and fish resembling Newfoundland tuna, kept company with baskets of tiny eels not longer than a pin. Finally I found a tray containing what looked like big rainbow trout, weighing four or five pounds each. Seeing these fish so far from home, and in a country where I did not know they existed, I was naturally curious, and in what little Italian I could muster, I undertook to ask the proprietor of this particular booth where they came from. As near as I could make out he said "Adriatic Sea." Then I tried to tell him that we had fish just like that in America, but I did a very poor job of getting that over. Obviously he thought I was trying to tell him that the fish came from America, which of course implied that they must be very stale by the time he was able to display them in Venice. His irritation was evident, and his response voluble. I was completely snowed under by a barrage of Italian words. It was clear that my effort to explain what I was really trying to say only provoked him the more. A crowd gathered and soon a swarthy sweater-clad fishmonger stepped forward. Fortunately he understood my personal variety of Italian, for he began gesticulating and jabbering at the proprietor, who was badly worked up by this time. Slowly a look of comprehension broke over the vendor's dark face. He grinned and nodded as he accepted a pack of American cigarettes, and we bowed ourselves into the background where we wandered and gazed among the busy fishmongers, but confined our comments to each other.

The ancient maritime city of Genoa is one of the strongholds of communism in Italy. On May Day of 1950, when I was poking about the city, a big Communist parade got under way. A long line of swarthy laborers, men and women, in trucks, astride bicycles and on foot, paraded the narrow streets, wearing red scarfs and hats, singing communist songs and passing out pamphlets and literature. A young fellow rode up and down the line of paraders shouting something through a megaphone.

"What is he saying?" I asked my English-speaking guide.

"He is repeating something about the evils of America."

"What evils is he talking about?" I inquired.

"He doesn't say," said the guide, with a weary smile.

After the paraders had dispersed it was our good fortune to again see the fellow on the bicycle, and at my request the guide hailed him and we had a talk with the guide acting as interpreter.

"What were you shouting through the megaphone?" I asked.

"I was saying down with the evils of America," he promptly responded.

"What are the evils?" I said.

Without the slightest show of embarrassment or interest he frankly responded, "I don't know."

"Then why were you saying it?"

"My boss told me to. That was my job."

"Why are you a communist?"

"Well, they tell us we are going to have a lot more to eat and that everything is to be divided equally between all of the people."

I knew that the Republic of Italy, not much larger than the State of Oregon, had a population of over 46 million, and I asked him, "Do you plan to stay here in Italy and share all the property with so many millions of people?"

"No," he said, "I want to get away from here."

"Then you want to get over to Russia?"

"Oh, no," he promptly responded, "I want to go to America. That is a great country. In America there are opportunities for everybody. I want to be an American."

With that I gave him a pack of American cigarettes which he eagerly accepted. We shook hands and parted the best of friends.

One night at Nice the white moonlight flooded in across the open balcony of our bedroom, and shone upon me with such brilliance that I could not sleep, and I arose to gaze on the placid Mediterranean Sea. As I stood on the balcony I saw a boat glide silently out from shore across the glittering track of moonbeams, and I watched the two fishermen spread their net. They maneuvered the heavy gear with great skill, left a circle of floats drifting on the tide, and then pulled noiselessly back to shore. I was interested to learn what would be the result of their night's labor, so I crept forth again in the violet dawn, hoping to see the men come back to draw in their catch. I had not long to wait before the little boat appeared again. The fishermen rowed out toward the ring of floats on the water, and I could hear the dip and drip of the oars in the vast quietude of early morning — that, and the hushed lapping of the waves on the shore, with an occasional faint faraway call, and the bark of a dog in the distance. I hoped to see a heavy catch, but the fishermen were not successful. Only a few small fish floundered in the great net as they pulled away. But I shall not soon forget the sight of that pale dawn, the pearly sea, and the far street lights which gleamed in a long twinkling line clear to Cap d'Antibes. A pallid star fainted in the west, and in the east, morning broke in dim streaks of lacy light above the distant hills. I shall long remember that setting of tranquil beauty, and there came to my mind Romeo's lovely, eloquent lament:

"Night's candles are burnt out, and jocund day stands tiptoe on the misty mountain tops."

By the Waters of Our Forefathers

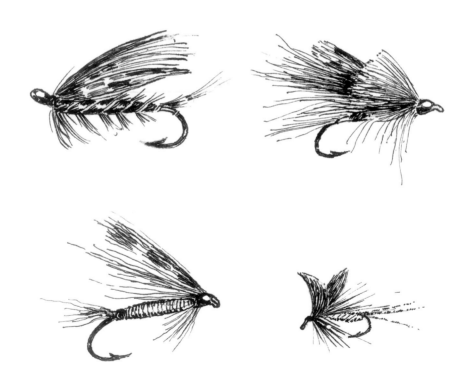

When I was in England fishing the chalk streams, I made the mistake of referring to the trout as "German browns." I was promptly informed, with no little display of feeling, that they were brown trout, not German browns. Almost since the days of my first trout on Herman Creek I have dreamed of fishing the Itchen, that famous chalk stream of southern England. It seemed to me that to fish there would be the supreme experience of a dry-fly fisherman's life. Yet, the very day my turn finally came for "a rod" on this historic stream, we were obliged to sail for home on the *Queen Mary*.

But I did enjoy many a pleasant June day on several other streams and lakes of the British Isles. My approach was usually the old one of talking myself into the privilege of fishing in waters where, except for being a member of the great brotherhood of mankind, and of the ancient fraternity of anglers, I had no right whatever to be.

Save in some of the more remote sections of Ireland, Scotland, and Wales, all the fishing waters of the British Isles are controlled either by individuals or clubs, or by guest hotels. At the hotels the fishing is by ticket for a particular date and hour on a particular beat. A large section of a stream is called a "water." A smaller portion of it is called a "beat," and the right to fish it is called a "rod." One or more rods are allotted to a definite beat of a particular water at a given time and from one designated bank or the other. Because there is heavy and persistent fishing, the trout are shy and, as most of the streams are clear and placid, it requires some skill to float a dry fly to a rising trout with any hope of capturing him. However, as in all things, there are exceptions. One day in our little British automobile driven by a competent chauffeur, my wife and I found our way to the picturesque village of Hungerford. There under the sign of The Blue Bull, we had lunch of cold pork pie and characteristic warm beer. That morning I had been unsuccessful in talking myself into a fishing excursion and while we ate lunch I was lamenting the fact to my wife. Then the pink-faced waiter who had overheard part of the conversation kindly volunteered the information that there was a small stream running just back of the inn, thence under a stone bridge and through the town where I was welcome to fish. With no expectation whatever of even seeing a trout, I set up my rod while my wife sat on a bench in the shade of a blooming hawthorn tree at the edge of the stream. Without getting out of my business clothes, I cast a May fly over a likely pool. In a flash a brown trout weighing almost two pounds had the fly, and a few moments later was flopping on the grass at our feet. Within a distance of seventy yards I caught five nice trout in little more than as many minutes, and I had confined my fishing wholly to the strip of water back of the inn above the bridge.

Then there was the day when I fished a little stream a few miles from the village of Hook in Berkshire. It was shallow and clear, and I had but little luck. Usually while I fished, my wife drove about the countryside with the chauffeur, and returned to pick me up at an appointed place and hour. I had no more than started to fish the stream when I snapped one of the tips of the little two-and-three quarter-ounce Hardy Marvel rod, given to me by my fishing friend Judge Douglas. This was a keen disappointment and the fishing was poor, so I ambled back to the bridge where the car was to meet me. I sat for some time on the grass at the edge of the stream in the shade of an old stone bridge, and let the fly dangle idly on the dark water beneath the arch, where it seemed to become fouled. I gave the line a pull and was astounded to find that there on the end was flopping an exact duplicate of the trout I had taken behind the inn at Hungerford.

By far the most pleasant experience I had fishing in England grew out of my bold tactics above mentioned. We had come to a pretty green valley through which purled as inviting a stream as I have ever seen. It flowed under one of the innumerable arched stone bridges that one finds all over England. It circled the lawn in front of a charming red brick manor and meandered through the meadow. I called at the house and was greeted by the butler, In response to my standard request that I might try my luck fishing there, he explained that "the Master" was away, but would return about two o'clock that afternoon and that I might then renew my request. Following his advice, I met the owner, Mr. T. Marson Till, at the appointed hour. "The Master" was the typical English squire as we had always pictured him in our mind's eye, rosy faced and comfortably round. He was clad in a velvet smoking jacket and his dogs leaped about him as he came forward across the lawn. At first I thought he was completely deaf or that if his hearing was not impaired, he had determined to hear me out before turning on his heel and closing the conversation, as his face registered no change of expression whatever. I talked as earnestly and convincingly as I knew how, telling him of my consuming desire to fish his water, my great distance from home, and my love for his delightful country and its people. Not until I got through did he speak. First he asked me to repeat my name. His next question was "What kind of rod do you use?" Seizing the opportunity to revive the unilateral discussion, I told him that I had several rods with me, three Leonards, a Powell, a Hardy, and a Heddon. Then I launched into praise of the British Hardy rod which was entirely sincere, but somewhat to my astonishment, he tersely remarked that the American rods were by and large superior to the British makes and he wanted to know if I would show him my tackle. So we pulled out the rods and set them all up. One after the other he grasped them and made a few false casts to test their action. He obviously began to warm up to the subject. Next he told me that I must meet his wife. Back to the house we went, and he presented me to the courteous and charming lady herself. They asked me if my wife was with me. Yes, she was in the car at the gate, so there was a further round of introductions. Then Mrs. Till suggested tea and the butler brought out an attractive tea table and set it up on the green lawn in the shade of a great elm tree. We had tea and dainty sandwiches, and felt much as if we were characters in an Anthony Trollope novel. We lacked only the village curate to make the setting complete.

After tea Mr. Till invited me to look over his elaborate assortment of salmon and trout flies and a vast amount of other tackle, and his gracious wife showed us through her beautiful old house. It was especially interesting to us as being typical of the smaller English country estates. It consisted of an old part of brick and timber built in the early 1600's to which had been added a large modern section of many rooms, each with its fireplace and unmistakable air of easy living and cultured interests. Family portraits of real distinction and excellent oil paintings adorned the walls; delicate furniture from the great days of Lord Chesterfield appeared on every hand and gleaming silver stood ready for service. Amongst all this were, to my wife particularly, eye-catching antiques, such as rare samplers, hand-done bedspreads and a great row of charming little Staffordshire china houses, which adorned one whole mantel shelf. We were amused to see the very luxurious beds which had been provided for our host's spoiled and pampered dogs in a room adjoining the warm kitchen, and to observe the tame Muscovy ducks tramping in and out of the house quite unrebuffed.

After this ceremony Mr. Till finally got back to the subject of fishing. He told me that I was welcome to go ahead with my proposed assault upon his stream and pointed out the more likely spots where I might raise a trout. With the formality or strangeness once broken, he was the very soul of cordiality.

The afternoon was hot and the water was glassy, with the result that I had no luck, although I did spot a number of good fish. In the meantime Mrs. Till and my wife had found much in common in books and architecture. While I fished they compared notes on their mutual favorite, Jane Austen, and drove about the little hamlet of Boxford with its thatched cottages embowered in roses, and its ancient graveyard close by the church solemn with yew trees and cypress and banks of myrtle.

My genial host insisted that we return the next day for luncheon, following which he would join me in fishing other portions of the stream. Return we did, and I had a grand time picking up several good trout. The upshot of the matter was that we became warm friends and have since exchanged letters and books. I sincerely hope we may find ourselves together again, either in England or America.

Our experience with the Tills is quite typical of those contacts which Americans often make with their British cousins. It is true that they are inclined upon first meeting to be reserved, but when the ice has been broken, they are as friendly and cordial as any people on earth. We had somewhat similar experiences not only elsewhere in the British Isles, but also on the European continent, particularly in France.

That "Little Bit of Heaven," Ireland, can be a very exasperating country to a traveler without much time on his hands. Usually he cannot wait for a change in the weather and the rains come down with unvarying persistence. He soon takes on the damp odor of soggy woolens which assails his nostrils wherever he goes. But strange to say, by the time he has become reconciled to the musty smell, his unpressed clothes and his wet feet, he begins to like it for there is a peculiarly soft and refreshing quality about the atmosphere of the Emerald Isle. In that gentle land the sky is always freshly washed and, though it is often gray, silvery clouds pile up in feathery banks, and the whole earth is a green velvet carpet. Everywhere are little white stone huts with pungent smoking chimneys and masses of flowery rhododendrons and enormous wild fuchsias blooming on every roadside, and acre upon acre of shining green holly, laden with heavy clusters of brilliant berries. What a display it is when the berries are red and how we longed to be able to gather them for our Christmas holidays! It is a bower, an intimate and embracing realm where one cannot long remain a stranger.

When one's car stops on the road, the pretty rosy-faced children crowd around it, and their parents stand in the doorways, eager to speak and to share. Though they are obviously pathetically poor, they make a friendly, happy group. Here and there peasants are seen cutting peat or turf, as they call it, from the bogs and trundling it in carts drawn by sleepy-looking lazy horses. These nags are surprisingly well nourished in that impoverished country and are treated to the best the farmers have in food as well as in kindness. The whips carried by these humped-over drivers were especially amusing to us; usually a crooked stick with a piece of string dangling from the end, or a tattered wisp of bush with which no horse alive would ever realize that he had been struck.

One hears much laughter and local banter, although, particularly in County Kerry, the dialect is so broad that it is extremely hard to understand. Time and responsibility mean nothing to these people. Over and again I made appointments with a boatman or gillie for a definite hour of the day only to find that I was lucky to have him show up at all, particularly at any time during the day of the appointment.

The villages are quaint and definitely foreign. The principal streets are lined on each side with two-storey stores which have living quarters above them for the family. The proprietor, whether merchant, banker, or blacksmith, lives on the second floor of his own establishment and conducts his business on the ground floor. Usually Americans think of such quarters as cheap or undesirable, but we found this not to be the case at all in Ireland. We went to spend an evening with our friends, the Conveys of Castleisland, and after finding the local bank over which they live, rang the bell at a side door where we were welcomed and led upstairs to a pleasant apartment of several rooms with a storey above which was reached by a fine old winding stairway. We found that our friends lived in great comfort and we sank into soft easy chairs and basked in the snugness of a glowing peat fire, while their handsome little children danced Irish reels and sang folk songs with neither embarrassment, nor the slightest evidence of forwardness or conceit.

No two buildings in the villages of Ireland are the same color. They are painted in soft shades of green, pink, blue, lavender, yellow, or white. At a common level between the first and the second storey of each building, appears the name of the proprietor in huge letters, O'Brien, McCarty, Sullivan, O'Toole, Flannigan, Casey, Monnihan, and so on through the whole category of good old Irish names.

I learned that a hotel near Killarney controlled a strip of salmon water so I purchased a ticket and made arrangements to fish it. I was directed to appear at the hotel precisely at nine o'clock the next morning. By a little after eleven the gillie showed up, and not more than an hour later the chauffeur put in his appearance, so off we went in a deluge of Irish rain, stopping before long at a farmhouse near the river. There we huddled under a cowshed to protect us from the downpour while we had lunch. My gay companions brewed the customary tea, and helped themselves very liberally from the picnic basket. Then we set up our tackle.

The gillie said "U nee a straw cas u na." On the Continent I had picked up a few words of French and Italian and I was able at times to understand at least a little of what was being said, but it was wholly beyond my power to understand a County Kerry Irishman speaking English. I asked him to repeat his statement, which he did a time or two. I answered "no," but when I observed his apparent disappointment I promptly reversed the response and said "yes." His broad smile convinced me that my second guess was better than my first. I mulled the matter over in my mind for some time and concluded that what he was trying to say was that I would require a strong "cast" which is the English and Irish synonym for leader.

So in spite of the gray clouds and intermittent showers, hyphenated now and then by glimpses of blue sky and splashes of sunshine, the gillie, the chauffeur, and I walked down through the fields and meadows to the stream. As we sloshed along a muddy lane, the chauffeur said something about the excellent appearance of the corn. I could see only a field of rye, waving green and rank in the downpour, but patient inquiry conducted under the handicap of his Celtic brogue finally developed the fact that in Ireland corn, such as we know it, is unknown. All grains and cereals are called corn. The rye was corn and so was the field of wheat across the fence.

The stream ran placid and clear between grassy banks, but like all the other waters of the British Isles at that time of year it was extremely low.

I was equipped with a fly rod, and a light free-running casting rig with a multi-hooked lure. The gillie carried an enormous Green Heart salmon rod, not less than twelve or fifteen feet in length, which must have weighed six or seven pounds. With this miniature telegraph pole he vigorously flayed the stream until he broke the tip. For a time I fished with the fly rod, and left the casting rig lying on the grass, but I raised no salmon, although we saw one or two big fellows breaking the surface. When I decided to put by the fly rod and cast the lure, this tackle had vanished. Then I saw the chauffeur down the stream. There he stood beating the water with it, with the broad and vacant grin of an imbecile on his florid face. He was obviously delighted, but I could tell at a distance that a terrible thing was happening. He had failed to release the drag. I could hear the grind of the gears, and before my very eyes, he stripped them. In addition he had lost the handle of the reel somewhere in the wet grass. He helped look for it with a light heart, but we were not successful in finding it and there it probably lies to this very day.

By that time I lacked some of my usual enthusiasm, and I went back to the base camp to pick up my fly rod again. There I discovered that the gillie had taken my reel, line, leader, and fly and had put them on his big salmon rod which he had stuck together after a fashion by poking the broken tip into the middle joint ferrule. He was too busy with his angling to be free to talk to me. All this was exasperating beyond measure, but I could see that there was no harm in the simple souls. They were delighted when I was, and obviously looked upon the whole trip in the nature of a junket for one and all, but I was unable to adjust myself to their happy mood. By the time I could talk the gillie out of these adjuncts, and re-rig my rod, the fishing was about over for the day. Nevertheless I made emergency repairs to the casting rig, and just before dark I was able to hook and land my first

Atlantic salmon, a small fish weighing about six pounds. Small though it was, it did give me quite a thrill before yielding the spirit and being gaffed by the gillie. An estimate of the cost of this fish if the whole trip were charged to his expense, would probably be about one hundred eighty-seven dollars. We carried the salmon to our friends, the Conways, who received it with pleasure, and told us that fish in Ireland were always expensive anyway.

The jolly miller who lived on the River Dee was a very old friend of mine, for I had known him since Mother Goose days. When I arrived in the British Isles I poured over my map and found that there are two Dees — one in Scotland and one in Wales. It is the Scottish Dee and its sister stream the Don, which flow into the sea near Aberdeen, that are world renowned for their periodic runs of Atlantic salmon. There is a definitely orthodox method for fishing this river, and innovations are hotly resented, as they would be in any country so steeped in tradition as Scotland. It was here that my old friend Charlie Miller, a great fisherman like Spen Biddle, but now gone to his reward, astonished and disgusted his gillie by catching salmon in an unconventional manner. On that river the practice is, and has always been, to drift the fly throughout the full run without any movement or agitation whatever, but Charlie, who never knew the meaning of the word orthodox about anything, used his own partic-ular system. He fished with a wet fly as he had always fished for steelhead in the Northwest. He let his fly sink well below the surface and worked it across the current with little jerks as it swung in at the end of the run. He was the only fisherman who had any luck that day. He caught three fine salmon. These he displayed at the inn. There was no enthusiasm. The next day he started out with his stolid gillie walk-ing beside him. He had always heard that the Scotch were an austere race but he had not believed them to be this rigid. They went forward in silence and not a word was said as Charlie rigged his tackle, though the air was heavy with disapproval, and when at last he cast his fly and prepared to fish as he had the day before, the gillie could keep mute no longer. He pulled up short and said tersely, "We don't wur-rk the fly on the Dee, sir." Even Charlie, whose nonchalance sel-dom forsook him, was taken aback.

I had no opportunity to fish the Scotch Dee, but I did spend a fine day on the Dee in Wales. We were sojourning in the romantic old walled city of Chester, and a drive of forty or fifty miles took us into Wales where the quaint little villages and rugged scenery were delightful, and the brick buildings, with upturned eaves, made us think of oriental pagodas. The Welch Dee is a picturesque stream, tum-bling down through a verdant valley, here boiling over stones and there spreading out in placid flow along clean gravel bars. We got no fish, for the stream was too low and clear, but we took much pleasure in talking to the candid and friendly Welshmen who stopped to watch as I cast my flies on the river. Their language, a mixture of Celtic and English, is as hard to understand as rural Irish, but there was never any mistake in interpreting their kindness and good spirit.

We found unusually low and clear streams throughout Scotland. I got no fish on our trip to Kinloch Rannoch, though we reveled in the ride over the moors, where rosy children waved to us, and dour peasants stood silent and appraising by the roadside. Strange long haired highland cattle gazed at us from the stony pastures, and mossy-faced lambs cuddled by their mothers in the shelter of the rocks and hummocks of the heather-carpeted hills. We came eventually to a romantic and remote highland inn, presided over by a handsome host in well-pressed kilts who made us welcome. We found the patrons of the inn intensely Scotch but interested, and with a distinctly proprietary attitude, in the British Royal Family. They had the greatest respect for Queen Mary and told us with relish a story which particularly pleased the duty conscious Scotch.

They related that one day a member of the Royal Family who was to dedicate a hospital the following morning came in and flung herself down in exhaustion, exclaiming "I am tired to death and I hate hospitals!" Whereupon the great Queen rose with dignity and said severely, "You are a member of the Royal Family. You are never tired and you love hospitals."

It is obviously Queen Mary who has put royalty in the enviable position it occupies in England today. One needs but contemplate the countless empty thrones in Europe to realize the greatness of that accomplishment.

Truth and Consequences

My wife read the manuscript up to this point and said, "Your book is probably all right, though it isn't true to nature." "Not true to nature!" I exclaimed, "why, every single word of it is exactly true, what do you mean?"

She went on, "You only give one side of the picture — everything perfectly lovely. I could give you a list of twenty items, not one of which you would dream of putting in that book, and they are all equally true."

I replied that I would like to see such a list, only to be handed, the following day, a strange compilation from which I now quote excerpts. I will even expatiate on a few of her suggestions. It read in part:

> Why don't you tell about —
> The time I shook the snake out of your bed roll?
> When we slept through the storm in that dirty old
> miner's cabin, full of rotten potatoes?
> The terrible day on Sheep Creek?
> When you paid that Chinaman in Canton a quar-
> ter, or something, to eat that nasty fish alive?
> When you took away that little boy's fishing rod,
> and used it yourself?
> The time the cat ate the tail off that big fish, and
> you were mad about it?
> etc., etc., etc.

The list was completely incoherent, but it had a few constructive thoughts scattered among unpleasant facts, so this chapter is based in large part, on her ideas, without much regard to literary style.

Terrible Day on Sheep Creek

I had heard, through an acquaintance who runs the pool hall, that excellent fishing was to be had on a small stream about forty miles across the desert from home, that the roads were good, and that few fishermen knew anything about the spot. I thought it strange that I had remained in ignorance of a stream with such remarkable potentialities so near at hand, and decided to fish there the following Sunday, planning the trip largely for the pleasure of our foster daughter, Ruth Morrow, an ardent and tireless angler. So, true to plan, we packed folding chairs, table, and lunch kit, and started off, with me in oppressively high spirits, so my wife claims. The sun beat down in glaring fury on the hottest day of the summer, and we bumped along across the desert with blinding white alkali dust flying up and choking us. The road soon dwindled to a trail, full of rocks and bumps, and the scorching bare hills buzzed with what my wife insisted were rattlesnakes. True, we were in typical rattlesnake country, but really all she heard was the incessant clicking of millions of grasshoppers. The relentless sun pursued us until we finally drew up in the shade of a few parched cottonwoods, the only trees to be seen for miles around. A dreary, turbid stream dawdled along nearby. The filthy earth under these straggling trees had been the feeding ground for bands of sheep from time immemorial, and rusty tin cans and trash, shamelessly littered the landscape, while lying stretched in the only good patch of shade were two bloated, wooly sheep, dead these many moons. Swarms of angry blue-bottle flies roared above them, or shot like hornets through the trees and the air hung heavy with a powerful aroma. It was discouraging indeed, but my spirits were still high as I settled my wife, in every comfort possible, in the stream itself. I placed chairs and table in the shallow water, and left her, bare footed and ensconced with fly-swatter, knitting, and a good book, while Ruth and I took sandwiches from the picnic basket and started for the creek.

Well, we worked up that wretched stream for hours, and fanned it vigorously with our flies, while the heat hung like a volcano over our heads, and the blue sky turned to brass, but never a fish did we see. We ate our lunch and then went on, still hopeful, but a little later, when I turned to speak to Ruth, I was just in time to see her reel, stumble and fall in a heap. I rushed back and found her in a dead faint. I laid her in the dust, put wet cloths on her head, and fanned her while I stood between her prostrate form and the outrageous sun, until she revived, and we were able to make our painful way back to the trees. There we found my wife, morose and uncooperative for cows had also taken a fancy to cool off in the stream whence she peered out angrily at us from amongst the legs of nearby bovines. It was decided that we must depart at once, violent though the heat still was. But misfortune continued to dog us, for, in the hottest and dirtiest spot on the trail, while I chopped at a stump against which the rear wheel of the car had jammed, I gave a glancing blow with the hatchet, and gashed a deep cut in a new tire.

To make a long story short, we reached home at last. There stood the big house cool and shadowy among the leafy trees, and when we entered, it was eloquent with the quietude of peace, and the soft murmur of the air conditioner. We got Ruth to bed, smeared her blistered lips with camphor ice and doused her limp body with sunburn lotion. The next morning my wife couldn't speak above a whisper, due to a terrific cold which she had taken, and I had a bad dose of poison ivy.

How to Make a Smoke House

I had supposed that every fisherman knew how to smoke his fish, but my wife insists that such is not the case. Because of the enthusiasm invariably aroused by the sight of a plateful of our smoked trout, and the inroads made upon it by our guests, I will follow her suggestion and describe the process, for the returns on the investment of time and trouble are out of all proportion to the effort required. Many of the more permanent types of smoke house are so constructed as to admit the smoke through pipe or trench from an adjacent source such as a stove or disconnected smudge. They admit of innumerable variations and refinements but are not considered here. What follows deals with the simplest type of temporary device.

One who goes into the woods expecting to smoke trout should carry with him the following items:
a light single-bit axe or a heavy hatchet
a reasonable quantity of six penny nails
several yards of soft iron baling wire
a pair of wire clipping pliers
a short handled shovel or spade
two squares of chicken wire netting about four feet in diameter
a quantity of gunny sacks, old blankets, sheets, canvas, tarpaulin,
or light building paper for walls and roof
a flour sack
a long, strong, sharp butcher knife
a pair of rubber gloves
three or four pounds of ordinary table salt and a pound of brown sugar

If the smokehouse can be built on a gravel or sand bar, the likelihood of the spread of fire will be reduced. If it is built on ordinary earth, the surface accumulation of grass, leaf mold and pine needles should be removed for a width of not less than a foot clear around the smokehouse. When one's base camp is located near a stand of small trees, four saplings spaced about four feet apart will suffice for the corner posts. Or the posts can be provided by driving pointed saplings into the ground, to extend about five feet above the surface. Three and one-half or four feet above the ground, attach cross members of light material to the posts around the entire structure as though building a one rail fence. Then stretch a shelf or rack or netting across the members between the corner posts. If the netting shelf is not large enough to accommodate all the trout to be smoked at one time, stretch the other section between the posts eight or nine inches above the first. Nail or wire strips of sapling, or light split rails, on the top across the four posts, and cover the entire frame on all sides, and across the top, with such material as you may have brought along for that purpose. The smoke will discolor the material, so, if sheets, blankets or tarpaulin are used, they should be of little value. If gunny sacks are to be used, they should be split down one side and across the end. The covering material should de placed on the frame in such a way as to eliminate smoke leaks, preferably by providing a generous overlap where it is brought together at the front. Nails, bits of wire, or short, clean, tough, sticks, two or three inches long, may be used to pin the front overlapping flaps together. The front overlap can be parted to enable one to place the fish on the netting racks and to build and tend the fire.

To prepare the fish for smoking, one should provide a work table of boards, slab, bark or saplings, upon which to dress the fish. A bench, box, or the surface of a big clean barked log will suffice. Into this shelf, or improvised table drive a small headed nail. When the fish have been cleaned, press the head down on the nail so that it will slip through the eye sockets. This will hold the fish firmly in place while being butchered. With one end of the butcher knife held in each hand, press it into the flesh just back of the gills, and down to the backbone. By pulling the knife forward, and down, against the backbone, one can peel off half of the fish in the form of a fillet. Turn the fish over and repeat the operation on the other side, whereupon there will remain only the head, backbone and tail. Cut each fillet into two or three pieces, depending upon the size of the fish. Then mix a sufficient quantity of salt and brown sugar, three parts salt to one of sugar. A prick of the hand by a fishbone, particularly when one must next handle the salt, and finally stoke the fire, can make a nasty irritating sore, so use the rubber gloves, both when butchering and salting the fish. Sprinkle a liberal quantity of the blended salt and sugar, both on the flesh and the skin sides, and around the edges of each fillet, and place the chunks in the flour sack. Hang up the sack of fish and allow the surplus moisture to drip away, and the salt and sugar to work into the flesh. I find that the best plan is to allow the fish to hand overnight. Some prefer soaking in brine but I prefer the dry method.

When ready to start the smoking, cut a substantial quantity of fuel from green, deciduous trees, such as aspen, willow, vine maple, alder, birch, or oak, being careful to avoid conifers like fir, pine, tamarack, spruce, and hemlock. Place about ten inches apart, in the very center of the smokehouse floor, two sections of green wood, cut from a small tree, with a diameter of four or five inches. This will prevent the spread of fire. All of the fuel, including these diminutive logs should be about one foot long, so that the fire can be contained in the middle of the smokehouse floor and kept away from the inflammable sides. In preparing the fuel, include the trunks, branches, and leaves of the trees and bushes. Bits of branch, in full leaf, will help smother the fire when once well under way. With an ample quantity of fuel at hand, build a small fire between the side sticks, for which purpose you may use any dry material, even from conifers. When the fire is burning brightly, smother it with the smaller sticks of green wood, twigs, and leaves. Then spread the fish on the racks starting the operation by placing the chunks skin side down. This will preserve the juices until the smoking produces a shiny film. Close and fasten the front flaps, and see that the walls are held firmly to the ground with pegs or rocks. Keep the fire smoldering, but replenish it from time to time with the green, sap bearing, sticks and leaves, and it will simmer and sizzle for hours, and develop a great smudge in the tight smokehouse. Occasionally the fire may burst into fame, whereupon it should be beaten down. The smoking should continue for twelve to fifteen hours. If the process runs into the night, bank the fire well before crawling into your sleeping bag. Ere the job is completed, your eyes may sting from sticking your head into the smokehouse when turning the fish, or replenishing the fire, but nobody suffers very long from that ailment.

When the fish has been thoroughly smoked, it will be a fine shiny brown on the outside, and deep pink inside. Place it in a porous bag or, loosely in a paper carton, and it will last for several weeks. Upon returning home, keep the pack in a cool dry place. If it develops a tendency to moisten, showing a few moldy spots, rub them away with a cloth soaked in vinegar, and it will be none the worse. As a *hors d'oeuvre*, or for a cold lunch, smoked trout is a treat par excellence, and if one brings home enough to enable him to be generous with his friends, they will be bound to him with hoops of steel forever after.

That Bear Hunt

Some of our friends were planning a bear hunt, and invited us to go along. I do not hunt big game, but the fishing should be excellent, so Fred Moes and I planned to fish while my wife and Helen Horton gathered huckleberries which were abundant in the very vicinity where we were going. The plan sounded perfect, and in due course the men packed guns, fishing rods, duffel, spirits, and wives, and the caravan headed for the famous John Day country. There bears and wild game have now taken over the territory, once trodden by little eohippus, the famous prehistoric three-toed horse. In the valley late-summer haze dimmed the sharp outlines of the higher altitudes, the rich colors of the ready harvest were a feast for our eyes and everywhere birds were flocking and preparing for their long flight south.

Towards evening we drew up at our destination, a flat, needle-carpeted bench on the breaks of a vast pine forest. The air was clean and fragrant, and the brawling John Day River tumbled over its rocky bed only a few feet from our camp. I set up our folding trailer, with its double beds, while others laid out their sleeping bags. After supper we sat about the blaze and watched the darkness fall. The stars came out, and the glow from our fire built a pleasant forest room with a black wall of trees snugly encircling us. There in the flickering light and shadow we sat speculating as to how many sharp eyes were peering at us from the protection of the dark woods. We told tales of adventures, and when the embers faded we went to bed, "shut up in measureless content."

With the earliest trace of dawn the hunters were up, rattling around the fire, cooking their breakfast, and then they disappeared into the misty woods. The rest of us proceeded as planned. Fred and I took off for the lower river, and a good day's fishing, while the women set out with their pails to gather huckleberries. It was almost dark when we returned to the camp. The women had been lucky in finding berries, told us about seeing a porcupine and reported finding a dried snakeskin lying on a rock. The hunters had returned too, footsore, sunburned, and badly discouraged. Never a sign of a bear had they seen. Fred and I had a different story to tell, and here it is.

The hills that form the rugged canyon of the John Day River are steep and high. It wasn't much of a job to scramble down to the stream, but in the late afternoon, when Fred and I, laden with heavy baskets of trout, had to climb back up again, on our return to the cabin, we often slipped on the dry pine grass which covered the open, sunny slopes, stumbled over the rocks, and were quite weary when we finally reached the bench and found the faint trail. So we sat down to rest and catch our breath in the shade of a clump of bull pines. Suddenly we heard a terrific growl, and glancing up, saw, facing us, not thirty yards away, a big brown bear with mouth wide open displaying rows of vicious white teeth. Although we had often seen bears at a distance when going about through the woods, none had ever before manifested any interest in us, but rather were glad enough to hurry away on our approach. But this was a very different bear, and as we leaped to our feet we were genuinely frightened. The big brute would approach, stand on its hind feet and flay its forelegs, armed with long, curving talons, snarling and growling as though prepared to devour us on the spot. It would advance with thrashing paws, back away again, circle about among the logs and rocks, getting closer to us, and appearing more vicious at every sortie. Except for our jack knives, we were wholly unarmed, but without thought, each apparently acting on the primitive instinct of self defense, we opened our knives and waited for the attack; for when we attempted to back away into the clump of trees, the bear rushed to within thirty or forty feet of us and we knew that retreat was useless. Then it occurred to me that the bear might have been attracted by the smell of our fish, so I pitched my laden basket toward the creature. The situation grew worse, for the animal became even more excited. About the time I began to contemplate my past sins, and to wonder what luck I might have in crashing the Pearly Gates. Following the expected attack, I heard the snapping of a twig overhead. I glanced up and saw, not twenty feet above us, in the small trees, two half-grown, fluffy cubs. We realized at once that the big she-bear was merely trying to protect them. She was not interested in eating us or our fish. She only wanted us to leave the scene promptly and without further ado, a desire with which we were in heartiest accord, we backed no further into the trees, but gingerly side stepped, trying to make ourselves as ingratiating as possible, and after a few minutes, which seemed like hours, we got out of the neighborhood. I made no attempt to recover my fish basket and its contents, but I have no doubt Mother Bear called her babies from the trees to eat my trout. When we did get back to the cabin and related our tale to the bear hunters of the party, they merely grunted and said, "You can't beat the luck of a fisherman."

How to Make Oregon Grape Jelly

I said, "making jelly certainly doesn't belong in a book on fishing." But my wife instantly brushed that objection aside with the remark, "Of course it does! Everybody wants to know about that, and besides you can eat it with fish any time." I will admit that the results she achieves are successful and delicious, and as the luckless fisherman can often fill his empty creel with berries as he walks back toward camp, I give her recipe herewith.

Recipe

Pick nice big berries that aren't too ripe but are good and juicy. Wash but don't bother to pull off stems. Measure and add one-fourth as much water as there are berries. Put in kettle and mash up a bit and cook till soft. Strain through a jelly bag. Boil juice five minutes and next add one cup sugar for each cup of juice and stir till dissolved, then boil without stirring and test as you would currant jelly. Don't cook too much at a time.

How to Debone a Trout

So often we have watched with a shudder, while guests at our table have hacked and lacerated a beautifully cooked trout, that we are certain very few people know what to do with that epicure's prize when, in all his beauty, he is laid out on a dinner plate. It is a sickening sight to see a man chop off a segment full of bones and push it into his mouth. His thoughts must certainly be on casting out rather than on tasting. So, for the additional reason that removing the backbone, ribs and all, is so very easy, and will add so immeasurably to a guest's enjoyment of the fish, I give the simple rules by which this can be done.

Every member of the species *salmo* and *salvelinus*, which include all trout, char and salmon, as well as most other kinds of commonly shaped fish, has a fine, easily observed median line down each side, from just back of the gill to the exact center of the tail. A fish's muscles are so formed that they readily part at this line. When that is understood, the trick of removing the flesh from the skeleton is simple enough. Turn your plate so that the fish's tail is pointing toward you, and the head toward the elaborate centerpiece, with whose arrangement the hostess has expended such painstaking effort, and over which she is now peering at you. With the fork in the left hand, hold the fish on the plate, and with the knife, held in the right, cut down the median line from head to tail. Then with the knife blade, press the flesh, between the cut and the back of the fish, off to the right. Push the flesh from the left side of the fish away from the ribs by counter-pressure of the knife, with the blade turned at an angle against the ribs. By thus working both sides of the fish, from the head toward the tail, half of the flesh, entirely free of bones is removed. Now, with the knife sever the backbone at the point where it joins the head, and with the thumb and index finger of the left hand pick up the backbone where thus cut, and draw it gently toward the tail, while at the same time, with the knife in the right hand pressing the flesh away from the ribs. I have not consulted Emily Post to determine just how you would proceed if left handed, but I am inclined to the view that the dictates of etiquette would be satisfied were the knife and fork shifted to the opposite hands.

At any rate, by successfully executing this maneuver one can eat the fish with an air of complete self-assurance, his hostess will be pleased, and the spirit of the trout may glide away through the still waters, contented and serene.

Cursorily Speaking

On a rare morning in June with the placid waters of Wallowa Lake sparkling in the sunshine, while the wooded shores smiled down upon us, my wife and I were idling about in a light skiff. Repeated casts had failed to raise a single trout, and my light fly rod was lying in the boat. With no thought of catching a fish, my wife picked up the rod and idly dangled the fly out behind the boat. Neither of us was paying any particular attention to the lure as it bobbed along upon the surface of the clear water, for we were engrossed in the sheer beauty of the scene. A kingfisher rattled across the lake, uttering its raucous cry, the mountains brooded over us and all was serene. I was rowing the boat in lazy fashion, and we were chatting of many happy things, when suddenly a big trout gulped the trailing fly. We were aroused to instant action for the fish stripped out a quantity of slack line and then splashed and wallowed at the top of the water. I maneuvered the boat in such a way as to pick up the slack in the line and my wife began vigorously cranking the handle of the reel, at the same time pulling and lifting the rod. Before I could fully realize what was going on she called out, in triumph, that classic question, "What shall I do now?" as she held my delicate rod in a dangerous arc, with the big plunging fish snubbed directly against the tip with not an inch of leader to spare!

She claims that I roughly snatched the rod from her grasp and uttered that classic response, "Get the hell out of there."*

* From John Taintor Foote's marvelous fishing story, "A Wedding Gift."

CHAPTER

As it was in the Beginning

"The may fly is torn by the swallow.
The sparrow speared by the shrike.
And the whole little wood where
I sit is a world of plunder and prey"

— Tennyson

A fisherman has much occasion to be alone with his thoughts, and unusual opportunity for observation as he walks in the solitude, little disturbing the lives of the wild creatures that hurry by on their accustomed business. He notes the furtive movements of the rabbit, timidly hopping among the ferns, the watchful action of the weasel as he slinks along the shadowy stream bank, the caution of the beaver who plops below the surface of the pool, the startled toss of the deer's antlered head, and he comes to the definite conclusion that all animate things live in constant fear and that all are predators — men, beasts, fish, and fowl. Through centuries of development, men have learned to conceal some of their fear and avarice under the veneer of civilization. But a fish is the same primitive thing it was in the beginning. That the influence of fear through the ages has been upon mankind is not too difficult to analyze, though it is curious how few even educated men have been willing or, perhaps more correctly, able to look facts in the face and concede that their actions are largely based on fear, born into them with the first stir of life.

From the time when the first prehistoric man cowered in his cave, trembling with terror at the voice of thunder and the flash of lightning, fear has marked him for her own. As the centuries rolled on, these alarms impelled men to conjure up vengeful spirits which they blamed for the storms, floods, bitter cold, scorching heat, the blood lust in savage beasts, and all the ills that beset their helpless primitive lives. So they thought to save themselves by placating the evil forces through sacrifice, supplication, and much mumbo-jumbo, erecting rude symbolic idols of wood or stone, forerunners of all our churches and cathedrals. Gradually there developed ceremonies and rituals calculated to assuage the wrath of these spirits which had by then become gods.

Thus religion was born. Eternal punishment in the life hereafter for heresy and disbelief was taught by a few of the more shrewd who capitalized on this universal fear by providing, for a fee, some mystic Open Sesame to the joys of Paradise.

The leaders among our cave-dwelling ancestors may be credited with laying a firm foundation for the many present-day forms of organized worship. Without questioning the teachings of their childhood and the accepted beliefs of those about them, without feeling the inclination to analyze their motives and usually in the utmost good faith, men bow their heads in prayer and supplication to a God of whom they are afraid and who, they have been taught to believe, will deprive them of eternal salvation if not appeased. In brief, that same fear which impelled our aboriginal forefathers to bathe their crude images in blood and to mutter their incantations to the wind and the sky exerts a powerful influence over our behavior today. Although man has now largely outgrown his fear of personal violence, he is ever apprehensive, not only for his destiny throughout eternity, but for his very existence here on this earth. He fortifies himself against hunger or want by straining his every energy toward the accumulation of worldly goods. He accepts as laudable ambition that urges to excel, so that he may be more sure of his place in the sun than his neighbor. He is greedy from sheer necessity. The urge to kill that he may eat, and the impulse to overwhelm and subjugate, still actuate his daily conduct. All of humanity, as every living creature, reacts to the same irresistible impulse.

On one of those delightful days in late fall when Indian summer has gathered unto itself all the balm and sunshine of the fading season, lie down on a grassy slope at the edge of a placid lake, look up past the towering trees and beyond the purple peaks and flinty spires into the hazy, distant blue. All seems serene. There are no distracting noises or even the faintest suggestion of conflict or strife. Peace reigns supreme. Suddenly the quiet waters of the lake are broken by the splash of a rising trout as he gulps a hapless insect. A martin teetering from the topmost branch of a nearby willow sweeps out and, in midair, catches a dragon fly that glided too close to his perch. Some busy ants find and promptly attack and devour the little green worm that dropped from the branch overhead. The statuesque heron, which has been standing so patiently among the sedges at the margin of the lake, plunges its sharp bill below the surface with lightning speed and comes up holding fast a struggling minnow. That lazy little frog, sitting on the lily pad and blinking at the sun, suddenly thrusts forth his long sticky tongue, impales a bluebottle fly, and is himself promptly devoured by a watchful garter snake. Back in the thicket, a wily fox pounces on a partridge that has just finished its meal of grubs and grasshoppers and the sleepy looking owl is already thinking about the squirrels and mice he will enjoy for supper as soon as the sun goes down. If all the still, small voices in the autumn's hush could be heard as their millions and millions of little lives are brought to such violent ends, if each could utter its death cry in accents no louder than a whisper, the whole world would be swallowed up in a vast wave of sound.

Two factors emerge: one that fear is both a blessing and a curse, the other that everything that lives must eat or be eaten. Without the impelling force of fear, all living things unaware of lurking danger would vanish from the earth. Eat or be eaten was the first dimly grasped philosophy. More than two thousand years ago, Diogenes observed that self-preservation is the first law of nature. The impulse exists equally among men and fish. Indeed few have pondered upon a fact which scientists have recognized for many years: that man came into existence upon the earth carrying the unmistakable marks of a much earlier life, already ancient, and that he was the inheritor of rich gifts from a far more lowly creature than himself, one in fact with whom he is not too pleased to claim relationship — a fish! Now the fish is a humble creature, but time was when he was the very lord in his own world, for no living thing trod upon the land. There he swam, sovereign of all the sea, vastly superior both in form and skill to any of his neighbors. In the gloomy depths of the Silurian Ocean two hundred million years ago, he evolved essentially his present perfect form, that torpedo-like shape which man has imitated in his boats, planes and submarines. He developed his firm shiny scales from the soft folds of his tender, vulnerable skin into a beautiful protecting iridescent armor; he developed a skeleton inside his body instead of without, like those of his fellow ocean dwellers, the shell fish, lobsters, crabs, and oysters. But most advanced and precious of all, he grew a backbone, jointed and with nerves. He as the original owner of a spine, yet the humblest of all creatures to possess it. From such simple origin all blooded creatures profited, and the idea once developed has never been abandoned by an expanding universe. So we anglers whose ancestors first stirred in the prehistoric slimes are particularly indebted to Brother Fish for two great gifts: a skeleton on the inside and a pliant, nervous backbone. One needs but to ponder for a moment on the statement, so heavy with disapproval — "he has no backbone," to realize how priceless mankind inherently considers that possession to be.

Patient, plodding study has uncovered the fact that the smartest fish left their ocean world for the rivers, or perhaps more likely, they became the smartest, once having found themselves out of the surging, teeming seas. In the ocean currents, abundant food drifted by and the fish had only to remain stationary to eat and fill their bellies, if they were so fortunate as to escape being eaten in their turn. But once in the more dangerous and sterner environment of rivers and streams, they were forced to develop a capacity for finding food and for seeking protection by dashing to cover when danger threatened, two accomplishments by no means trifling. Civilized man is still struggling to master these identical problems and his often conspicuous lack of success should lead him to think more highly of his finny fellow creatures.

But *Homo sapiens* can take heart from the fact that there in the stream ended the college education of the fish. He developed neither ingenuity nor capacity for reasoning; he did no more than follow a blind guiding instinct that preserved him in his own simple world. He is just a fish and so he will no doubt remain to the last, ready to fight for his life in his proudest moment, yet merely a drifter on the waters of the world, a shiftless fellow, a cannibal, a devourer of his own progeny and a fierce and implacable enemy.

Simple as the life of a fish may be, there are traits and tendencies that have given him a character which the fisherman can observe for himself as he wends his way along the banks of streams where trout lurk and wait for insects to drift by.

Little trout like little children are always ready to eat, and on sun-flecked surface and shallow pool the slaughter of the innocents goes on. The larger trout like the maturing individual is more deliberate, usually confining himself to regular feeding intervals and places. His appetite is enormous. Many an angler, enjoying the good fortune to fish a strip of water where heavy trout are ravenously feeding, finds them still gulping food even when they have become too full to swallow, grabbing voraciously for more, with insects and minnows actually spilling from their mouths when they are landed.

No fly-fisherman possessing any experience at all has failed to note that for some inexplicable reason every trout in the stream will start to feed at precisely the same moment. The surface will literally boil with rising fish for fifteen minutes to a half hour, whereupon the rise will stop as suddenly as it began, though the water may still carry abundant quantities of insect life. John Alden Knight, the author of the Solunar theory, claims to have solved the problem, and each year puts out a little pamphlet purporting to indicate the precise hour and moment of each major and minor feeding period everywhere on this continent. I have experimented much with these tables, and without in the least desiring to disparage their ingenious author and the painstaking research by which his theory was developed, I am much more impressed with such factors as water temperature, weather conditions, the height of the barometer, the stage of the stream, and the periodic hatching of aquatic insects than with time of day or phase of moon.

Many frustrated anglers who have tried in vain to coax to their lures a big trout visible through the clear water, cling to the idea that a fish can become worldly wise and will shun a fly after having been hooked a time or two, thus learning by bitter experience of its deceitful nature. There is nothing to this notion. The fish has not become "fly shy," nor has he learned any lesson which will protect him for long. Of course an escaping trout, having been hooked, may become so frightened as not to rise for some time thereafter, but this is not because he has learned any particular lesson. It is simply the old primeval fear bred in him through the centuries. On the other hand, if a light fly has broken off in the mouth of a heavy trout and the fish has not been yanked about in the process, he is apt to rise again at the very next cast. More than once have I taken a good trout and retrieved from his mouth a fly which I had lost in the preceding cast.

A little reflection will satisfy the student of fish life that trout are grossly stupid, possess but the tiniest of brains, and have no capacity for thought or speculation. A trout may have been hooked more than once on artificial flies, but it is not within his power to say to himself when a lure is next drifted over his particular lie, "Oh, oh, there is another of those annoying flies. I have been hooked a time or two so I know all about them now, and I am not going to be fooled again." What actually happens is clear enough. The trout does not take the fly for any of several good reasons. If he is large enough to have adopted a particular time and place to feed, the fly may be presented at the wrong time or the fish may be in the wrong place. More likely the fly does not look to the fish like anything he wants to eat. Or, as is the trout's definite habit, if he at the moment is feeding upon a particular insect he will decline all others regardless of how tempting they might appear to the angler. What is most likely to be the case is that the fly is poorly served, striking the water with a splash, is of an unattractive pattern, or is accompanied by an obviously visible and conspicuous line. If a trout is naturally feeding upon one of the many types of mayfly, the most delicate of the Ephemeridae, he sees no splash when the insect touches the water or any clumsy cable trailing out before or behind. Trout, like all other living creatures, are greedy; but they are likewise extremely timorous. If the shadow of the angler is cast across the stream, he has put the trout down in that area for some time. If the fly is too large, if the cast is awkward, or if the line and leader are clearly visible to the trout, he will instantly be frightened. He may still lie in the pool within sight of the angler, but any impulse which he might otherwise feel to seek his dinner will have left him for the time being.

Contrary to popular belief, mature trout, both in stream and lake, will select a sheltered place against a rock or behind a log where he prefers to lie throughout the whole span of his years, and another place not far distant where he prefers to feed. The watchful angler will find him in one or the other of these spots at the proper time of day or night. Even in lakes where it is often thought that trout cruise about at random, the fact is that having selected their abode, they confine their foraging excursions to that particular area. As trout in a stream attain great size, they become more deliberate in their feeding habits, often declining even the most attractive food throughout the day, leaving the deep pool and feeding on the shallow riffles at its foot only after dark.

A little trout will rush at his food, splashing the surface in his eagerness, often leaping into the air. But a big trout will rise leisurely and suck in the insect, leaving hardly more than a dimple on the face of the water.

Then there is the matter of sound and hearing. Fish do not hear the ordinary noises above the surface of the water, but they are extremely sensitive to any vibration on carried through it. As you move along the edge of the stream, sing or shout if you will; but be very careful when traveling the overhanging banks that the shock of your tread is not carried to the fish below; and when you are moving among submerged rocks and stones go as gingerly as possible so as not to set up undercurrent vibrations. On a lake, clumsy rowing, killing a fish by beating it against the gunwale of the boat, or scraping or shuffling about over the floorboards, all communicate frightening vibrations to the fish.

When a big trout is feeding he will lie in the same area hour after hour and day after day. As the insects float over him, he will rise to look them over, and will move slightly to the left or right for a particularly dainty morsel, but often he will let any number of the very insects upon which he is feeding drift by if they are too far away from his natural lie. Therefore, in floating a fly over a likely piece of water do not be discouraged if the trout falls to rise on the first or even several successive casts. The experienced angler will keep placing his fly a little closer in or a little farther out until it is floating directly over the fish, whereupon, in all likelihood he will be rewarded with a strike.

Regardless of the abundance of food on the water, even including the very type of insect upon which trout would normally feed, they often decline to rise at all on an excessively hot day. When such conditions are present the angler had best loaf under a tree until the sun has set and the shades of evening gather, keeping a weather eye on the stream, for just before dusk on a summer day he is apt to encounter a rise so startling as to convince him that the stream contains a hundred trout for every one which he suspected lived in its purling water.

During the spawning season, usually in early spring with the rainbows, and in late fall with the eastern brook trout, they can be readily taken, promptly rising to almost any lure presented. This is not because they are eager to feed, but rather because they are seemingly annoyed by the presence of a multicolored nuisance which disturbs the process of their spawning. At these times the trout are thin, the males develop unusually large heads and they are worthless for the table. The sensible and considerate angler leaves them alone.

Another fallacy currently accepted by most anglers is that a hooked trout possesses sufficient intelligence to dive immediately under an overhanging root or between the stones or into a tangle of moss or weeds for the express purpose of rubbing the fly from its mouth. To accord a fish credit for such intelligence is not to know him. What the fish does when executing such a maneuver is merely to repeat what he and his ancestors have always done when startled or frightened — rush for cover. If in the process the angler loses a fly, it is simply his hard luck and cannot be credited to any great sagacity on the part of the fish.

Then there is the erroneous notion that trout possess such a fine sense of discrimination that they will take a fly when attached to a 3X leader, but refuse it when served on a 1X. In other words the argument amounts to a claim that more and better fish will be taken on a light leader than on a heavy one. Only this summer I was fishing with a friend on Silver Creek. He can handle a fly far more expertly than I, but when we met for lunch and compared notes, I had a good many more and considerably larger fish than he. I had been using a 3X leader while he had been fishing with a 1X. To his mind it was the light leader that had given me the advantage. But I disagreed with him, so we exchanged leaders, continuing to fish the same water after lunch. My catch for the afternoon was again much better than his, with more and heavier trout. What was the answer? Simply this. Use the type and weight leader that best fits the fly with which you are fishing at the time. A size six or eight fly at the end of a 3X or 4X leader is preposterous, for it is wholly out of balance. The fly then cannot be presented without a slap or splash and usually twists around the end of the light leader before it ever touches the water. On the other hand, a number fourteen or sixteen dry fly on a 1X leader is even worse. There will be a heavy knot at the eye of the fly and it will not ride the water cocked up to simulate an insect, but will lie on its side, float upside down, or may even be thrust entirely above the surface by a coil in the stiff leader. Not only that, but when the heavy leader is cast, it will override the light fly and the mess will strike the water in a tangle terrifying enough to frighten away any trout in the vicinity otherwise disposed to feed.

On the day above mentioned I noticed while fishing the stream in the morning that the trout were feeding on very small insects, so I used a tiny dry fly, which to present properly it was necessary to use a light leader. On the other hand my companion, apparently feeling that the trout were feeding on larger insects, used a larger fly, and quite correctly a leader heavy enough to complement it. By midday when we had exchanged leaders, the hatch of tiny insects was over, but the trout were occasionally rising to larger bugs such as blue dragon, caddis and stone fly. Consequently my heavy leader and large flies again scored, while my companion, thinking to take trout in the afternoon on the small flies and light leader which I had used in the morning, had little success. He had failed to take note of the obvious fact that the trout had entirely changed their diet. It was just as simple as that.

But let us view the question from another angle. Those who maintain that a light leader will catch more and heavier trout than a heavy leader should at least be logical. We know that little trout, because of their voracious appetites, youth, and inexperience will strike at almost anything that touches the water, including a fly tied to a heavy leader or even to the end of the line. But as trout grow older and larger, they become more particular about their feeding, and the angler is confronted with the necessity of serving his proffered fly in as delicate and lifelike a manner as possible. Up to that point the light leader proponent would appear to have the best of the argument. But the trout continues to grow and if he is a rainbow, decides either to make a journey to the sea, returning to the stream as a husky steelhead, or to take up his abode in an ample, deep pool where he attains great size and becomes monarch of all he surveys.

Now, if it is to be argued that a trout gains wisdom with years, and learns to discriminate between the light and the heavy leader, shunning the latter, it would follow that when we go after steelhead or really big trout, we must use a leader no heavier than 3X or 4X. I maintain that if we undertook this, it would be a lucky angler indeed who could bring to gaff any steelhead or trout weighing over two pounds. The facts are that big trout such as steelhead, Kamloops, heavy rainbow, sea-run cutthroat, Loch Leven and brown trout attaining substantial size, readily strike large flies and lures. They should be and in fact must be fished with heavy leaders, 1X, OX, or even heavier. The fish will take the fly or lure just as readily on a heavy leader as on a light one, but in the latter case he will not only take it, but keep it. Don't be talked into the notion that only light leaders catch big fish. Neither light nor a heavy leader will do any good if the fly attached to it is the wrong pattern or size, is clumsily or improperly served, or is fished in the wrong water or at the wrong time.

As a final test, take a 1X leader and a 3X leader. Fill a five-gallon pail with water. Select one of the leaders and stretch six inches or so of between your two hands, immersing it in the water. Have a look at the leader so submerged, and then do the same thing with the other leader. See if you can detect any difference in their appearance. You will not be able to do so, nor can the trout.

In Scotland particularly, and in several other localities where I have fished, a popular method is "dapping." This consists of flicking the fly on and off the surface of the water in quick little jerky movements whereby only the fly and no part of the leader or line meets the water. A fly "dapped" or flicked onto the water, instantly retrieved and flicked again and again, will often raise a trout when other methods fail.

Volumes have been written about what is generally thought to be the only correct way of floating a dry fly is casting it up and somewhat to the right or left, allowing it to float back with the current as the line is retrieved. Many fish are taken in this way. But after years of trial and error, I am convinced that by far the better way to work a dry fly, particularly on larger water, is to float it downstream toward the rising trout, waving the rod and paying out line as the fly pursues its course along the current, the method taught me by Spencer Biddle and more exactly described in the chapter, "Yellow Tail in Salt Water."

A patient angler comes to know fish but not to love their character, for they are particularly cruel, vicious, and greedy. They are shy and fearful from the necessity for self preservation, but they are merciless to all in their power. Their strike is savage in the extreme and it is well for mankind that water is their habitat and that their average size is small, for they would be ferocious foes.

The obvious deduction to be drawn from this philosophizing should be helpful, if not flattering, to the angler — that by studying himself he may learn to know his prey. For certain traits and characteristics are universal throughout nature — the same for man and for all else that breathes. Every living creature will protect itself, fight for its life, and employ all the advantages of its environment to the fullest extent. The tiger lies in the bamboo jungle concealed by the very stripes that seem so conspicuous when he paces his confining cage in the zoo. He knows when to wait and when to spring, when to tread softly and when to roar and terrify. The young of every kingdom are impetuous and incautious, the mature wily and contriving. Try as he may, mankind cannot throw off the yoke which binds him to his mute and often savage brethren. That thought may well discourage the stoutest heart for it is a fetter more obvious, more powerful than most of us realize.

But there is a solace by no means inconsiderable in all this rather gloomy meditation. The God of nature has bestowed one inestimable gift upon mortal man. He alone of all His children can praise His splendor, he alone can marvel at his majesty.

So I conclude this chapter with what I call the Angler's Psalm because so often these words have come to my mine when I have lain on my bed of boughs beneath the stars after a day of fishing.

"When I consider Thy Heavens and the work of Thy fingers,
the moon and stars which Thou has ordained,
What is man that Thou art mindful of him?
For Thou hast made him a little lower than the angels,
and hast crowned him with glory and honor.

Thou madest him to have dominion over the work of Thy hands;
Thou hast put all things under his feet;
All sheep and oxen, yea, and the beasts of the field;
The fowl of the air and the fish of the sea,
and whatsoever passeth through the paths of the sea.
Oh, Lord, our Lord, how excellent is Thy name in all the earth."

CHAPTER

Ways and Means

Fishermen have always been gullible and superstitious. Even today these qualities are conspicuous among primitive tribes, and, as late as the seventeenth century, some of the most civilized of anglers, entertained strange ideas about the origin of fish. Izaak Walton, the dean of modern fishing, reports that pike come into existence through certain types of marsh grasses which turn to fish, and that eels are born of particular mud slimes into which God mysteriously injects the stir of life. Although he modestly credits these startling opinions to one Gestner, he seemingly adopts them as his own, for he proceeds to discourse upon the subject at some length.

I well remember the days of my childhood, when I would collect several horse hairs culled from the shafts of the grocer's wagon, and place them in a bottle of vinegar, with every expectation that they would eventually turn into snakes. And indeed, as I look back on it now, we were not altogether certain that we did not believe in salamanders living in fire, and phoenixes rising to a fresh youthfulness out of ashes. But I was amused years later when I read a sober statement, in *White's Natural History of Selbourne*, that it had been definitely established that goats do not breathe through their ears!

But fishermen have redeemed themselves by their ingenuity, for they have invented innumerable ways of capturing fish. In this connection, I must relate the story told to me by my friend Bill Deems.

Some years ago Bill was invited by a group of natives to join in a fishing trip for sharks off the coast of Brazil. The party proceeded to the fishing waters on a crude raft called a djangada, which was equipped with a sail and facilities for boiling pumpkins! As he tells the story, a portion of the raft was paved with large flat stones. Upon these a fire was built, and over it a huge kettle was placed, containing pumpkins about eight to ten inches in diameter. The gourds were thoroughly heated in boiling water and when the curious sharks began to mill around the raft, cutting the surface of the sea with their menacing triangular fins, a piping hot pumpkin was tossed overboard. Because of its bright color, the morsel would be immediately gulped. The greedy shark would soon flounder to the surface and expire belly up, literally scalded to death from within, and would then be dragged onto the raft. One could hardly call this sport fishing, and it was surely tough on the sharks, but probably as good treatment as the man-eating brutes deserved. I have never seen this sport mentioned in all of my reading on fish and fishing.

Some of the fish-eating Indian tribes of British Columbia have invented a method of inducing sea-run fish to enter the stream, which they insist is infallible. When the anadromous fish are reluctant to start their inland journey to the spawning beds, the Indians whittle a fish out of a piece of wood, paint it in lifelike colors, anchor it in the stream with its head facing the current and the tardy fish come swarming in.

A good many years ago, in England, a method for taking fish from the deep sea, called "bulter" or "trot" was developed. It is still used to some extent in the capture of large fish, such as cod, ling, coalfish, halibut, rays and hake. A strong line of unbelievable length, often as long as eight miles, is equipped with as many as four thousand hooks bated with squid, herring, and other small fish, and is weighted down toward the bottom of the sea. When being dragged through a school of fish, they are caught in astonishing numbers.

Even a federal judge, when he gets into the subject of fishing, may lay aside his black judicial robe, forsake the austerity with which he is accustomed to grace the bench, and recognized that "a little nonsense now and then is relished by the best of men." Not only is this illustrated by the discourse and the jingles on the oiled mouse in Judge Douglas' book *Of Men and Mountains*, but as well by a note which I received from him the other day. He wrote that, in a letter recently addressed to him by his friend, the Honorable Alfred P. Murrah of Oklahoma City, Associate Justice of the Tenth Federal Circuit, the following appeared:

> "The art of catching large cat fish with bare hands
> is called "noodling." Large cat, weighing some-
> times as much as one hundred pounds, are usually
> found where the river has undercut the shady
> bank. These large fish lie up in under the bank
> here the water is both cool and still. The fisher-
> men locate the fish by diving or feeling their way
> in the likely places. Once located, they scratch
> their under-belly somewhat like you would
> scratch a hog, and the fish makes a somewhat
> similar grunting noise. After the fish is "tamed,"
> the fisherman runs his bare hands through its
> gills and starts to the surface. Then the fight
> starts, and believe me, it is a fight. I have known
> fishermen to have been literally dragged down
> the stream for as much as one hundred or one
> hundred and fifty yards before the fish finally
> tires. On one or two occasions, I have known men
> to lose eyes and parts of hands in the battle. The
> fish are very good to eat when cut up into steaks
> and fried in corn meal.

Now, if you can top this one, we will stop the music. I confess that it doesn't even approach yours on charming a trout in a clear water stream, but I suppose by now your fertile imagination has conjured up another Himalayan story."

Along the Riviera at Nice, I saw a strange device used in fishing from the shore of the Mediterranean Sea. During the afternoon the pebbly beach that fronts the promenade was crowded with lovely French damsels clad or more accurately, unclad, as only they dare to appear. Even on Coney Island, such a spectacle would surely have induced a police raid. When the last of the sun-kissed beauties had tripped daintily back to her nearby resort hotel, and the sparkling blue sea caught the slanting rays of parting day, a weather-beaten old Frenchman showed up on the deserted strand with a coil of heavy fish line about his arm. Tied to the end of the line was a little piece of wood, shaped somewhat like a diminutive barge. It had been whittled out of a scrap of lathe or thin board. The device was about five inches long and perhaps an inch and a quarter wide, and one quarter inch thick. The line was attached to the front of the board which had been whittled to a point, and the under side carried a lead plate to keep the lure weighted to the bottom of the sloping sea beach. In the middle of the upper side of the board, placed about three quarters of an inch apart were two parallel long gang hooks sharpened to needle point. On the pointed front of the lure just behind the hole where the line was tied, a bit of mussel was attached by a string. The hopeful angler whirled the lure about his head, and, with a mighty heave, cast it far out into the sea. He allowed it to remain there for a moment and then began to retrieve it with little jerks, repeating this operation again and again. Although I made a feeble effort in what I called French to learn what he was fishing for, and how the thing worked, I was wholly unsuccessful, but I got the impression that he was fishing for flat-bottom fish such as flounder or turbot. Apparently if a school of such fish happened to be in the immediate vicinity when the lure settled to the bottom they would probably flop about, find the bait and, when reclining over the sharp hooks, would be snagged when the rig was jerked from beneath them. With characteristic patience the angler fished in this way until dark, but got no fish during the time that I watched him.

Let's Eat

Long before the Faithful Twelve, many of whom were fishermen, followed the Nazarene about the country along the shores of the Sea of Galilee, fish of many kinds constituted an important item in the diet of many peoples. But relatively few knew then, or know now, how to prepare and serve the innumerable types of shell and other fish in any but the most familiar ways. Elsewhere in this book will be found one of my favorite recipes — trout filets cooked in deep fat. To this I must add another. It is for boiled trout served cold. As few cooks serve this dish, I give the method for preparing it. Before cleaning a trout weighing one and a half to two or three pounds, scrape it thoroughly with a knife, not to scale the fish, but to remove its natural coating of slime. Then clean it in the conventional manner, cut into chunks of convenient size and tie them loosely in a cloth in order to keep intact. Prepare "court bouillon" as follows. Take a sufficient quantity of water and season it to taste with salt, pepper, a clove of garlic, a slice of onion, a few small bay leaves, a pinch of thyme and the juice and rind of half a lemon. Place the fish in this liquor and simmer for twenty-five or thirty minutes, depending on the size of the chunks of fish. When done, remove the fish from the water and lift away the skin which will be loosened by the cooking. Take out the bones, place the fish in the refrigerator to chill and serve on crisp lettuce leaves with mayonnaise, lemon juice and a garnish of green parsley. When sauterne wine is substituted for the lemon a finer zest is added to the dish and if one prefers the fish hot, it can be served with well-seasoned egg sauce after de-boning. Either method will produce a delicious entree.

Throughout the European continent, and particularly in France, Switzerland and Belgium, one sees "trout a bleu" on the menus of the better restaurants. We received our introduction to this delicacy one day when dining in Brussels. The waiter took our order and soon appeared at my wife's elbow so that we might inspect the fish before being cooked. She did not notice his approach and turning suddenly, saw him holding a big trout wildly flopping in his net and thrashing frantically about in its efforts to escape. She involuntarily gave a startled scream at which she was much abashed and the waiter, net in hand, beat a hasty retreat, but he evidently did not take her outcries to indicate disapproval, for the trout was cooked and served with smiles of satisfaction all around. To prepare "trout a bleu," the fish is dropped alive into a kettle of boiling water, containing about the same ingredients as those above mentioned, but because the fish has not been killed before being subjected to this fatal immersion, it turns a brilliant steel blue, and when served still looks as natural as life, though having taken on this strange electric hue.

My friend Nils Teren, President of the Oregon Pulp & Paper

Company at Portland is a big man, radiant of health and good will. When it comes to fish, he is a true epicure. The following in his own words, is his recipe for 'Gravad' Salmon so popular in Sweden.

"After the fish has been thoroughly cleaned and split lengthwise, remove all the bones and the head and fins. In other words, filet it but do not remove the skin. Take fine table salt and mix in sufficient ground white pepper to make the salt a light gray color. Rub this mixture thoroughly into the raw meat and if the fish is large, sprinkle some of the salt and pepper mixture outside as well. Cover the inside of one piece quite heavily with dill and put the other piece on top with the small end of the top filet resting on the wide end of the bottom filet. Then roll the two filets in waxed paper which should be folded at the ends to prevent air from entering. Place the fish on a large tray and place a wooden board on top of it and weight it down with some heavy objects. The fish should be kept at a temperature of 60 to 65 deg. Fahrenheit. If the fish is put into an ice box, the preparation takes a very long time. In a temperature of 60 to 65 deg. the fish should be ready in two days. After that time the paper is removed, the meat is cleaned with a moist towel and the skin is removed. For serving, the meat should be sliced very thin. The sauce is the most important part and is prepared as follows. Thoroughly mix one tablespoon French mustard, one tablespoon vinegar and one tablespoon granulated sugar. To this mixture add three tablespoons olive oil, one at a time, mixing thoroughly after adding each tablespoon of oil. Add some finely minced dill to this mixture. This amount of sauce should be sufficient to serve three or four people."

The Chinese usually keep fish alive until they are ready to cook them. We once were guests at a typical Chinese dinner in old Peking, that lovely alluring city which seems to have changed very little since the romantic days of Marco Polo. There beauty and stern reality still walk side by side. We entered the establishment through a shadowy courtyard where ancient trees grew in great porcelain tubs, with the walks all about set in mosaics of fruits, flowers and little fish, and we were led to a huge vat where a number of sad-eyed carp swam about in melancholy fashion. Here we were directed to select our fish which we did, and were then escorted through the quiet courtyard toward the restaurant itself. This pleasing prelude left us wholly unprepared for the scene of confusion which followed. We were led into the building through a black cavernous kitchen, where bustling Chinese, stripped to the waist, worked at the glowing spits, and squawked raucous orders to their minions. Although nothing can equal the dignity and quiet poise of the high-class Chinese, neither can anything approach the racket and derangement of a Chinese boss who must keep his crew on their toes.

We hurried through this pandemonium, where it was certainly reasonable to suppose that several unfortunates were having their throats cut, and found our private dining room. It was dark and gloomy too; but the fitful light of the horn lanterns was sufficient to enable us to see that we would not be the first to use the cloth spread on the table, nor the only patrons to recline upon the rumpled couches against the walls of the room on which we were supposed to rest between courses. But our minds were soon occupied to better purpose, for a procession of busy servants began to carry in a confounding array of food: Peking varnished duck, thousand year old eggs, bird's nest soup, shark's fins and other courses, all really delicious. The Chinese are superb cooks. Among all these viands our fish arrived, laid on a fragrant bed of greenery in a jeweled pewter platter accompanied by secret sauces and condiments, so that his end was by far the noblest moment of his existence. We ate with chopsticks, or tried to, and our punctilious host, following the ancient custom of the country, would taste every item of each succeeding course by placing it in his mouth. Having found it good, he would pick up another identical morsel with the same chopsticks and place that in the mouth of my finicky but submissive spouse.

In America prawns are usually fried in deep fat, but in Japan they are treated in many different ways. They are particularly delicious served cold with the shell removed and smothered under a sauce somewhat akin to that used here with the conventional seafood cocktail, or in an exotic variation of mayonnaise. I shall always relish the sight of this superb dish when I recall the delightful evening when my wife, my daughter Mary, and I dined on the roof garden of the old Grand Hotel in Yokohama. Everything about the service was fastidious and exquisite, cool breezes drifted up from the bay, and delicate sunset colors illumined the western sky and transformed the city below into a fairy scene, toy like and foreign. Rickshaws glided smoothly along with their dainty passengers, and swarms of kimono-clad cyclists moved up and down the darkening streets.

The American menu often includes lobster, but rarely in any other form than broiled or thermidored. In Panama, Ancon, Colon and elsewhere in Central America, lobsters, which are somewhat smaller and far more delicate than those of the Atlantic seaboard, are served cold with mayonnaise. They are boiled with appropriate seasoning, shelled and the meat of the tail cut in long diagonal slices. Dipped in mayonnaise they are hard to beat. The final perfect touch is a Planter's Punch — all this in a breezy cool hotel, with exotic flowers banked around the veranda, and silent well-trained servants ministering to one's every wish.

No one who spends any time in New Orleans fails to dine at Antoine's and to enjoy the famous Oysters Rockefeller. If the diner has been previously initiated to such a delicacy he is also sure to order pompano baked in a paper bag, supplemented with the chef's famous creampuff-like potatoes, the whole preceded with a sazarac and topped off with a Crepe Suzette cooked on a chafing dish at his elbow. It adds to the fun when the house lights are flashed off as the brandy is lighted, though nothing can enhance the transcendent cuisine itself.

Yet of all the many kinds of seafood which I have enjoyed, I believe the palm must go to the yellowtail steaks which the master of the greasy little Tormenta fried in butter in his tiny galley and served to Spen and me when we were fishing in the Bay of Ensenada. The yellow tail has very firm meat, and partakes somewhat of the quality of veal, but the flavor is all its own, unexcelled and unique.

> I submit a list of eating places for which I will assume the responsibility of a Duncan Hines:
>
> Omar Khayyam's in San Francisco - excellent Turkish food, Shish kebabs and pita bread.
>
> Harry's Bar in Venice - lobster, seafood, miscellaneous entrees and snacks, cocktails and cosmopolitan atmosphere.
>
> Hotel Wagons-Lits in Peking - Chinese pancakes and incomparable afternoon tea.
>
> Durkins on the waterfront in Boston - Huge lobsters - ribs of roast beef 16 inches thick - noise and atmosphere.
>
> Hotel Bali at Den Passer - heavenly mangosteens served by a soft-spoken, barefooted, sarong-clad waiter with a hibiscus over his ear.
>
> Hotel Des Indies at Batavia - rice taffel, an amazing feast of sixteen courses.
>
> Hotel La Concha at Key West - pompano and coconut ice cream.
>
> Mitlas in Mexico City - pavo (turkey) with hot sauce.

Alfredo's in Rome - fetocini (noodles) and caneloni.

La Tour d'Argent in Paris - superb pressed duck.

Cafe Roger la Grenouille in Paris - frog legs, snails and uproarious, disorderly fun.

Sloppy Joe's in Havana - juicy, thin-sliced ham sandwiches and Daiquiri cocktails.

Ermitage or Harmonies in Berne, Switzerland - fondue: a chafing dish concoction of melted Swiss cheese in spiced white wine on chunks of bread, all diners eating from a common dish with long-tined forks.

Butler Arms at Waterford, Ireland - gammon and spinach.

Little did I know that the frog in Mother Goose was merely served old-fashioned ham when he called for his gammon. Many other interesting and exotic eating establishments throughout the world, famous for one dish or another could be added, but I prefer to conclude with a little place right here at home.

Now, Haines is a very small town in Eastern Oregon, not far from Baker. Highway 30, the Old Oregon Trail, runs down the one business street. The Pine Cone Barbecue is located in an unpretentious building on the very edge of town, on one side of which is a garage. On the other side is a tiny restaurant with one L-shaped counter and benches for not more than fifteen people. It has no adornment except a horrendous juke box in one corner and a few pots of ivy on shelves, but the food is delectable. The menu is brief: barbecued sandwiches, ham, beef and pork, chicken pies, chess and other pies in season (only one kind at a time), tea, coffee, milk, ice cream and candy bars. The prices are suited to the purses of cowboys and clerks from the nearby stores, and there is shade to be found in a grove where tourists who do not want to crowd into the little restaurant can draw off with their families and stretch their legs before resuming their way down the highway. A secret recipe for barbecue sauce is like nothing else in the world, and the chicken pies (full of chicken too) are like those mother used to make, only a whole lot better. Travelers could easily pass by so unpretentious an establishment, but it will pay them to stop. They will find not only delicious food, and sense the feeling of the Old West,P but they may rub elbows with the rustic citizenry.

CHAPTER

The Diamond Hitch

Even today, particularly in the remote vastness of Central Asia and in many of the primitive outposts of the unconquered West, pack animals carry much of man's commerce and worldly goods. Camels in northern India and Tibet and throughout the deserts of Africa; yaks and sheep in other parts of Asia; horses and mules both in Europe and in much of the western hemisphere; burrows in Mexico and South America. Placing goods on pack animals is no mean trick, particularly if they are to make the contemplated journey without mishap. Out in the Northwest the popular method is the employment of the diamond hitch.

Packing horses and mules for a trip through the wilderness is usually accomplished by the use of pack saddles and alforjases. The conventional pack saddle in general use is a crude but efficient affair. It consists of two oval-shaped wood pads which straddle the back of the animal. To these are affixed, fore and aft, sturdy cross pins some two inches in diameter, usually constructed of hickory or oak. These cross members resemble the letter X, one at the front and one at the rear of the saddle, which is held to the beast by a broad fabric or horsehair cinch equipped with heavy straps and buckles. The alforjases, large oblong canvas bags, are provided with loops of rope at both ends and when filled are equally balanced as to weight on the cross members of the saddle so that they hang against the sides of the animal. Bedrolls, sleeping bags, boxes and such other duffle as need to be packed are then nested across the top of the saddle and in front of and behind the cross members. Guns, fishing rods and similar items are placed in the V of the saddle or on either side of the cross pins. Then blankets, a tent properly folded, or a heavy canvas tarpaulin is placed across the finished pack and all are bound snugly together with a long pack rope to one end of which is attached a wide cinch which terminates in a stout wooden hook. It is the last vigorous pull, when tying the pack that completes the diamond hitch. By this pull the parallel ropes at the top are spread and the diamond effect is accomplished. As the pack is tied on prior to the final pull, the ropes are comparatively loose, thus affording enough slack so that in the tie off the diamond is spread out upon the top.

The trick is to so adjust the cinch and pack rope as to bind all together in a firm load. When the diamond hitch is properly "thrown" it is bound so as to present on the top of the pack, a diamond-shaped arrangement of the rope. This all sounds very easy, but to anyone other than an experienced packer it is quite the reverse. Inexpert arrangement of the rope, or a few pounds additional weight on one side or the other will shortly develop a tendency in the load to shift to right or left as the animal moves along the trail, or bucks his way through jack pines, trees and brush.

Some years ago when my brother Joe was even more of a tender-foot than I, we essayed a pack trip of several weeks into the high mountains. Bob Wanker, who operated a stock ranch in the foothills not far from the point where we entered the forest, supplied two saddle horses and a pack horse with equipment.

On the memorable day of our start Wanker did the packing and as he went about it he instructed me on each step of the procedure. I watched him with absorbed interest and listened to his detailed instructions as he threw the diamond hitch and snugged up the pack. It seemed simple enough. I was sure that I understood it.

Well, we got to our first camp without mishap. The horses were accustomed to mountain trails, were as tractable as Easter bunnies and did not even shy when a big brown bear which we startled out of a huckleberry patch blundered away across the rocks and logs.

We established a delightful base camp on the margin of Echo Lake, reveled in excellent trout fishing and outdoor cooking and enjoyed the sleep of the just on pine boughs in our little pup tent. We required no refrigerator for on the north side of the lake deep snow banks extended to its very margin. By deeply imbedding the fish in snow we could keep them almost indefinitely.

I realized that in a few days, we must cross a high granite ridge where the trail was little more than a scar in order to get down to our next proposed camp on Tombstone Lake. So, though professing to my brother that I had thoroughly mastered the diamond hitch, I surreptitiously practiced it on every occasion with a match box and a piece of string. Even that night after we had retired to our little pup tent and Joe was asleep I continued my practicing by the light of the dying fire or a tallow candle. Yes, I was sure I had it down pat.

We arose early on the day when we were to move camp, put in some time on the lake where the trout were rising in a most enticing manner and then got our horses in and went to work on the packing job. Try as I would I simply could not get the ropes to even faintly resemble the design which they should present. The rope which was to go under the alforjases would slip up between them and the saddle. The part that was to be passed diagonally across the pack would not stay in place while I struggled to impose the cross-tie. Cooking utensils, bundles and personal effects would slide off and out of the pack. But I kept manfully at it and finally got the mess tangled onto the horse in such a way as to enable us to make a start. The load shifted a little as we went down a hill, but most of it didn't fall entirely off the horse — until we were fording a stream. Then the whole thing let loose. I shall never forget the look on the face of that pack horse. He stood his ground valiantly in the very center of the stream, but turned his head and looked

sadly back at me with an expression which for all the world said,
"Oh, what a guy. Oh, what a mess."

With some floundering about and considerable derision directed at me by Joe we got the stuff together, dried it out after a fashion and tried again, this time with a little more success, for we finally did get to our campsite on Tombstone Lake.

For a time after that experience I gave up trying to throw the diamond hitch and was willing enough to compromise with the "Hallock Hitch," a process of twisting and winding the ropes about the pack and saddle in any way at all that would keep the load fairly intact. It worked pretty well too, except that one of us had to bring up the rear in order to salvage such items as persisted in falling out of the pack.

But I was not ready to admit total defeat, and I continued to practice with a match box and twine, being then resolved to save my final effort for our departure from the last camp at the Taylor-Green cabin which was only a half day's return trek to the Wanker ranch. I gaily envisioned us riding in with everything snug, and a good diamond hitch holding the pack.

By the time we broke camp that morning at Taylor-Green cabin I knew that I was master of the situation. Furthermore, there was a convenient hitching pole right by the cabin on which I could stand in making the tie and exerting the final pull. One of my troubles had been that with a high pack and me standing on the ground I could not execute the maneuver with knowledge of what was going on top. This hitching pole would solve the problem. I got everything on the animal in good shape. We had consumed most of our edibles so we filled the alforjases with trout packed in snow and tucked bundles, bags, and parcels snugly on and around the saddle, covering it all with our heavy canvas tarpaulin. I cinched up the pack rope, wove it here and there across and around the pack in what I knew was the proper manner and then, standing on the hitching pole some three feet above the ground I summoned Joe from the cabin where he was gathering up a few personal effects to place in his saddle bag.

I shouted, "Now, Joe, watch this. I know I have got it at last." So absorbed was I with my endeavor that I did not hear the faint tread of horses coming up the trail. "Here goes," I cried. With that I gave a mighty heave on the rope, thinking sure to see a diamond develop snugly on the back of the pack at last. But something had gone amiss. There was nothing whatever to resist the pull. Off came the line and down I went, falling backward off the hitching pole, while most of the pack slid off the horse and fell to the ground on the other side.

With a roar of laughter, Wanker and two of his cow hands rode in on the scene.

"Well, Blaine," he choked between whoops of laughter, "I see you are now an expert with the diamond hitch. I wouldn't have missed the show for a million dollars."

We returned to the ranch about on time, but it was Wanker who repacked, threw the diamond hitch, and led the pack horse back to his barn.

As we drove away with our goodly supply of trout I heard the neighing of a horse. Looking over my shoulder I beheld the patient pack animal with neck outstretched and lips curled back, giving me the horse laugh if a horse ever did.

C H A P T E R

Fishing in Oregon Waters

S eries of Articles Devoted to the Gentle Art of Angling.

1. BROOK TROUT and the COLUMBIA RIVER GORGE

By way of preface, let me remark that this series of articles, devoted to the gentle art of fishing, appear here somewhat against my better judgment. They have been penned, not by a scientist learned in all the Latin classifications and anatomical arrangements of the many finny creatures, but by a simple fisherman who loves more the sound of gurgling brooks and the sight of open blue sky than the doubtful joy of a knowledge that his Latin classifications are correct or his theory on genus, as disclosed by fin arrangement or scale markings, is faultless.

These articles will abound in biological errors. A fish's caudal fin I shall be pleased to call by its unlovely sobriquet, his tail. Perchance I may confuse the *Salmo irideus* with the *Salmo gairdneri*, and the char may even be referred to here, without further apology, as a trout; but underneath it all I hope my patient reader may catch some useful hints on angling, or, not being a fisherman himself, may end by holding in higher regard those prevaricating, though harmless, individuals who are so classed.

The other day a friend of mine remarked that since the fishing season had closed he supposed my days off must hang very heavily upon my hands. Somewhat to his surprise I replied that the fishing season never closes. And such is indeed the case, especially here in Oregon. Fish of ten inches or more in length may be taken on rod and line the year round, with no violation of the law, and this without regard to kind. Salmon, trout, char, bass, grayling and any of the many varieties of bay fishes may be taken by angling at any season of the year, subject only to the qualification as to the first three named, of their measuring ten inches or over.

It is a popular idea that the fishing season opens in the spring of the year, and, to most purposes, so it does. About the time when the first wildflowers venture a peep at the uncertain weather, and after the last snow patches have disappeared from the hollows of the lower woods, we read on the calendar that it is the first of April. The State says we may now go "a fishing." And though we have been fishing often during the preceding months of winter and early spring, we have gotten into the habit of calling this first April day the opening of the season.

Let us then begin our fishing with the first of April. We have looked forward to the date, recognizing in it our first chance to catch a mess of early brook trout. And here, at the expense of appearing inconsistent, permit an amplification. The trout here referred to is not that gorgeous little fellow popularly known as the eastern brook trout; and the latter, the brook trout of the East, is not a trout at all. Sounds like a paradox, doesn't it? One might well ask the conundrum, when is a trout not a trout? And the answer would be, when it is a char. To be more exact, while the small trout of our Oregon brooks, the cut-throat or black speckled trout (*Salmo clarkii*), the mountain and western brook trout (*Salmo perperatus*) and the rainbow or red-side (*Salmo irideus*) are really brook trout, since they are true trout living in brooks, the so-called eastern brook or red-spotted trout (*Salvelinus fontinalis*), which is not a native of our streams but which is always referred to by that misnomer, is actually no trout at all. He is a char.

Some day after you have eaten your lunch at noon, step over to First and Alder Sts. and observe the trout in the tank in Constantine's market. There, side by side, you will see the native cut-throat and his eastern brother, the brook trout. This fellow with his pink and gold spots, his red belly and fins, and his peculiarly mottled back, is the *fontinalis* or char.

The story runs that our pilgrim fathers, eager to learn if the many streams which they found on this new continent would afford trout fishing such as they had left in Merrie England, soon discovered this brilliant little fellow, and, though he was quite dissimilar to the brown and Loch Leven trout at home, promptly named him brook trout. Although probing scientists later proved this fish to be a char and not a trout, the name stuck, and today he is quite generally known as the eastern brook trout.

But enough of *fontinalis*, be he trout or char. We started out this April morning for a mess of brook trout and these we will get; real bona fide trout of our western brooks. It remains only to be said that our trout, all of them, have teeth on their tongues, while the char has not.

It is April. On the higher levels little rusty patches of snow still lie, though already, in the broken glades, white trilliums glisten against the deep moss and the first anemone has pushed up a round, heavy bud full of promise.

There are no flying bugs about, though many such in the embryo; fat larvae and grubs, can be found if we but know where to look. We may well expect to find the particular brook decided upon still milky from snow water and clouded by spring freshets.

Where shall we go? We want to catch some little trout, within a few hours of Portland. We think of the famous old Columbia Gorge, with its many dashing water courses. There is Herman Creek, near Cascade Locks; Eagle and Tanner Creeks, near Bonneville; Pierce Creek, Dry Creek, Williams Creek, Bridal Veil Creek, Latourelle Creek, Gordon Creek, Trapper Creek, Cedar Creek, and many others. All good. But my own little pet brook for early April fishing I have purposely refrained from mentioning. Being particularly fond of this tiny stream, I am loath to let you in on my secret. It is quite the prettiest, coolest, daintiest little rill that I know, and each year it affords me quite a respectable creel of small cut-throats. So I have learned to consider it, with its accompaniment of blossom and brake, my own tiny April domain. But I know this is selfish indeed, so I turn it over to you in its wild loveliness. Young's Creek! We shall try its purling waters.

This creek tumbles down through the rocky defiles of Sheppard's Dell, near Bridal Veil, and finds its way to the Columbia about a mile west of that point. But it cannot be ascended from its mouth. In places the water plunges sheer for many feet, and the footing is uncertain. So we will follow the Bridal Veil Lumber Company's logging road till we get up onto the bench land to the right of Bridal Veil Creek. Then take the road to the right over the divide, and a few minutes' brisk walk brings us to the rough little stream. If we are lucky enough to be first in, and are not discouraged by brambles and rough walking, we should take a fair catch of pretty cut-throats.

It is too early for fly-fishing. We will have ample opportunity to indulge that later. This is a plain case of bait. Come with a bait box full of fresh, clean angle worms. To toughen and prepare them for bait, place in a clean earthen jar, half-filled with moss which has been dipped in water and squeezed nearly dry. On this drop a teaspoon full of milk and a light sprinkling of corn meal. After worms have been left in the jar for twenty-four hours they will be found bright, tough and lively.

For brook fishing use a short, light, rather whippy rod, about seven feet long. A long rod is very unwieldy in the brush, while a short casting rod is too stiff. Fifteen or twenty yards of medium-weight, oiled silk line is plenty for this fishing. The reel is the least important item. Use a three-foot light leader single hook loop. Very often the only line out will be the leader. A half dozen No. 8 hooks will complete the outfit.

Fish slowly and carefully and keep well out of sight. This point cannot be too strongly emphasized. These little trout are extremely wary, and any sudden movement of the fisherman sends them off in a flash to hide under some rock or sunken log till they are reassured.

Fish the deeper pools under overhanging banks and beside submerged rocks. Pinch a split shot onto the leader above the hook, and lower it into the likely places, being careful to keep it moving slowly with the current.

Freshets and swollen streams cause the banks to cave off here and there, and the fish eagerly watch these places for worms and grubs. They are hungry and vigorous in the early spring, and will bite readily, although rarely will they take food from the surface.

The day is spent working along the stream from pool to pool, taking a fish here and losing one there.

Budding nature greets us upon every hand, and if we do not bring home three wild flowers to every trout, we have missed the essence of the excursion.

We will clean our little catch before we leave the stream, being careful to keep them away from the water as much as possible. Fish cleaned dry keep much better than those washed and packed in wet grass. A few fresh ferns lining the basket keeps the fish cool and firm. Garnish the pack with water cress, and if my humble little stream has not yielded a full complement to your yawning basket fill the top with wild flowers.

With this offering you should be able to buy permission for another and reconcile "her" to the idiosyncrasies of a fisherman.

2. DESCHUTES RIVER and the RAINBOW TROUT.

The question has been often put to me by enthusiastic anglers, "Where can I go for a Sunday fishing trip, that I may get a mess of trout and still lose no time from work?" And I reply, "The Deschutes." This too with very little consideration for the so-called "fishing season." Big fish can be taken from the Deschutes the year round.

Even today but a comparative few of the cult realize what an angler's paradise this wild stream really is. Tumbling from the high-mountain meadows and draining a myriad of crystal lakes at the very top of the Cascades, the Deschutes River rushes north for nearly the entire length of our good old State, finally roaring into the Columbia east of The Dalles, where its turbulent waters are soothed and blended into that great flow to the sea.

In every pool, behind every sheltering rock, along every choppy riffle for this whole distance of more than two hundred miles lurk gorgeous rainbow trout eager to attack the proffered lure. This stream at our very dooryards. Two nights on a sleeper, a whole eighteen-hour day on the river, and we are back on the job, refreshed from the jaunt and richer by a full creel and a full heart.

There are at least three kinds of game fish in the Deschutes. The beautiful, gamey rainbow (*Salmo irideus*) or red-side, as he is locally known; his less sportive though more powerful cousin, the Dolly Varden (*Salvelinus malma*) who is a char as distinguished from a true trout; and the rather inconspicuous though really good fish, the grayling.

Each of these fish commands our respect for its different fighting qualities. The lordly surges and spectacular leaps of the trout excite keenest admiration. The vigorous power and sullen resistance of the char compel us to respect this voracious fish and cause us some uneasiness for the safety of our tackle. As to the grayling, his skillful dodges and quick turns in white foamy water give us many a thrill, while his ability to grab, in swift current, a spoon hook three times the size of his tiny square mouth is a source of constant wonder.

From the first of April till well into the winter fish can be taken from the Deschutes, and I have no doubt the bait fisherman can get them even during the winter and early spring when the stream is swollen and cloudy. The very cream of the season, however, extends from about the first of May, when the caddis flies hatch, till the last one disappears toward the end of June. At this time the merest novice can get fish, and they are in the pink of condition.

Then caddis flies emerge from their pebbled shell where they have spent the larval stage of their brief career, and hang in great numbers upon the willows and brush along the banks of the stream. It is then that the fish lie close under the banks, waiting for the flies to drop. And it is then that the fishing is at its easiest and best.

Start your day's work with plenty of No. 4 and No. 6 Caddis flies, tied especially in imitation of this insect, and don't forget to soak up a half dozen six-foot leaders for immediate use. The fish are large and powerful, and your tackle is bound to suffer. I have learned to pin my faith on the big hooks at this season of the year. Nothing smaller than No. 6.

Approach the stream with caution. Although the fish are close in, they are by no means as bold as this might seem to indicate. They are close to shore because the flies are there, but for this very reason they are even more shy than usual. Do not expect too much of the big, fine-looking pools. The fish are not there in May. Leave them for the September fishing. Cast your fly lightly into the comparatively still water above some low-hanging willow or on the river side of a half-submerged rock near the shore. Keep well out of sight and let the fly float naturally along with the current. Do not attempt to keep it on the surface. A big trout seldom takes his food from the very surface of the water. However, do not allow the slack line to pull the fly; let the fly pull the line. By all means keep your eye or the hook. These red-sides are as quick as lightning when they strike. But do not expect a wild rush. It is only the little trout which splashes at the fly and leaps out of the water before it is hooked. Your big trout moves rapidly up to the partially submerged fly and sucks it into his mouth with lightning-like rapidity, though with hardly a flutter of the surface water. The strike of a big trout is known in the fisherman's vernacular as a "lump." When the water appears to lump up in the vicinity of your fly, strike quick and hard. The fish can spit out the fly with quite as much dexterity as he can pick it up, and he loses no time in doing so when he finds that he has been fooled.

Your line is brought up taut against a firm, quivering something out there under the willows. For a second it remains stretched motionless. You wonder if you have hooked a snag. But only for a fleeting second are you in doubt. Then follows a battle royal. The big, brilliant fish leaps clear of the water time after time. He rushes madly out into the current, and you must check his heavy surges. He dashes back to the home pool with such marvelous speed that to recover your slack line is a problem. When he makes one of these home runs it is best to ignore the reel for the time being, and haul in line off the rod with your free hand.

But gamey as he is, the fish cannot last long against such heavy odds, and with luck you are soon able to dip him up in your landing net, and a beauty he is indeed.

And so the day advances. You land some of them, and more you lose. Many a lusty fellow takes or breaks a hook and leader, and many another works the hook from his mouth in the fight.

During the heat of the day the fish are close under the banks in the shade of the willows. In the afternoon they move leisurely across to the shady side, and if you happen to be on the wrong side of the river then, you had best crawl under the trees and take a nap. The evening's fishing will tax your strength and nerve.

When the last rays of the sun have left the river, pick out a long, choppy, deep riffle with foamy, broken water at its head, and whip out forty or fifty feet of line. You will now have to wade well out, and cast all the line you can handle. A 9- or 10-foot rod, with plenty of backbone, is needed for this work. If you are going to buy a rod get a good one. A hand-made Hardy, Leonard, Thomas or any other of the standard rods. A cheap, whippy rod is worse than none at all. For long, accurate casting you should have a tapered line of at least thirty yards.

The fish are now in the open water and you are not hid from them as you were in the morning. A long cast, therefore, is indispensable.

Use two flies. If they do not strike a Caddis, try a McGinty. It is a great taker for evening fishing on the riffles. Cast the head of the riffle and work down. As the bait comes quartering in off the current at the toe of the swift water, look out. Your fly is under the surface. You are handling lots of line. Your footing in the swift water is precarious. This is a test of your nerves.

Watch the fly! Or the spot where you think it is. Any quiver of the waters, any slacking of the line, any lumpy swirl, the faintest gleam of red or silver, is the sign. Strike! You may miss him—you may be fooled, but you cannot afford to wait for the jerk. If you do, you have waited too long. Your fish is quicker in the swift water than he is in the still places under the willows. The lump, the gleam of silver, the slack in your line; they mean that a fish wants your fly. Try to take it away from him. You will find that he is the quicker. Your very act will send the hook home to the bony substance of his hungry mouth.

Then the fight all over again, with variations, until your fingers grow cramped from gripping the rod and your shoulders ache from the weight of the heavy creel.

Finally the shadows lengthen and the light fades from the water. A breeze springs up from the south. The fishing is over for the day. You dry your wet feet and legs by the uncertain heat of a sagebrush fire over which you have brewed a tin pot of coffee and fried a scrap of bacon. The purple shadows gather deep in the hollows formed by the high rim rocks. The ragged summits of the bare hills are silhouetted against a far sky studded with millions of tiny brilliant stars. The day is done. And it has been a good day. You are tired but happy, and as you doze in the little station building out there in the big still night, waiting for your home train, you offer up a silent little prayer of thankfulness. You are glad to be alive — and you are not ashamed to be a fisherman.

3. STEELHEADS AND THE ROGUE RIVER.

I recall having read in one of Henry Van Dyke's exquisite little fishing stories a line which he modestly credits to our long-deceased and much-respected brother, Ike Walton, but which I truly suspect originated in his own fertile brain. Musing on the excellence of a luscious wild strawberry which he finds ripening on a sunny bank, he volunteers that "doubtless God could have made a better berry — but doubtless God never did."

And now, on this particular spring morning, when the call to go "a'fishing" is strong, the thought comes that doubtless God could have made a finer trout than the steelhead, but doubtless he never did.

I think it will be admitted by all who have taken steelhead (*Salmo gairdneri*) trout on light tackle that they are easily masters of their kind. The rainbow, especially of a pound and a half or two pounds weight, is a worthy adversary. He can rush and leap and sulk with a style all his own, and be as game, every inch, from the tip of his stub nose to the end of his square tail. A big cut-throat in small water is worthy of your best efforts. Even the cannibalistic Dolly Varden, with his slower though more ponderous surges, will come in for his share of credit as a game fish.

But to the steelhead, the powerful, lithe, quivering steelhead of the Rogue River, belongs the title of king.

I refer to the Rogue River steelheads because to me they typify the perfect trout. Perhaps this is purely imaginary. It is possible, and for that matter quite probable, that the fish of the Rogue River which we catch in the fall with a fly are the same fellows who visit our northern streams in January and February, or, if not the same fish, then at least of the same family. True they are all of the genus *Salmo gairdneri*. True they are all steelhead trout. But I cling nevertheless to the fancy — if it must be called such — that the trout of the Rogue are the finest trout in the Pacific Northwest.

Along toward the end of December, and in greater abundance during January, the steelheads of our northern waters ascend the many tributaries of the Columbia and the coast streams. At this time very fine specimens are taken from the Sandy River, Bull Run Creek, Beaver Creek, Clatskenine River, Hood River, Nehalem River, Salmon Creek, etc., in Oregon, and from the Klickitat, White Salmon, Washougal, Lewis, Cowlitz, and many other rivers and creeks in Washington.

In these streams and at this season the fish, for some inexplicable reason, readily strike a bait of fresh salmon eggs. For this fishing a short, light casting rod with a free-running reel is used, and the bait — a luscious chunk of roe probably half as large as a man's thumb — is tied is tied onto a number two or three hook with red thread.

Why the fish take this lure remains an enigma. They are evidently not feeding. This is apparent from the condition of their stomachs, which are absolutely empty and have contracted to the point where they are hardly distinguishable from the intestines. Probably they strike the eggs in a vicious desire to mutilate and rid themselves of unwelcome fish babies in the embryo who have dared to invade their particular spawning water. But even though such may be the case, I know from my own experience that steelheads in the White Salmon have been taken on a grasshopper bait, which would seem to explode that theory, and the fact that the anadromous Rogue River fish, which does not feed in fresh water, eagerly strikes a gaudy fly in the summer and fall, renders it still more perplexing.

There are two recognized seasons or periods during the year when steelheads can be taken in the Rogue. The upper river yields fish from as early as the middle of June clear through the summer and late into October, while on the stream below Grants Pass the steelheads will not strike before probably the first of September. It was my good fortune last year to make one of a party of three who spent several days in July on the famous stream at "French's," some seventeen miles from Medford.

Our excursion properly began — the enchanting part of it at any rate — when we emerged from our rather cramped sleeping quarters on a southbound Southern Pacific train to find ourselves weaving in and out through the very heart of magnificent broken hill country, sprinkled with fine fir, cedar and hemlock, and covered underneath with a mixed growth of laurel, chaparral, manzanita, and great ferns. If our fishing ardor cooled during the hot night, in proportion as our temper and our temperature ascended while tossing in those stuffy berths, the freshness and beauty of that morning in Cow Creek Canyon, with the click of the rails marking off the rapidly decreasing distance from our Mecca, caused that ardor to reascend to a much higher level.

It is experiences such as these which add to fishing excursions their inexplicable charm. It is this full appreciation and enjoyment of the lovely bounties of God's great big out-of-doors which endears to the fisherman his hobby. Perhaps he himself doesn't fully realize this. At least he doesn't stop to analyze it. But be he at heart a true fisherman, then unconsciously will he drink in the wholesome, happy, healthful influence of open sky and trees and sunshine, the songs of birds, the perfume of fragrant growing things, the ripple of wild water and the joy of life. Indeed your true fisherman "finds tongues in the tree, books in the running brooks, sermons in stones and good in everything."

From Medford an accommodating Ford trundled us across a rolling valley country of fruit orchards, ripening grain fields, vineyards and broken glades, from whose patches of laurel and chaparral little coveys of quail would rise and whirl away.

Then French's, a modest, rather isolated farm, on the very bank of the river, and then — the river itself. And such a river it is indeed. Imagine a mountain brook with all its eddies, its riffles, its tumbling, broken water and its deep, still pools magnified a hundred times, and you have the Rogue. Imagine, too, the fish of the brook equally magnified, and you get an idea of the size of the monsters of the tribe piscary which (unless you are a dexterous fisherman like myself) are quite apt to take your proffered lure. I almost completely prevented such a catastrophe. But my two friends, who were less skillful, actually found themselves on several occasions in the embarrassing situation of having allowed a big steelhead to seize and retain their flies, which necessitated their playing and landing the creatures in order to recover their property.

Before this experience on the Rogue I entertained a modest idea that I had some notion of fly casting. After fishing with and watching my two companions, both masters of the art, I have concluded that I know more about pragmatism or the fourth dimension.

In order to catch a Rogue River steelhead one must first locate the likely water. This is really quite important. The fish do not lie in every pool, nor on every riffle. On the contrary, you may walk a long, long way and may pass many otherwise likely places before you find proper steelhead water. But finally, when you do find a loam, swift, rather choppy stretch flowing over seamed bedrock, at a depth of from four to twelve feet, get ready for business. The first requisite is supplied.

Now as to the fly: A No. 6 is perhaps the best size. There are many favorites. A Grizzly King, Silver Doctor, Brown and Gray Hackle, Queen of the Water, or Royal Coachman; each may prove a winner. I know of a Rogue River fisherman who, by way of experiment, took seven consecutive steelheads on as many different flies in one afternoon.

Use the heaviest quality of gut leader. A steelhead, once he feels the sting of your hook, is as wild and reckless a fighter as you can find in any water that flows.

Now wade out. Not up to your ankles or your knees or your waist, but up to your neck if need be. Get out where the big fish can be reached. Find a reef of bedrock if you can, which will afford shallower water for your footing. If you can't, hang on to the bottom with your toes. The famous "Big Kelly" of Rogue River says he doesn't believe in deep wading. He says he can't cast after the water begins to run into his ears. He refuses to go any deeper than his neck.

Now cast. If you can whip out forty feet, then whip some more. Forty won't do. Neither will fifty—nor sixty. When you get out seventy feet of line, you are beginning to reach the fish. At this distance your fly is quite submerged. It ought to be. Your steelhead wants it from four inches to a foot below the surface. Let the fly swing down and in across the tail of the flow above the lower broken water. Watch the line. THERE: It straightens out in a flash! A broad swirl twists the surface water way out where your line disappears. The tip of your rod is jerked down, and the reel sings. Now mind your footing. It's well that you have plenty of backing. Already the tapered line is clear out and twenty-five, fifty, seventy-five feet of the backing flies from the reel. Then a mighty splash! Seven pounds of quivering, angry, stubborn fish is contesting with you his right to live. He knows more wiles than a politician, and he tries them all. Time after time he leaps clear of the swift water and scatters diamonds with his lusty tail. Over and over again he lets you coax him to more favorable water, only to rush with renewed vigor back into the swirl.

But the best fish that swims cannot fight for long against that constant strain of good bamboo and a firm wrist. Little by little he yields, until finally, from sheer exhaustion, courageous to the last, he rolls over and without further protest allows himself to be lifted from the water at your feet.

Now, at close range, you can see how it was that he proved so formidable an adversary. Every line in this lithe creature suggests strength. His fine body, from the end of his nose to the tip of his tail, is just one highly developed, powerful, exquisitely efficient muscle. Unlike most creatures whose force must be applied through different limbs and parts working more or less independently, his whole effort is expressed in the one muscle, which is the fish himself.

I will say here for my two friends, those gentlemen who wielded the fly so marvelously, that at this juncture of the performance they lifted the prize from the water, very gently extracted the hook from his bony mouth, gloated over his beauty and his fighting qualities for a brief moment, and returned him to the stream, a wiser fish and none the worse for his experience.

I say my two friends did that. I did not. My fish (I use the word in its singular sense); the one I finally did land after days of failure, could not have purchased his ransom with all the wealth of King Midas.

The Chapter "Fishing in Oregon Waters" first appeared in *The Oregon Sportsman*, Volume III, Numbers 3, 4, & 5, 1915

The Measure of a Man

Our acquaintance of the city seems to be a charming fellow. He is gracious, considerate, courteous and well-groomed. He plays a good hand of bridge, enjoys the opera, knows something about books, has seen a bit of the world, and is looked upon as a leader in his community. He is, in fact, the typical well-to-do American.

But take him out on a fishing trip, live side by side with him for a week, and what is he like? I know of nothing which will give his measure more quickly or more accurately than close contact in the woods.

Does he grumble and complain when the fish will not rise? Does he shirk the jobs of rustling firewood and of helping make down the bough beds? Does he carry his share of the duffel without complaint as we struggle over the hill to our next camp site? Does he willingly take his turn as cook or dishwasher? When we are to boat the lake, where one man casts while the other rows, does he rush for the seat in the stern or does he cheerfully take his place at the oars? When he rows does he flay the water with awkward gouges and splashes, or does he pilot the boat quietly and smoothly to the edge of that little bay where the fish are rising in such tantalizing fashion close to the shore grasses? Particularly, does he hog the best pools and riffles on the stream, keeping ahead throughout the entire day, or does he respect the traditional custom of leaving to his companion who is lucky enough to be first on the pool the undisputed right to fish it through undisturbed? If he cheerfully assumes and willingly performs his share of these tasks and fully measures up to these standards, he is quite the man he appeared to be in town; but if he does not, I have taken him on our last fishing trip.

I know and love at least four men who have never failed in any of these respects through the many years that we have fished together. Two of them, already mentioned at length, Spencer Biddle and Judge Douglas, are fishing companions par excellence. The other two are Fred Moes and Dr. H. J. Horton, known to his friends as "Bill." If an all-wise Providence has provided a happy fishing ground for departed anglers, and if I may hope to rate a place there, I do not want to go unless these friends will be there too. Were he here today, another man whom I cherish would have been mentioned long ere this. But seven years ago the good book of his life was closed forever.

Woodson L. Patterson was one of the first to take me under his wing when I came to Baker many years ago. He showed me the places where the big trout lay, and where the water fowl and upland birds were most abundant. He, perhaps even more than any of the others, was the very soul of cooperation, courtesy, and infinite patience, on our many outings. In addition to these qualities, he possessed a highly cultivated mind. "Arcturus with his sons" was his familiar, and he walked daily with the greatest of the poets. He never quite became converted to fishing dry with a short, light fly rod weighing not more than three and a half or four ounces. But with his old Divine nine-and-a-half-foot, six-ounce rod which he used during all the years that I knew him, he could float a fly as delicately as anyone with whom I had ever fished, an admission which from a man who considers himself fairly adept with a fly, should be taken for what it is intended — one of the highest compliments that one fisherman can pay to another.

It is our campfire that converts the wilderness into a home, and claims the spot as our abode. While we move through the woods one part is no more friendly than another. As yet there is no particular intimacy between us and the pleasant wildwood all about. But, the moment we select a place to stop and build a fire, the spot instantly becomes our forest home. The little wisp of smoke climbs up among the trees marking our bivouac. The rocks and logs which were strangers but a moment ago now seem to look upon us with a kindly interest. At first the chipmunks and camp robbers remain somewhat aloof, but now they gradually close in and take advantage of our kindly indolence by snatching a crumb or two from the edges of our scattered lunch. So we linger around the blaze, poking up the embers and pitching in the charred ends of sticks. We suddenly develop an ability and a desire to squat about the fire as our ancestors must have done eons ago. We are loathe to leave, and when we do move on we look back over our shoulders as though departing, never to return, and mayhap some of us never will.

Bill Horton is always the first to build a fire and to construct a little wall of stones across which we can balance the handle of the frying pan and suspend the coffee pot. Fred brings in from windfall, thicket, and glade, a surprising quantity of firewood, placing the larger sticks in one pile and the twigs for kindling in another. Both men are good camp cooks, and each is an expert with a dry fly in his own right. With these men there is no grumbling, no complaining, no task too hard to perform, no burden shirked, and an unbounded enthusiasm for nature and fishing.

As we loose the boat from its mooring on the sedgy bank one or the other reaches for the oars. If we are fishing a stream the best water is first tendered to me. And if I land a good fish both men will applaud my efforts and admire the fish's mottled beauty with more enthusiasm than if they had done the job themselves. No matter how early I may arise, nor how late I may sleep in camp, I wake to the aroma of coffee; and before I have dashed the chill drops of the morning ablutions from my face, Bill and Fred are frying crisp bacon or ham with eggs cooked precisely as I like them. Sometimes they serve

a plate of baking powder biscuits or bannock bread, cooked in a frying pan, tilted at an acute angle before the glowing embers, and shifted from time to time in order to give the batch a uniform golden
brown. But what is more, these men often seem to be thinking just
what I am thinking at the time. They will suggest the very next jaunt
that I was about to propose, whether it is a trip across the ridge to a
nearby lake or to a particular stretch of the stream, or just a lazy afternoon sprawling in the shade of the pines. In the fall Fred and Bill are
my companions when we hunt the pheasants that haunt our nearby
fields, and the ducks that come whirling in over our ponds and
sloughs at the first definite change in the weather. Many a time when
we know that Rusty is about to flush a big China cock in a patch of
tules, or out of a fence corner thicket, one or the other will call, "Your
bird, Blaine. Let him have it."

When we shoot ducks over the same strip of quiet water in
Powder River where we have hunted together for many years, one or
the other of us will be designated captain. The captain calls the shots,
either "Right, left, and center," if we are huddled in a row under the
overhanging bank and a big flock of ducks heads our way, or "You
take him," if a single floats in over the decoys. When either Fred or
Bill is captain, most of the singles are called for me. Yes, a man's true
character will show up very soon on a fishing trip or afield with gun
and dog.

As time has rolled on, our program for getting back into the great
wilderness areas, scattered so generously throughout the Northwest,
has changed with the ever-increasing improvements in outing equipment provided by forward-thinking manufacturers, and as well by
the years that have taken toll of our endurance and strength. At first
we would go forth for a week or two in the woods with nothing more
elaborate than the packs on our backs, which contained a blanket
apiece, a frying pan, a coffee pot, a few tin utensils, and a meager supply of staples — coffee, sugar, canned milk, flour, baking powder,
beans, and prunes. Young bodies and hearty appetites were more
than enough to offset what today, traveling in that way, would seem
a real hardship. Later, when we rode horseback through the mountains, a pack mule helped to carry more equipment, and we included
with our duffel a little tin reflector for baking, sleeping bags, and folding cots — all considered the last word in outdoor luxury at that time.
Then came the automobile, and our horizon was vastly extended.

Years ago my wife frequently went along on our trips. In our
eagerness to fish the moment we arrived at a selected camp site, we
wasted scant time upon bed-making. Often we merely spread out a
blanket or two upon the ground, sometimes among the rocks, and
occasionally upon an ant hill. Many times interesting variations

would be added to our camping days, such as fighting yellow jackets, and frightening curious cattle away from our camp.

One night when we were lying thus, looking up at the stars, our old dog Pete was doing a little prowling on his own account. Presently he flushed a rabbit and gave chase. There was a wild scurry and dash to our very bed, where Pete killed and crunched the creature to a medley of my wife's horrified screams and the rabbit's expiring whimpers.

The advent of the station wagon afforded even greater luxury. But the time comes in the life of every fisherman when he looks more kindly upon the tamer varieties of outing. So Fred and I now have a comfortable little cottage on the verdant banks of Eagle Creek, just one hour's drive by automobile from Baker, where Bill is often a most welcome guest. The stream runs just beyond the spacious shady porch of our cabin from which, were we so disposed, we could pick up a trout or two by casting right from our comfortable canvas armchairs. Not twenty feet from the veranda, the stream has accommodatingly carved out a long, choppy riffle with deep green water in the middle, and a froth of white bubbles at its head. Many a time we have taken enough trout for our evening meal from this riffle alone. The fish are not large. They run from eight to fourteen inches, but occasionally we do pick up a two- or three-pounder. Not content with this, however, we have developed a series of ponds or small lakes, all of which are stocked with trout. On the largest lake we can cover all the water from our light rowboat, and though we can fill a basket with lusty fish in short order, we usually spend many hours just drifting about on the placid water, enjoying its reflections of the glorious mountains which encircle our little valley.

A half mile or so below the cottage, the stream tumbles through a rocky gorge, with many cascades churning between the boulders and numerous deep-green, foam-flecked pools. It is along this stretch that we seldom fail to land one or more really big trout. In late summer, nodding bushes laden with wild black raspberries border the stony trail. It is rare when we do not see one to a half dozen deer gazing at us from the open glades as we go to and from the cottage, and ruffed grouse scuttle to cover in the thickets along the creek. Little red shiny wild strawberries nestle in the grass in our very dooryard, and in spring the whole country is painted with brilliant wildflowers of innumerable variety, and in great profusion.

Yes, much can be said for bough beds out under the stars, and for fish or game cooked over an open fire, but when one passes the three-score milestone, a good wood range and a big oblong iron griddle for hot cakes in the morning, running water out of a faucet, comfortable chairs for backs made weary from floundering about over slippery boulders, and deep soft beds, where one lies between fresh sheets and goes to sleep to the murmur of the nearby chattering stream, are luxuries that do offer strong appeal.

So with the closing pages of this book, and the last days of another too-short summer upon us (but one nevertheless with its full complement of trout), I look forward to the next weekend, and the little white cottage with the red roof under the friendly pines. When autumn closes in and the leaves turn, when the crisp air bites through our jackets and the days for fishing are over, I know that I shall be sitting before the fire in that snug cabin, sunk in my own reveries. And I know of what I shall be thinking — old friends and many waters. I shall fervently acknowledge my many blessings to my Maker. Surely He will not hold me sacrilegious when I exclaim from my heart,

"My rod and my gaff, they comfort me."

About the Author

Blaine Hallock (1884-1954) was born, raised, and educated in Oregon. He practiced law for many years in Baker, Oregon, describing himself as the "lawyerly fisherman". Besides being a great writer, Hallock was also a gifted poet and oil painter. All of the drawings in this book are his.

Blaine Hallock's childhood newspaper, The Pendleton Sun, is included in the children's writings of the national archives.

He wrote about fishing in several journals, and left this unpublished manuscript to be recovered from a box in a barn some 60 years after his death. His fishing stories cover much of his lifetime, and take readers on adventures across the globe.

An early proponent of catch-and-release fishing, Blaine was an avid and vocal supporter of water and land conservation, serving on several commissions to that effect.